Cyberspace, Data Analytics, and Policing

Cyberspace, Data Analytics, and Policing

David B. Skillicorn

CRC Press
Taylor & Francis Group
Boca Raton London New York

CRC Press is an imprint of the
Taylor & Francis Group, an **informa** business

First edition published 2022
by CRC Press
6000 Broken Sound Parkway NW, Suite 300, Boca Raton, FL 33487-2742

and by CRC Press
2 Park Square, Milton Park, Abingdon, Oxon, OX14 4RN

CRC Press is an imprint of Taylor & Francis Group, LLC

Library of Congress Cataloging-in-Publication Data

Names: Skillicorn, David B., author.
Title: Cyberspace, data analytics, and policing / David B. Skillicorn.
Description: 1 Edition. | Boca Raton, FL : CRC Press, 2022. | Includes bibliographical references and index.
Identifiers: LCCN 2021020499 | ISBN 9780367642761 (hardback) | ISBN 9780367647766 (paperback) | ISBN 9781003126225 (ebook)
Subjects: LCSH: Computer crimes--Prevention. | Criminal justice, Administration of--Computer network resources. | Police--Data processing.
Classification: LCC HV6773 .S565 2022 | DDC 364.16/8--dc23
LC record available at https://lccn.loc.gov/2021020499

ISBN: 978-0-367-64276-1 (hbk)
ISBN: 978-0-367-64776-6 (pbk)
ISBN: 978-1-003-12622-5 (ebk)

DOI: 10.1201/9781003126225

Typeset in Nimbus font
by KnowledgeWorks Global Ltd.

Contents

Preface

As the 2020–21 pandemic showed, cyberspace is pervasive in social life, education, business, and government. It is also becoming pervasive in crime because so much value is in play in the online world and in the interface between cyberspace and the physical world. Criminals have been quick to take advantage of the opportunities provided by cyberspace, although the skill required to take advantage of some of these opportunities is still great enough to limit the damage. New kinds of crimes have evolved to take advantage of cyberspace directly, while other, more conventional crimes have changed in the way that they are carried out.

Law enforcement has, to some extent, been left behind by these developments because they have weaker incentives than criminals do, and they work within much tighter constraints. These include a slowly evolving legal system, and the way in which law enforcement organizations are siloed, at the national and often regional level.

However, law enforcement have an advantage if they can work out how to leverage it: data analytics can be used to understand the workings of large and/or complex systems (in this case crimes and criminals) based on the observable data about them. Law enforcement has always been good at using data. Using data analytics requires a substantial change in the way that data is leveraged, from a primarily query-driven mindset to one in which the data plays an active role.

This book addresses both the role of cyberspace and the role of data analytics in a way that is accessible to both frontline law enforcement and analysts. It is not an academic book, but there are notes providing a path into deeper background for those who are interested.

Acknowledgments

I am also grateful to all of my students – in teaching them, I learn myself; and many of them have directly contributed to my thinking about this area. Thanks also to Clifton Phua for comments on drafts, and to Ross Jansen-van Vuuren for help with chemistry.

I would also like to thank my editor, Randi Cohen, who has helped at every stage, and made the publishing very smooth.

List of Figures

List of Tables

Chapter 1

Introduction

Law enforcement is being changed by the development of two related technologies: cyberspace, the globe-spanning communication and interaction infrastructure, and data analytics, an approach that extracts actionable knowledge from large amounts of data. Some of these changes are obvious, but many of them are subtle.

Because cyberspace has become the most important way in which governments, businesses, and individuals get things done, it has created opportunities for new kinds of crimes, and new ways of carrying out old crimes, at scale and speed. Cyberspace has become both a huge target and an enabler for crime.

Fortunately, the advantage is not entirely with criminals. Cyberspace also makes it easier to collect data, both about the actions of ordinary people, and the actions of criminals. Data analytics allows patterns to be found within large datasets, both the signals of particular criminals at work, and broader knowledge about the ways in which criminals operate. This compensates, in some ways, for the greater opportunities that cyberspace gives criminals. Law enforcement can be smarter, and so achieve better clearances rates, perhaps even at lower resource cost.

Criminals can find each other and learn from one another more quickly and more easily than ever before. Although law enforcement can also benefit from better communication, it faces hurdles that come from borders at all scales from cities to nations, and the differences among jurisdictions that these borders create.

These new technologies have been disruptive, and both criminals and law enforcement are struggling to understand how to use them in the best way from their mutually adversarial perspective.

Most of those involved in law enforcement and intelligence will be aware of some of the effects of cyberspace and data analytics, but most will not be familiar with all of these effects. Indeed, the environment is changing so fast that it is difficult to keep up. This book is designed to help you fill in gaps in your knowledge, and to

DOI: 10.1201/9781003126225-1

get a broader perspective by stepping back and looking at the issues in a synthesized way. Although the focus here is on law enforcement, many of the same issues arise for intelligence, financial intelligence, customs, corrections, and cybersecurity.

Chapter 2 introduces cyberspace and its properties that have had the greatest impact on the landscape of crime and criminals. Chapter 3 introduces the new kinds of crime that cyberspace has enabled and the way in which existing crimes have changed because of the existence of cyberspace. Chapter 4 shows how the ability to communicate at speed and mostly independent of geography has made it easier for criminals to cooperate.

Although cyberspace has created opportunities for criminals, the news is not all bad. Chapter 5 shows that cyberspace has provided new opportunities for law enforcement as well, in particular the collection of data at unprecedented scale and new ways of extracting actionable knowledge from it, an approach that has come to be called data analytics. Chapter 6 describes the ways in which data for analysis can be collected, and the subtle and often difficult issues that arise from data collection. Chapter 7 describes, at a high level, how these data-analytic techniques work and what they can be used for. Chapter 8 describes some case studies that show how these data-analytic ideas can be applied to real law enforcement situations. Chapter 9 describes how the communication possibilities of cyberspace have changed law-enforcement cooperation despite the boundaries between different jurisdictions.

Chapter 2
Cyberspace

Cyberspace has pervaded our societies and our lives, and continues to have a major impact on individuals, families, groups, businesses and governments. Crime has been changed by the existence and use of cyberspace, and so has the fight against crime.

In a perfect world, law enforcement would be proactive in understanding the potential for new and adapted crimes, developing new tools and approaches to address them, and training personnel in how to understand these new crimes and use new capabilities against them.

The advantage, however, is with criminals. They have fewer restrictions on their actions and they are self-funded; whereas law enforcement lives with a legal framework that often fails to keep pace with changing technology, and with budgets that increase only slowly and are hard to redirect. Criminals can communicate globally, learn from one another, and mount many crimes from anywhere. Law enforcement enforces the laws of particular jurisdiction, and faces practical and legal hurdles for sharing information.

In this chapter we outline the properties of cyberspace that have changed the playing field for both criminals and law enforcement.

2.1 What is cyberspace?

Most people encounter cyberspace via the *World Wide Web* (WWW), the system of web servers and web browsers that gives us access to the world's knowledge.

The World Wide Web was developed as an information-sharing system, but it is also increasingly the mechanism by which we act in the world, as the browser-server interface has been enriched to allow us to do banking, book travel, and upload videos, as well as to interact with one another on social-media sites.

DOI: 10.1201/9781003126225-2

The World Wide Web is only a subset of the *Internet*. The Internet consists of a wide variety of nodes:

- *personal computers* and workstations;
- *phones*[1], devices that are so closely tied to us that they act almost as human surrogates;
- *Internet of Things* devices such as CCTV cameras, smart light bulbs, thermostats, fitness trackers, door locks, and door bells;
- cyberphysical systems that operate factories, pipelines, water supplies, and electricity grids;
- web servers that power our World Wide Web interactions;
- compute servers that carry out substantial computations for organizations that need them;
- clouds, which carry out substantial computations or store large volumes of data, and which are shared between many different users who can use them on demand.

As well as these nodes, there are networks of pipes that connect them. The networks have two parallel forms: the cell phone networks that connect highly portable devices; and the wired and wifi networks that connect most other devices. These networks are, of course, connected to one another in multiple ways.

The individual pipes vary widely in their capacity and operation. For example, Bluetooth networks carry data over a few meters; wifi networks carry data within a single space such as an office or house over a hundred meters or so; coaxial, cell, or optical fiber connections carry data over a few kilometers; and much higher capacity connections carry data between cities, and underneath oceans.

Networks contain switches that direct the traffic along the paths from its sources to its intended destinations. These switches are just ordinary computers, optimized for the tasks of directing and moving data, and so they have all of the capabilities and issues of other devices on the Internet.

Alongside the Internet are some less well-known parts of cyberspace.

1. Many militaries have their own networks which use the same kinds of devices and network technologies as the rest of the Internet but are not directly connected to it. These networks are often "air gapped" from the Internet, so that they have no direct connections. In practice, this separation is not as strong as it seems because there are multiple channels that allow information to cross the gaps (although they mostly require sophistication to exploit).

   For example, software on these air-gapped networks must be updated somehow, so there is necessarily information flow into them. The Stuxnet malware was inserted into an air-gapped network that ran Iranian uranium centrifuges using USB keys. These had been loaded with software updates on systems that were attached to the Internet. When these USB keys were attached to computers on the air-gapped network, they installed malware on the centrifuge controllers.

There have been several experiments in which USB keys were dropped in the parking lots of secure installations, and non-trivial numbers of them were taken inside and plugged into secure computers by unthinking Good Samaritans.

Computers on the air-gapped network can also leak information that can be detected because their operations necessarily cause changes in the physical environment around them. Information leakage has been detected in physical mechanisms such as the sound they emit, their disk operation, their screen display, and fluctuations in their power use.

2. Cyberspace contains content that only exists transiently, and so cannot be found using search engines. For example, when you authenticate to your bank, the bank displays a page showing your account balances. This page is created on the fly, and can only be seen by you. As a result, it is never indexed, and so cannot be found other than via the bank's front page and then authentication. Such content is stored in back end systems, such as databases, but it only is assembled and comes into existence as an entity on demand, and only for a short time.

   Cyberspace also contains content that is always present but is not indexed by search engines and so cannot be easily found. Anyone can create such a page with some care.

   This collection of pages with limited accessibility is called the *deep web*.

3. Cyberspace also contains a subspace called the *dark web*[2]. This consists of data that is explicitly hidden in two different ways.

   The first kind of content is hidden because it requires access via a particular mechanism. The most well-known of these mechanisms is based on the *Tor router*. Anyone using a specialized browser or plugin can have their web access requests directed to the Tor router. The router uses a set of volunteer nodes to move the traffic around randomly. When the traffic exits the Tor router, it can go to a special set of websites whose URLs end in '.onion'. These websites cannot be connected to directly; only from a Tor router node. Thus this part of the dark web is a separate world wide web that is not directly searchable, and can only be accessed, as it were, from one particular direction.

   The Tor router framework makes it difficult (but not, in fact, impossible) to know which browser is talking to which web site. Although originally designed for privacy, it provides an opportunity for illicit activity that is hard to track and so has become popular with criminals. Dark-web web sites can sell illegal products and disseminate information without attribution.

The second part of the dark web consists of nodes which, as it were, only speak their own private language. Ordinary Internet traffic that reaches them is simply discarded. In order to convey data encoded in their own private way, totally new mechanisms are required for communication. For example, to reach such a dark-web web site, a totally different kind of browser is required. This kind of dark web activity is much harder to track since it is close to impossible to tell what observed data movement means – it is like listening to a conversation in a foreign language. Fortunately, considerable skill is required to use such a specialized subnetwork and it is beyond the capability of many criminals.

Cyberspace has its origins in an academic and defence network called the *Arpanet* which was designed to connect trusted parties and to work in a distributed fashion so that it could survive a nuclear attack. Cyberspace's explosive growth in both size and functionality has been built on this foundation. There was never a point when the basic operating principles of cyberspace could have been redesigned to be more appropriate for its scale, since at every step, new pieces had to be able to work with the older pieces. Worse still, the decentralized design of cyberspace meant that there was never (and still is not) a centralized body capable of making and enforcing design decisions. The result is a system that is forced to operate in ways that make little sense for something that is so critical to most aspects of modern life. In particular, security has had to be retrofitted wherever possible, but within difficult constraints.

2.2 The impact of cyberspace

The existence of cyberspace, and its continuing evolution, has had an impact both on crime and on policing. The most obvious property of cyberspace is its *scale* – suddenly we can reach at least half of the world's population via email or text messaging, and we can find out personal details of a large fraction of that half from web sites and social-media presence. A spammer can send an email to 100,000 people at virtually no cost, and a tweet can make its way to 100,000 people with a single click. We can also access a large fraction of the world's knowledge, including things that we might wish criminals couldn't find out.

The second obvious property of cyberspace is *speed*. Groups can collaborate on a design or a plan in real-time, working collaboratively on the same document or presentation. Problems with supply chains can be reported almost instantly. Our speed of action also has some negative consequences: we can retweet or click on a link in an email faster than the moment it takes us to judge if doing so is a good idea. A cyber attack can be carried out on hundreds of computers within a few seconds.

Cyberspace is also *pervasive*. In the U.S. people spend more than 11 hours per day looking at the screens of their phones and computers. Cyberspace interactions are the way we work, communicate with one another, and entertain ourselves. They are also increasingly the way that we spend money.

This rapid growth of cyberspace, and its intrusion into almost all areas of life has come with a cost. The embryonic form of the Internet, Arpanet, connected research labs and universities, where the users were knowledgeable and accountable. As a result, security issues were hardly considered. Subsequent developments privileged convenience over security at every stage. As a result, the components of cyberspace have no overarching security design; rather security is a series of minimalist hacks to prevent the worst misuses. This provides many opportunities for misuse by criminals, as well as accidental destruction. Security is, in any case, not the kind of property that can be retrofitted. You cannot decide to make a system 10% more secure and then design a series of changes to make it so.

Cyberspace has a huge sunk cost problem. Making a security improvement in even one small way requires agreement from the entire system, since cyberspace is a connected system. The pipes that connect systems must all speak the same language so that the nodes at each end can communicate with one another, and the nodes must all agree to at least provide minimal common services to one another.

The original Arpanet was also designed to survive a nuclear attack so, by design, it worked in a distributed way, with no central control of its operations. This has continued into the Internet today. The management system that decides how data is routed through networks and what happens when pipes are congested or broken is a distributed one. There is no overarching body or organization that runs cyberspace. Decisions involve independent bodies, large network providers, large social media and search businesses, Internet service providers, and national governments. Their interests are not necessarily aligned, and proposed changes require extended, and often unproductive, negotiations.

There have been several research projects aiming to redesign cyberspace from the ground up, but all have foundered on inertia and the relative success of the current system. New organizations and governments regularly propose restarting an Internet 2.0 project but, so far, without much success.

Because computers are infinitely flexible, it almost always makes sense to implement new functionality by taking a general-purpose computer and programming it for the required functionality. The result is that the entirety of cyberspace uses only a handful of different: processors, operating systems, connection mechanisms, and clouds. Cyberspace is full of monocultures, the same basic tools used in millions of different settings. This creates huge vulnerabilities; an attack or exploit that works against one kind of tool can be replicated to work against many others.

2.3 Identity and authentication

The ability to act in cyberspace gives each individual great power, and such actions should come with accountability. The inherent security weaknesses of cyberspace make accountability difficult. Even knowing who carried out some action ("attribution") is difficult, let alone holding them responsible for it.

But there are clearly some actions that cannot be allowed to happen without a robust link between the online action and the person carrying it out. Making this link is called authentication.

Cyberspace has mechanisms to authenticate individuals to do various things: use particular computers or phones, connect devices to networks, download software, access particular parts of websites, shop online, or change systems or networks, but the mechanisms we use to decide who is allowed to do what are weak. This enables many kinds of criminality because actions cannot be tightly tied to the individuals who carried them out.

Security practitioners frame authentication in terms of three potential modalities: something we know (a password), something we have (a credit card) or something we are (a biometric such as a fingerprint). Passwords are by far the most common authentication mechanism, but they are becoming almost unworkable. The computational cost of breaking a password using brute force calculation is low enough that good passwords must be long – perhaps a minimum of 15 characters at present. This is at the outer limits of what people can remember, and the situation will only get worse. Strong password requirements backfire because users use a password they can remember at multiple sites, which means that breaking it at one site potentially pays off at other sites.

A strategy based on something we have is common in the physical world using objects such as physical keys or fobs for cars. Credit cards are another physical-world authenticator, but their use requires a second factor, the PIN associated with the card.

Authentication using something we have has limitations. It is easy to forget the object (leaving our keys at home), preventing authentication, and objects can be lent to someone else, destroying the link that authentication is supposed to establish.

It is hard to use object-based authentication online because of the need to have some way of detecting the presence of the object from within cyberspace. This can be done by, say, requiring the object to be plugged in to a USB port or to be close enough to be detected by Bluetooth.

Some object-based authenticators such as credit cards have quickly turned from something we have (the card itself) to something we know (the card number and CVV) to make online shopping easier.

Biometrics look, at first glance, as if they might be much better authenticators. A wide range of properties of our bodies have been considered as possible authenticators: fingerprints, blood vessel patterns, irises, faces, voices, or ear shapes. These have the advantage that we cannot forget them, we always have them with us, and we cannot lend them to others.

However, there are multiple serious problems with biometric authenticators. First, just as for object-based authenticators, there must be a detector for the biometric at every point where authentication is needed. So far, this has only been reasonable for fingerprint and face detection. Second, there are always people who do not have a particular biometric (missing fingers or fingerprints, missing eyes, and so on) and so an alternate mechanism must also be available at every point of authentication. Third, many biometrics are easy to spoof: fingerprints with silicon moulds or simply pressing on the detector using a thin plastic sheet, high-quality photos of irises, and so on. Fourth, if a biometric authenticator is compromised, there is no way to issue a replacement. Fifth, some biometrics can change relatively quickly. For example, voices change when we have a cold, fingerprints change when if cut our finger, blood vessel patterns change if we take up vigorous exercise, and so on. These problems are difficult to avoid and explain why biometric authentication has not taken off, despite the weaknesses of knowledge- and object-based authentication.

Authentication is usually only required at a few places in each person's actions in cyberspace: getting access to their phone or computer, accessing their local network, signing in to some kinds of web sites, and purchasing online; but these moments are rare in the totality of their actions. Most actions are only weakly associated with a real identity, unless an explicit authentication was required immediately before the action. It may be possible to determine that this particular account, email address, credit card, or phone was used in a particular action; but it is much harder to tie that to the presence and involvement of a particular individual. It is easy to disavow actions: "my password must have been stolen", "my credit card was stolen", "someone must have used my computer while I was at lunch", and criminal prosecution standards of beyond reasonable doubt are mostly unattainable.

Authentication is a developing area, with two-factor authentication being extended to multi-factor authentication (which sometimes means using more than two factors, but usually means two-factor authentication with a choice of which two factors to use out of a larger set).

Risk-based authentication is also increasing in popularity. At its simplest this means taking into account factors other than identity in deciding how risky each particular authentication event is, and so how much explicit authentication the user must provide. For example, if the access is from the same computer that the user has used before, then a single authenticator may be sufficient, but if not then more is required (a second factor, some challenge questions, or something else).

This idea of measuring how potentially risky the access is can be extended to other features: not only the IP address of the device requesting the access but also the browser being used, and the operating system being used and its version. Google has developed a form of this idea that they call *Beyond Corp* in which many aspects of the connecting device and user are evaluated, and access is allowed in a fine-grained way. This includes authenticating based not only on the static properties of the accessing device but also on temporal properties such as whether recent updates have been applied. Devices (and users) who have only been weakly authenticated can be granted partial access, appropriate for the level of confidence of the authentication system that they are who they claim to be.

Such systems raise the bar for criminals to pretend to be someone else because not only must they know some facts about the other person, they must also be able to simulate the device environment that they ordinarily use.

Despite these developments, cyberspace is, at its core, a place for anonymous activity. When an identity is associated with such an action, the identification must always be regarded with some doubt, especially in settings where there is an incentive to conceal or manipulate identity.

There is also a fundamental mismatch between the structure of cyberspace and the international Westphalian world of nations with borders between them, and each nation having, in principle, complete control of its own internal activities. Traffic in cyberspace travels wherever is easiest or least congested on its way from source to destination. This hardly ever has anything to do with which nation's territory the next switch, or the web server, or the cloud is located in. There are no customs officers examining the data crossing into or out of each country.

Criminals need not live, or make money, in the jurisdiction in which their crimes are committed. In fact, there are considerable incentives for them not to. Law enforcement, in contrast, work within a legal system that is country-specific (and often even finer grained than that) and with powers that largely stop at their national borders.

There have been some attempts to impose national borders in cyberspace. The most ambitious is China's so-called Great Firewall of China, which attempts to control the access of its citizens to cyberspace in the rest of the world, using a combination of access rules and an allegedly large group of human supervisors. Even this is not enough, and it is apparently reasonably easy to evade the firewall if desired.

Other countries have made contingency plans to cut their local piece of cyberspace off from the rest of the world, but it is hard to test these plans without an economic impact on the countries concerned, so it is hard to know if they will work. In any case, the countries that have gone farthest down this road contain far more cyber-troublemakers than the rest of the world, so cutting them off from the common cyberspace might be an improvement. For example, it is noteworthy that, when China shut down to deal with the coronavirus, spam across the world slowed to a trickle, only to come roaring back as China reopened.

The speed and reach of cyberspace also give all of us access to a huge pool of information and people. For criminals, this means that it is easy to find out how to commit certain crimes, to find potential collaborators, and to find those willing to sell the tools required for crimes, including toolkits for cybercrimes. Best criminal practices can be easily disseminated, and potential victims found. Geography is much less of a limitation than it used to be, so criminals can now act internationally almost as easily as they can act locally.

The effect can be seen in the waves of crimes of a particular kind that start in one place, spread all over the world within a short time, and then die away as the victim market gets saturated.

Speed and reach have an impact on law enforcement who can also access unprecedented amounts of information about the criminal landscape: who is active, what crimes are becoming popular, and what ways of addressing them have worked. Law enforcement can also share best practices in investigation. Although geography is also becoming less important for law enforcement than it was, the advantage is smaller for them than for criminals because of the different regimes under which police forces in different jurisdictions live. An investigatory step that may be legal and easy in one jurisdiction may require a warrant in another, and may even not be possible at all in a third.

It has always been true that there is an asymmetry between crime and law enforcement because law enforcement must try to prevent *every* crime, while a criminal is a success by committing *any* crime. This asymmetry becomes more obvious when the effort required to prevent, investigate, or (especially) prosecute a crime increases, while the cost to a criminal to commit one decreases (and especially when even an unsuccessful crime cannot be traced to its perpetrator so that attempts are free). Cyberspace has exactly this effect.

The final change that cyberspace creates is that data is valuable in a way it never was before. There has always, of course, been a market for stealing trade secrets, tender bid amounts, and strategic thinking for both businesses and governments; but scale and access has made these conventional crimes easier.

And there is a new kind of data stored in cyberspace, *personally identifiable information* (PII), which is valuable for identity theft, for people trafficking, and for blackmail and extortion. Before cyberspace, personally identifiable information of course existed but it was hidden away, piecemeal, in many different places that all required physical access to acquire. Finding the profile of an individual that might have taken a week of intense work fifty years ago can be assembled in less than an hour from online sources, and at much lower cost.

2.4 Encryption

Traffic in cyberspace travels from source to destination along pipes and through nodes and switches that cannot be controlled by either the source or the destination. Anyone along the path can see the contents of all communication and read it unless the content is concealed. That is why encryption is so important, and becoming so common.

Encryption maps readable content (the *plaintext*) into a form that conceals that content (the *ciphertext*) in such a way that the mapping can be reversed, but only by a recipient who has the right knowledge (called the *key*).

The encryption/decryption mapping must have the property that two almost identical plaintexts map to very different ciphertexts and two almost identical ciphertexts must have originated from very different plaintexts. In other words, no structures in the plaintext are preserved into the ciphertext, so that there is no way to infer the content from any pattern detectable in the ciphertext.

In its simplest form, called *private key encryption*, the sender has an encryption key, and the receiver has a related decryption key. The sender encrypts a message with the encryption key and the sender decrypts it with the decryption key. Ideally, anyone who does not have the key can only decrypt the message with an impossibly large amount of computational work.

One of the oldest forms of private key encryption is the *Caesar cipher*, in which a message is encrypted by replacing each letter by the one, say, four to its right in the alphabet, with wraparound (so 'a' becomes 'e' and 'z' becomes 'd'). Messages are decrypted by replacing each letter in the ciphertext by the one four places to its left. The number 4 is the shared private key but the sender and receiver use it in a slightly different way (+4 versus −4). Replacing symbols one by one makes encrypted messages easy to decrypt because it preserves the symbol frequencies. The letter 'e' is the most common in English, so the symbol that appears most often in the encrypted message is probably the encrypted value of 'e' and from that the offset can be trivially inferred.

The obvious extension is to make the mapping of each symbol depend on the entire set of previous symbols – called *polyalphabetic substitution*. This was the mechanism behind the Enigma machines used by the Axis powers in the Second World War, and it immediately made decryption so difficult that computers had to be invented before messages could be decrypted.

Private-key systems can be made hard to decrypt, but they have a serious weakness: there has to be a way to get the key(s) to both the sender and receiver safely. They cannot really be sent using a separate private-key system, because then those keys have to be distributed and the problem has just been pushed back a step. They should not be based on previous private keys for then, if the system were ever broken, the ongoing keys would also be compromised. In the end, there is little choice but to transfer the keys physically, with the risks of real-world interception and copying.

The development of *public-key encryption* avoids (mostly) the key-distribution problem. In public-key encryption systems, each person has a private key that only they know, and which is used to decrypt messages sent to them. There is also an encryption key, known as the public key, which can be used by anyone to encrypt messages for that person. The two keys have inverse effects – a message encrypted using the public key can be decrypted only by using the private key. Unlike private key systems, though, there is no accessible relationship between the encryption and decryption keys: there is no practical way to infer the private key from the public key.

The public key, as its name suggests, is not secret and can be told to anyone. Its only use to is encrypt a message in such a way that only the holder of the private key can decrypt it[3]. The private key, on the other hand, must be kept secret.

Public-key encryption systems make it possible to use encryption for almost all data transfers in cyberspace. They protect the contents of messages from being read by others even if the messages are intercepted. However, they do not prevent nodes and switches from observing the sizes and timing of data transfers which may also often be revealing. Looking at the "envelopes" of communication (without looking inside them) is called *traffic analysis*.

All public-key systems have the property that the private key has an inverse effect to the public key; otherwise the plaintext of messages could not be recreated from the ciphertext. Many also have the property that the public key has an inverse effect to the private key. In other words, data altered by applying the private key can be extracted from its encrypted form by applying the public key, the opposite sequence to their usual use.

When this is the case, the public-key mechanism can also be used for *digital signing*. Suppose that the owner of a private key applies it to a document. Anyone who knows the corresponding public key can apply it to get back the original document – but the fact that the result is sensible content and not gibberish shows that it must have been the holder of the private key who encrypted it. Thus documents can be produced whose author is knowable and the author cannot later repudiate such documents.

Encryption can also be used to generate a *digital hash*. In this case the encrypted version is of fixed size, and the process is one-way – there is no need for a decryption capability. A side-effect of the need of encryption algorithms to map very similar inputs to completely different outputs is that the mapping must use all of the pieces of the input as part of the process. Digital hashing produces a compact representation that depends on all of the content of the original data, but with the usual encryption property that all of the original structure has disappeared in the encrypted version. Knowing the digital hash, it is effectively impossible to recreate the original data.

Of course, because the target encrypted string is of fixed length there will be multiple original data strings that will map to the same encrypted string; but the structure of the encryption guarantees that these will be spread out through the space of possible initial strings. It also guarantees that knowing the encrypted string does not help to reverse engineer any string that will map to it.

Digital hashes are a special form of a *digest* of an original string. They are often used when downloading software. The software's author will apply a digital hash to it, and post the resulting digital hash string, along with the software for downloading. Someone who downloads the software can apply the same digital hashing algorithm to the software after download and check that the hash result is the same as the one provided by the author.

Digital hashes are used in law enforcement to create digests of, for example, child pornography images. When such an image is encountered, its digital hash can be computed and compared to the entries in a database to see if it has been encountered before by other law enforcement agencies. This comparison is done on the hashes, not on the original images, avoiding the need to have a shared dataset of the images themselves. Such a dataset would itself be a target for criminals.

One of the tensions between law enforcement and encryption arises because encrypted messages cannot be decrypted by law enforcement, without the decryption key[4]. This is not the result of wilfulness by the software or hardware manufacturers.

The essential, but poorly understood, point is that there is no backdoor way to read an encrypted message, other than by using the appropriate key to decrypt it. There is no halfway house where decryption can only be done by the good guys.

Encryption is used by everyone who wants to be able to communicate privately. Not all secrets are guilty secrets. Organizations need to be able to plan their strategies, tactics, marketing, pricing, and delivery without their competitors being able to find these out. Encryption has many innocuous uses, but of course criminals and terrorists take advantage of it as well.

The only way to allow law enforcement warrant-based access to encrypted content is to force everyone to place their decryption keys in escrow, where they could be accessed based on a warrant.

This scheme has major, and in the end fatal, flaws. First, there is no way to force communicators to acquire their keys in the jurisdiction that wants to be able to do decryption, and no way to know that other keys (from somewhere else) exist and are being used.

Criminals can encrypt their communications using the externally acquired key, and then again using the national (escrowed) key. It is not obvious that the inner layer of encryption even exists until law enforcement attempt a warranted decryption, and discover that the decrypted content is strings of meaningless symbols. Criminals can claim that the decrypted content is actually data, which often looks like strings of meaningless symbols, so it is not surprising that it cannot be "read". The claim is difficult to refute.

Second, and more seriously, the escrowed decryption keys would have to be kept somewhere and this repository instantly becomes a high-value target for criminals, and indeed other governments. Both cyber and physical security for the escrow repository would be critical. As well as defending it against outside attackers, there would also have to a serious defence against insiders using the keys for personal or political purposes. Very few countries would trust their governments to maintain such a repository of valuable information safely, or to grant access only under an appropriate judicial process. And, of course, its existence creates an inverse to the key distribution problem since all of these keys would have to be collected at the escrow location in a secure way that could not be intercepted.

The bottom line is that there is no halfway point in the debate about encryption versus non-encryption. Encrypted data is hidden from everyone but the decryption key holder; unencrypted data is visible to everyone in the world who cares to look for it. The second alternative is untenable – too dangerous to be acceptable to ordinary people – so law enforcement will have to deal with the fact that most data will be encrypted, and so most communication cannot be intercepted and decrypted.

Lessig[5] has argued that human social systems are constrained by four properties:

- Laws, where violations have financial or physical consequences;
- Norms, where violations are punished by relational consequences;
- Market forces, which act in a distributed way to limit how much any individual or organization can do; and
- Architectural constraints, which make only certain actions possible within any system.

The problems that cyberspace causes for law enforcement can be understand within this framework. Both laws and norms are only weakly effective in cyberspace, primarily because of issues around identity. When an action cannot be definitively connected to its perpetrator, the consequences from laws or norms cannot be brought home to the person who deserves them. As the New Yorker cartoon caption has it[6], "On the Internet, nobody knows you're a dog". Market forces provide some constraints, but many potentially problematic activities (sending emails) are free to users because there is no plausible way to charge for them, while others (accessing web sites) are free to users because businesses want consumers to access their information and interact with them, and so bear the cost of web servers and communication networks. Cyberspace has the common problem that those who pay for it, and those who use it are not the same people, so financial constraints do not work well. Architectural constraints are few because of cyberspace's origins and rapid growth, and its inherently distributed nature. Of all human systems, cyberspace is extremely unconstrained for something that is global in scale and reach, and through which so much of society's actions take place. It is not surprising that criminals have taken advantage.

2.5 Crime is changing

The growth of cyberspace has changed the face of crime in three ways. First, new crimes directed against cyberspace itself have come into existence: crimes that steal things that exist online, crimes that destroy online data or infrastructure, and crimes that can be monetized such as extortion, threatening to disable critical facilities, as well as crimes akin to vandalism – defacing web sites or denying access to online services. There are also crimes in cyberspace that are enablers of other kinds of crime: planting malware on computers, and selling tools and cybertools, including attacks in a box.

Second, there are crimes that are conventional but which happen in a different way (usually faster or at scale) because of cyberspace. These include scams and confidence tricks, crimes against the financial system, frauds, thefts leveraging online shopping, and distributing child pornography and related crimes of sexploitation and grooming.

Third, there are crimes that are conventional but have moved, at least partly, into cyberspace because they can more easily be carried out there. These include drug trafficking, speech crimes such as cyberbullying, obscenity, abuse and hate, and stalking. Of course, many crimes do not all fit neatly into the three categories, but the categories provide some sense of how the landscape has changed.

Money laundering, moving the proceeds of crime into the legitimate financial system, overlaps the second two categories. It is essential to so many crimes that we consider it separately.

Some of these cybercrimes exist because of the greater speed, scale, and reach of cyberspace. For example, finding someone gullible enough to fall for a confidence trick used to require a lot of work. Mass email has made this much easier, since it is now plausible to find the gullible one in a million at low cost. In fact, this has worked so well that scammers deliberately make their pitches seem implausible so that only the really, really gullible will respond to them. This reduces their own subsequent work required to qualify the targets and take advantage of them.

Other cybercrimes exist because of the security weaknesses in cyberspace. For example, stealing money from a financial institution relies on weaknesses in the design of web-browser security mechanisms, weaknesses in authentication designed by the banks themselves and the costs this imposes on ordinary customers, and weaknesses in each bank's own cyberinfrastructure itself.

Cybercrimes also flourish because of the anonymity with which users can act in cyberspace. Because attribution of any particular action is inherently difficult, and often time-consuming, it is extremely difficult to work out exactly who has committed a crime. Cyberspace makes it almost impossible to meet the standard of "beyond reasonable doubt" in connecting an individual to a crime.

The global nature of cyberspace also has two major impacts on the landscape of crime. First, it means that criminals can collaborate across the whole world, learning ideas and techniques from one another, and exchanging tools. Online learning enables anyone who wants to to learn how to be a better criminal, and to find others who can mentor or join in criminal activity.

Second, criminals can act anywhere while law enforcement live in a system of nations and national borders. From a law enforcement perspective, each country has its own legal system that delimits what is criminal, and perhaps more importantly, what kinds of data can be collected and shared about criminal activity. Criminals do not face these kinds of constraints and can carry out a crime in whatever jurisdiction makes it easiest, most lucrative, and hardest to detect or prosecute. They mostly need not live in the target country.

Of course, law enforcement has always cooperated on cross-border issues but these have often focused on physically adjacent neighbors with close and detailed cooperation, and then much less tightly coupled with supranational organizations such as Interpol for interactions at greater distance. Cyberspace does not really have borders, and a cybercrime is as likely to originate from some distant jurisdiction, with a different language and legal code, as from a neighboring one.

2.6 Policing is changing

The changing nature of crime because of cyberspace is creating many new challenges for law enforcement – but also some new advantages.

One of the biggest challenges is that crimes that happen in cyberspace or leverage it are often invisible. Of course, crimes with a direct financial impact are detectable but even then not immediately. For example, an ordinary person might notice that their pocket was picked almost immediately but it will usually take much longer to notice an illicit transfer from their bank account.

The problem of invisibility is even worse for data, because stealing data only requires taking a *copy* of it, so little trace is left because the data is still exactly where it was before.

Actions in cyberspace are routinely captured in logs of various kinds: communication sessions, web traffic, or even user commands issued. These can be a rich source of information about things that have happened, including bad things, but there are multiple issues. Logs are extremely large so finding the useful information is difficult, even after the fact. They are almost never watched in real time when they could provide an alert that something bad was underway (the false positive problem is what prevents this). The information they contain is relatively easy to spoof, since the Internet's basic communication mechanisms do not protect either the source or destination addresses of communication. The time stamps of actions captured by logs can also be altered to make it seem as if recent attack actions actually happened some time ago. Logs can also be altered retrospectively, or deleted altogether by a modestly knowledgeable criminal.

Legal frameworks and the procedures designed to comply with them often lag behind what criminals are actually doing, even when it is clear that their actions should be discouraged. This is especially true for what might be called brand new crimes in cyberspace, rather than just adaptations of conventional crimes to the new environment. Cybercrimes are often prosecuted using sections of the criminal code that were designed for real-world versions of crimes. These are not necessarily a good fit so that there may be questions about how best to prosecute even when it seems clear that a crime has been committed. For example, the provision in Canada's criminal code that makes it a crime to install malware comes from the Anti-Spam Legislation, but Section 430(1.1) of the Criminal Code (mischief to data) could also be applied. Neither of these actually seems to describe installing malware particularly well.

The problem is compounded because legislators, prosecutors and judges often do not really understand cyberspace and therefore have no sense of what is possible or the extent to which any particular action is consequential or not.

The scale and speed with which criminals can act in cyberspace also poses a challenge for law enforcement. For example, a spam email containing a confidence trick such as the Nigerian Prince scam can reach tens of thousands of people before anyone in law enforcement learns of it. Then it may take a day before warnings about it can be spread via the media, by which time some will have fallen for it. A day later the Nigerian Prince has transformed into a Middle Eastern businessman and the cycle begins again.

Law enforcement must also face the inherent asymmetry between being in the position of a defender and the position of an attacker. Criminals can exploit any opportunity they find to commit a crime, but law enforcement is expected by society to defend against all of them. In the past, the societal view of law enforcement understood that crimes could be detected after they happened, and then their perpetrators prosecuted, but there was much less that could be done to prevent crimes, other than basic hardening such as using better locks and safes.

This understanding has changed, perhaps because of an inchoate understanding by ordinary people that planning for crimes can leave detectable traces and data analytics could potentially be used to detect them. The issue was brought to a head in the movie *Minority Report* which depicted a world in which crimes were predicted in advance, and their would-be perpetrators arrested beforehand. The reasons why this is not even faintly plausible are subtle and so hard to explain to society at large; and often law-enforcement personnel themselves are not sure why this is an unworkable idea.

National borders also frustrate attempts to prosecute the criminals responsible for a crime in one jurisdiction when they live in another. The U.S. has made a practice of indicting cybercriminals, even when they have no chance of being arrested because they live in a jurisdiction where their actions are not criminal, where there is no extradition agreement, or even where their government is complicit in the cybercrime – but this "naming and shaming" is mostly a token gesture.

On the other hand, cyberspace does make collaboration between law enforcement within each country and across borders easier. Sharing of criminals' methods is straightforward, especially with the knowledge that something that worked in one place is likely to be tried in many others.

Modeling techniques using data analytics can also be shared so that successful detection tools can be used in other jurisdictions. This can range from something as simple as the signatures of malware up to the way in which cartels organize drug-smuggling routes.

The most problematic aspect of sharing is the sharing of data – about individual criminals and individual crimes. Privacy regimes, which differ substantially across jurisdictions, limit what can legitimately be shared. This is further complicated by differences in what constitutes a crime or a criminal and, at a practical level, the differences in the way that data is formatted in different police forces.

The availability of data is one of the major ways in which law enforcement can gain an advantage over criminals. This has a long history. More than a century ago, police forces started building files in which they captured the *modus operandi* of each criminal, relying on the fact that criminals, like the rest of us, have habitual ways of doing anything, including carrying out crimes. *Bertillon measurement* filing systems allowed individuals to be identified in a world where identity was a fleeting thing (as it is now online); and these measurements were quickly supplanted by fingerprints[7].

Large amounts of data about criminals and their activities is still being collected, and can be queried, to ask questions like "Has there been a crime with these five properties before".

The change in the use and usefulness of this collected data came with the insight that data analytics can increase the payoffs from such data. When data has to be queried, an analyst must think of a good question to ask. In contrast, in data analytics, algorithms build models consistent with the data and push these to analysts, whose role is to decide whether they are plausible and actionable. Less analyst cleverness is required, and the algorithms will detect and expose patterns that it might not have occurred to an analyst to look for.

This property of data analytics is an important part of *intelligence-led policing*. However, the inductive nature of the process is hard to understand, and may seem somewhat magical at first. Police forces lack sufficient personnel to take on the new roles that are required, and to be able to explain data analytics to higher levels of management.

Cyberspace has changed the way criminals act, and the crimes they commit. It requires complex changes by law enforcement to respond, almost always running behind and with budget limitations, as well as the inertia of having always done it this way.

Notes

[1]Technically, smart phones, but so few phones are not smart phones that it is hardly worth making the distinction.

[2]There is considerable confusion between dark web and deep web, so beware when you read about them.

[3]The public key can be left easily accessible, for example on the receiver's web site. However, although the public key's distribution is easy, it is harder to be sure that it is actually the key that belongs to the receiver, as it is supposed to. This issue requires a whole other infrastructure of *certificates* that exist to connect public keys with their owners.

[4]There have been cases where decryption has been possible without the decryption key, but these are the results of weak encryption mechanisms that failed to take account of increasing computational performance, or poor implementations of the encryption. This is one reason why use of a few standard encryption software packages is suggested, rather than letting each organization develop its own.

[5]L. Lessig, *The laws of cyberspace*, in: R.A. Spinello and H.T. Tavani, (eds.), *Readings in Cyberethics*, pp. 134–145. Jones & Bartlett Learning, 2004.

[6]New Yorker, July 5th 1993.

[7]J.E. Hoover, "Criminal identification", *The Annals of the American Academy of Political and Social Science*, 146:205–213, 1929.

Chapter 3

New opportunities for criminality

Cyberspace has changed the opportunities available to criminals because of the following properties, which we discussed in the previous chapter:

- The scale at which it operates, and the speed of actions that it enables.
- The weaknesses inherent in a system that was built for sharing in a trusted and accountable environment, but is now accessible to half the world's population.
- The absence of a single management system which in turn prevents consistent design choices about new functionality, especially security.
- The lack of authentication systems to associate each online identity with the real person to whom it corresponds.
- The connectivity it provides to find ideas, people, and tools.
- The fact that national borders play almost no role in its structure.

In this chapter, we explore how these properties of cyberspace have enabled new kinds of crime and so new ways for criminals to act.

3.1 Unprecedented access to information

For all of us, the world's knowledge is at our fingertips, including some of the less savory aspects of that knowledge. For criminals this means access to an encyclopedia of crime from which they can learn. When crime was limited by geography, teaching someone else how to commit a crime created a competitor, but now the student is probably going to commit the crime thousands of kilometers away. There is much less disincentive to produce criminal how-tos and post them online. Prisons are

DOI: 10.1201/9781003126225-3

notoriously places where criminals learn to be better criminals, but this role is being usurped by the World Wide Web.

Criminals can also learn from law enforcement in perhaps unintended ways. Law enforcement organizations have always produced reports about the kinds of patterns of crime they have seen, and often details about how these crimes were committed. When these reports were physical, their distribution could be controlled, and kept within the circle of other law-enforcement organizations. Now they are often posted online, where criminals, as well as law-enforcement professionals, can access them and learn from them.

Cyberspace has also become a place for criminals to connect. These connections can be used:

- To find other criminals. Historically, criminals collaborated with other criminals because of ordinary family or social connections, or because they provided a missing skill required for a particular crime. But these collaborators were almost inevitably local.

  Collaboration always brings costs: greater opportunities for betrayal, and more people to split the proceeds with, so there is always an incentive not to collaborate. The study of *cooffender networks*, criminals who committed crimes together, produced insights into the balance between the benefits and costs of collaboration for criminals.

  The ability to find others with missing skill sets online, and so beyond the natural circle of acquaintances and geography, provides greater opportunities for functional collaboration, and less incentive to simply collaborate with friends and family for crimes where physical proximity is not important. As in the regular working world this increases the demand for the very best individuals with each skill, and the corresponding rewards.

  On the other hand, it is difficult to trust someone who is only an identity in cyberspace, and easy to renege on a promised cut to someone who is far away, so there are practical problems with this kind of collaboration. So far, there has been more success with violent extremists recruiting would-be extremists online than criminals recruiting criminals.

- To buy tools needed to commit crimes, especially cyber tools. Some crimes require specialized hardware to commit them, and these tools cannot be bought from Amazon. However, specialists with either workshop skills, or the ability to use 3d printing can produce such tools, and sell them in ways that are hard to track. The tools needed for cyber attacks are even easier to buy online because they can be delivered digitally, and sellers spend as much effort to build one as to build 500. (This has the fortunate side-effect that a defence against one copy of a particular cybertool will work against all of the other copies. Sellers must choose either to make money by selling many copies of a cybertool knowing that its life span is probably limited, or selling fewer copies at a higher price expecting that its lifespan will be longer because of less frequent use by more knowledgeable buyers.)

- To plan. The ability to communicate quickly and constantly, along with ability to encrypt communication, means that criminal groups, and especially larger criminal groups, can plan and manage complex crimes in a way that would not have been possible in pre-cyberspace settings. For example, drug-trafficking networks often span several continents, a pipeline moving a valuable commodity which is easy to purloin at any stage. Communication enables close supervision using cyberspace which in turn means that stealing from the organization is more difficult. The ability to communicate also means that the pipeline can respond to law-enforcement actions by changing plans quickly.

The dark web has become an important place for these connections to take place because of a perception that it is free from prying law-enforcement eyes[1]. Web sites within the dark web are used for discussion forums, including teaching skills and making connections, and for marketplaces where both the physical tools of crime (lockpicks) and cyber attack tools can be bought.

Social-media platforms provide a place for groups to interact, but criminals do not seem to use them much, perhaps suspecting that they are open to observation, at least by the platform owners. There are a number of social-media platforms that support end-to-end encrypted communication, and these have been colonized by criminals who use them to plan and coordinate, knowing that it is exceedingly unlikely that their actions can be intercepted. One of the most popular at the moment (2021) is Telegram (telegram.org) which also makes messages disappear after a period of time.

Cyberspace has revolutionized the ability of criminal to communicate and collaborate, and so has changed many kinds of crimes. However, this capability is only available to criminals who are intelligent enough to use cyberspace, and to do so carefully enough that they do not make silly mistakes that expose their interactions[2].

3.2 Crimes directed against cyberspace

We now turn to the effect of cyberspace on crime itself. The first category is the most novel – crimes that exist only because cyberspace exists. In other words, the target of the crime is some aspect of cyberspace itself.

We begin with *enabling crimes*, crimes that do not make an profit for criminals directly but are a necessary step to allow other crimes to happen.

3.2.1 Malware

The first category of enabling crimes is implanting *malware* on target devices, which could be personal computers, phones, web servers, data servers, clouds, or Internet of Things (IoT) devices. This malware can be then be used to enable or carry out other crimes.

Malware includes all software that causes a system to do something that its owner did not want it to do, or at least give permission for it to do. Malware's effects can range from covert use of the resources of a system in ways we will discuss later, to complete destruction of the system. The key property is that malware gives a bad actor access to some part of the functionality of a system without the knowledge or permission of the system's owner.

Many devices run antivirus and antimalware software that is intended to detect attempts to insert malware into those devices. However, these almost always work by matching incoming software against the signatures of known malware so:

- They are always working to catch up with the latest malware. The providers of the signatures of known malware constantly scan the Internet for new malware and create new signatures when they find it. However, there is always a window when new malware could be inserted, before the signatures of the detection system have been updated to reflect its existence[3].

- The malware may come in many slightly different forms (*polymorphic malware*), functionally equivalent but superficially different, so that each form does not quite match the signature.

Antivirus and antimalware tools therefore offer quite limited protection against malware, especially from sophisticated attackers.

There are two different ways of getting malware onto a target computer. The easiest is to get the user of that computer to allow the malware to be installed without realizing that they are doing so. There are five common ways this can happen:

- The user installs an app or piece of software. Some apps available for download contain hidden malware that can execute quietly while the apps are doing what they are supposed to do (so there is no sign to the user that anything is wrong). There is no easy way for an ordinary user to decide when or whether an app contains malware, so we must rely on others, either malware detection software or the curators of the sites from which we downloaded it. For example, Google and Apple both vet apps available through their app stores for phones (although not always successfully); and Microsoft tries to limit the ability of ordinary users to download software except via their app store where they have also done some vetting.

  Simple hygiene measures can also help. There are some parts of the world that are more notorious than others for malware, and downloading from sites in these countries should be avoided. On the other hand, there is no reason why someone who wants to push malware cannot buy a website in a neutral country and so make it look less risky to download and install their software.

- The user visits a web site that downloads malware disguised as something else. When a web site is loaded into a browser, the viewable page that is presented to the user is a construct that has many different parts which have usually come from many different web servers. For example, the basic textual content may have come from one server, the images from another, and the advertisements from yet another. A user cannot control where these pieces come from (and cannot usually even tell) and so a web server can be compromised to serve malware disguised as, say, images without anyone noticing for a while.

  Not all of the content of a web page is static. Two-way communication requires the ability to collect data from the user via the browser and send it back to a web server, and this is done by downloading a small piece of code from the web site. A criminal can subvert the normal process to download instead, or as well, a piece of code which either is malware (but with limited functionality because it must run within the browser) or which downloads the malware separately, and installs it silently.

  The sheer complexity of what happens when a high-end web page is loaded makes it difficult to discover exploits like these; and the ability to have several tabs open in a browser at once creates extra vulnerabilities because actions can bleed from one to the other[4].

- The user clicks a link thinking it points to one place, while it actually points somewhere else. The link text for a hyperlink has no necessary association with the web site that it takes you to, so it is always slightly risky to click and follow a link. However, reputable web sites are careful about this, and browsers work hard to make sure that links in web pages are reasonably safe. For convenience, links are often embedded in other settings, notably inside documents and email messages, where it can be much harder to decide if clicking a link is safe. Any such a link may point to a site that downloads and installs malware.

- The user receives a phishing email. *Phishing* is the sending of an innocent-looking email that contains an attachment that will install malware when it is opened. Attachments are commonly used to pass documents from one person to another. Although a document seems like it should be just a container for text, many formatted documents can contain executable code. For example, a Microsoft Word document can contain macros which are designed to automate repetitive tasks such as formatting a letterhead so that it fits whatever paper size the recipient uses (letter vs A4, say), but which are powerful enough for arbitrary programming.

  Phishing emails can be sent at random, so at targets of opportunity, or sent to an entire group within a business in the hope that at least one of them will click on the attachment. Emails like this must seem faintly plausible since many people are now aware that they should not click on an attachment from someone they do not know. However, the From: addresses of emails can easily be spoofed, so such an email can be made to appear to come from a sender such as the Human Resources department, or even the CEO. Phishing is essentially opportunistic. It relies on a small fraction of recipients opening the attachment, either because of naïvety or distraction.

- The user received a spearphishing email. *Spearphishing*, as the name suggests, is an individually targeted form of phishing. It uses a carefully crafted email to send a malware attachment. The email is designed to appear so plausible, and perhaps expected, that the recipient will feel safe opening the attachment. Such emails are often directed at individuals who have access to the more powerful parts of business or government IT systems, so that the malware, if it gets installed, can do more damage.

  Spearphishing is more expensive for criminals because they must find out enough about each target individual to craft an email that does not set off a mental alarm in the receiver. This is difficult because targets who have greater access are usually more aware of security issues (although there have been some monumental exceptions). The email must seem to come from a trusted sender. The attachment must also appear legitimate, even after it has been opened because otherwise the recipient would realize that something significant has happened. Spearphishing is expensive, but the potential payoff of getting malware into a more carefully protected location means that is becoming more and more common[5].

The other way to get malware onto a system is to use a direct attack, exploiting weaknesses in the design of devices and, more importantly, the network connections between them. This is considerably more difficult than an attack in which the target unwittingly colludes.

Most computer systems and devices have security weaknesses. The attacks that leverage such weaknesses are called *zero day attacks* since they rely on a hole in security that can be exploited immediately.

When such a weakness is discovered, the discoverer usually informs whoever is responsible for the implementation of the relevant system, who produces a fix and makes it available, usually on a predictable release cycle. Those who are vulnerable can protect themselves until the fix is propagated by the implementer by adding extra security features, or turning off some functionality temporarily.

Security vulnerabilities are also made public so that sites know that they have an issue, whether or not they are immediately fixable[6]. These bulletins describe what software is vulnerable but do not explain how to exploit it. The unfortunate side-effect of this publicity is that criminals get to know of each vulnerability and may be able to exploit it before it can be fixed.

If the discoverer of a vulnerability goes direct to the implementer, and then the implementer releases a fix, the details of how to exploit the vulnerability may not be public. However, criminals reverse engineer the publicized fix to discover what the vulnerability was, so that they can exploit it at sites that do not apply the fix.

Sometimes weaknesses are not publicized by the discoverer but instead sold either to criminals or government signals intelligence agencies, both of whom can use it to attack systems, although with different motivations. The problem with zero day attacks is that their use gives away their existence, so that the underlying vulnerability will be fixed. They therefore have a limited shelf life.

In an effort to discourage discoverers from selling vulnerabilities, software designers are increasing offering *bug bounties*, payments to discoverers who report weaknesses to those who can fix them rather than to those will use them for attacks.

Systems, especially large and complex ones, may not have installed all of the currently available updates and fixes. Organizations fear that doing so may break their core business systems, and so they test them in protected environments first. This can take time. Sometimes large organizations simply do not have the resources to install every update or fix in a timely way. As a result, there will always be organizations that are vulnerable to attacks, even though these attack pathways are well-known, and fixes to them are available[7].

An attacker can look for systems that have not been fixed and either install malware on them directly or use them as stepping stones to install malware on more valuable systems. Devices such as printers are often ignored, but they are usually fully fledged computer systems and their functionality enables them to be useful stepping stones, all the more so as they are often invisible to defenders.

Large organizations also tend to have large numbers of zombie computers that are receiving no attention. Either they are no longer needed for their original purpose, or their task has been fully automated and forgotten. Such computers are juicy targets for bad actors since they may not be routinely updated and so contain vulnerabilities ripe for exploitation. The problem is getting worse as these zombie computers are actually virtual, that is they look like entire computers but they run within an existing physical computer. This makes them invisible and so easy to forget.

3.2.2 Crimes of destruction

Because so many organizations rely on cyberspace for their core activities, they are vulnerable to crimes that destroy their ability to act. These crimes can range from something similar to cyber vandalism up to crippling attacks that can disable an organization for weeks or months.

Most organizations, of all sizes, have at least a web site that explains what they do. Such web sites are powered by web servers which tend to be separated from the systems that run other aspects of the business. Web servers are often not well-protected from cyber attacks, perhaps because of the perception that they are a marketing function rather than a core business activity. As a result, they are often open to attack from:

- Opportunistic attackers. These are often the online equivalent of people who draw graffiti on walls. They are interested in their own reputations rather than, necessarily, the particular organization being attacked.
- Disgruntled customers or citizens. The attackers have some gripe with the organization and use the attack as a way to signal their displeasure.
- Protest groups. They may have no direct quarrel with the organization concerned but are looking for visibility and media coverage.
- Other nation's governments. They may use the attack to create an impression of incompetence or uncertainty in the organization. For example, defacing a government department's web site may create an impression of incompetence.

Remediating web site attacks is straightforward, and web-site attacks could mostly be avoided if organizations paid more attention to correctly configuring their servers.

Many organizations also have a portal that enables them to interact with customers (businesses), donors (non-profits), or citizens (governments). A more serious kind of destructive crime is a *denial of service* attack. Here the goal of the attack is to prevent the organization from carrying out the functions that happen at these portals: online shopping for a business, accepting donations for a non-profit, and filing taxes or renewing licences for a government.

The basic strategy is to keep the portal so busy dealing with fake useless requests that it is unable to find and deal with the real requests in the middle of the others. In the real-world this corresponds to sending many people into a store to mill around without buying anything, so preventing genuine customers from being able to buy anything either.

A simple denial of service attack requires an attacker to send lots of seemingly meaningful traffic to the target site. The obvious way to do this, send traffic from the attacker's device, used to work quite well but fails today for several reasons. First the target is most likely to be a domain (of the form multinational.com) rather than a specific target computer. An organization typically maps incoming requests for this domain address onto particular computers as they arrive, as a form of load spreading. This has the side-effect of forcing the attacker to be able to generate traffic faster than the entire set of target computers can deal with it, which is difficult. Second, if all of the attack traffic comes from the same address, the system under attack can dynamically change its *firewall*[8] rules to discard all traffic from that address, so the attack traffic never reaches its systems. This response can be automated: when traffic from a particular site crosses some threshold, discard it all temporarily.

A more powerful form of attack relies on the fact that the computer addresses used by network traffic are easy to spoof. The attacker can use this to create a multiplier effect that harnesses innocent computers to generate traffic to the target. For example, many kinds of traffic require the destination to either acknowledge a request or send a "Not known at this address" response. An attacker can send traffic to many innocent computers, spoofed so that it appears to come from the target of the denial of service attack All of the response messages will be sent to the target, and from many different directions.

This may still not generate enough traffic to overwhelm a target website. The third, and most effective method, is to use a *botnet*. Botnets are sets of computing devices, often Internet of Things devices, that have had malware inserted into them. This malware, rather than doing any direct harm to the infected systems, makes them controllable remotely by a botnet controller, which can direct any subset of the bots to carry out a particular task.

Those who have created botnets (sometimes called *bot herders*) rent them out to others who want to use them for a task where scale is important. Denial of service is one such task. This kind of large-scale denial of service attack where the attacking devices are geographically heterogeneous, and of many different kinds is called a *Distributed denial of service* attack (DDoS attack). These attacks are much harder to defend against because there is no simple firewall rule that can block the attack traffic while letting ordinary traffic through; and because botnets can be very large, large enough to overwhelm even large web platforms. Prices for a modestly sized botnet are in the tens of dollars range for an hour's use, and botnets with half a million nodes exist.

Since data now has value in a new way, another class of destructive crimes are those that delete data stored online. Organizations that are careful to maintain good and thorough backups are less susceptible to this kind of crime, but a surprisingly large number are not so careful, especially small- and medium-sized enterprises. Destroying data is essentially another form of cyber vandalism since the attackers have no interest in the data as such – just the impact on a target organization because of its destruction.

3.2.3 Monetized cybercrimes

The problem for criminals trying to monetize crime in cyberspace is that tracing money transfers within the financial system is much easier than tracking cash. Fortunately for cybercriminals, the development of *cryptocurrencies* has made more or less anonymous financial transfers possible.

Cryptocurrencies break the connection between the sender of a payment and its receiver. Although transactions are public[9] and tied to the actors involved, these actors are represented by cryptographic keys which are not necessarily traceably tied to individuals.

Monetized cybercrimes use cryptocurrency extracted from victims and paid to criminals, who can then turn it back into value within the conventional financial system.

Extracting cryptocurrency direct from the digital wallets of people who use it for other purposes is digital theft. Access to a digital wallet full of cryptocurrency requires a key, which like most encryption keys is represented by a long sequence of characters. It is not very practical to type this string in every time a transaction is made, so the strings end up stored on users' computers – where they become high-value targets. Attackers can either try to find the key, and then use it to empty the wallet by transferring the money to themselves; or insert a clipboard logger that detects when a long meaningless string is being copy/pasted and changes the destination address of a legitimate transfer so that it flows to them instead.

Cryptocurrency can also be used to pay ransoms in a way that does not link to the perpetrator, avoiding the perennial problem of collecting the proceeds of extortion and kidnapping. The most common cyber crime, and the most lucrative, is to install *ransomware* on a target's computer using phishing (or more probably spearphishing). Ransomware is specialized malware that encrypts the files on the target's computer, and then offers to decrypt them if a ransom is paid.

If the target's system has been properly backed up, then a ransomware attack is an annoyance; the system's files can be restored from backup and all that has been lost is some availability and the staff time needed to restore the files from backup. However, a startlingly large number of organizations, especially those of smaller size who lack dedicated systems staff, discover that they have not been doing proper backups, and so find themselves in a quandary when they are hit with a ransomware attack.

Like any extortion situation, organizations would prefer not to pay the ransom, but they may calculate that the cost of recreating a system with incomplete backups may be too high. Some organizations have found that this can take months.

Unfortunately, there is a further complication: the hacking tools necessary to carry out a ransomware attack can be bought on the dark web and used as a black box by unsophisticated criminals. They may not actually be able to decrypt the files, even if they wanted to. Thus organizations who opt to pay the ransom may find that their files remain encrypted anyway.

More sophisticated versions of ransomware attacks encrypt the files on the target system slowly in the hope that encrypted versions will be captured in the backups, as well as the running system. Fortunately, this level of sophistication in ransomware attacks remains rare. Ransomware attacks are also starting to be implemented via virtual machines (complete systems implemented in software) on the target computer to evade detection systems.

New variants of ransomware attacks are appearing. For example, ransomware is being extended to what might be called *embarrassware* – criminals combine encrypting files on the target system with exfiltrating some of the most potentially embarrassing data they find. The exfiltrated data might be examples of incompetence within the organization, customer complaints, inappropriate emails, or anything else that might increase the pressure to pay the ransom. They threaten the targets both with being unable to access their files, *and* with having their secrets made public. This dual pressure is designed to make targets more willing to pay the ransom. In another recent development, a psychologist's patient files were extracted as part of a ransomware attack, and each of the patients was individually asked to pay a ransom to stop their medical file from being released publicly.

There are limited defences against ransomware attacks. Tools exist that create files in random locations, and then regularly inspect their contents, watching for them to change. Since the user of the systems has no reason to touch them, any change is a signal that something, probably malware, is altering them. These files act as a tripwire, and an alarm can be sounded when changes are detected. The system can be shutdown before any more files are encrypted.

There is a growing market in ransomware insurance exactly because defences are difficult and attacks potentially so consequential. There is a vigorous debate about whether the existence of such insurance creates moral hazard, by encouraging businesses to cut corners on their cybersecurity. Pricing for such insurance is still fluctuating because it is such a new market, so pricing may, in time, reduce the apparent moral hazard.

Other forms of extortion are possible in cyberspace. For example, a denial of service attack can be followed up by a request to pay protection so that the DoS attack is not repeated.

3.2.4 Data theft crimes

Since data has value, there are new cybercrimes that involve purloining data. Organizations have many forms of data that could be valuable to someone else:

- *Intellectual property.* This includes all of the value that resides in a business that is, or will eventually be, protected by mechanisms such as patenting. This kind of data is valuable to an (unscrupulous) competitor. After patenting, the data is public, but an unscrupulous competitor from another country, especially one that does not support patent protection, may still be interested in the data. There will often be details that were not included in a patent filing but which would be useful to a would-be competitor.

- *Trade secrets.* This includes all of the knowledge in an organization that is not subject to patent protection. Many organizations also choose to keep knowledge that could, in theory, be protected by patent secret because its use by a competitor would not be obvious or detectable. This kind of data is more valuable to a competitor exactly because there is no other way to discover it.

  Governments, as well as businesses, are interested in knowledge held by other countries. Most national organizations restrict their data exfiltration activities to data that they perceive as relevant to their own national security, but others are not above passing useful data from other countries to their own national businesses.

- *Strategic planning.* This includes all of the knowledge of where a business or government plans to go, in terms of developing new products or new markets (for a business), or new weapons systems (for a government). The processes of decision making in other organizations are also of interest: board meetings (for a business) or political maneuvering (for a government). Knowledge of this kind of data enables competitors to plan their collaborations, or ways to undercut the planned directions or actions.

- *Tactics* – bids and tenders, marketing, release dates. This includes all of the knowledge of short-term actions planned by a business or government. Because of the timing, this kind of information is harder to exploit; but a business can undercut a competitor's bid if it knows what the amount will be, or release a product slightly earlier to get first-mover advantage.

When each organization's data was held in filing cabinets, extracting it was a difficult task, especially in volume, but data stored in online systems is a much easier target.

The general approach to stealing data is to use malware to gain entry to systems where the data is kept, and then find a way to transfer it out to the perpetrator's system, a process called *exfiltration*.

Unlike other kinds of malware, the intent of exfiltration malware is to remain undetected: obviously until the data has been exfiltrated, but also afterwards since otherwise the target organization may then change its actions. So exfiltration software may delete itself once the exfiltration has happened, and may work to clean up the traces it might have left in log files.

Exfiltration is more difficult for an attacker than many of the other crimes we have discussed. Large organizations have many computer systems with different purposes: some may be the personal computers of individual staff, other are web servers, or run the back-end systems such as payroll or stock control. The valuable data may be kept in a database server. A malware attack using, say spearphishing, may successfully introduce malware to one of the organization's personal computers, but then a path or chain has to be constructed from that compromised computer to the one that holds the valuable data. This requires a potentially sophisticated and complex process which is beyond the capabilities of many criminals. Of course, many pieces of confidential information are passed around using internal email or are stored on personal computers, so some kinds of data are easy to exfiltrate.

Organizations can defend against exfiltration attacks by having all of their document creation and editing tools insert special strings into every document within the organization, and then having firewall rules that forbid any data transfer containing those strings from leaving the organization's domain. This is not foolproof, but it increases the sophistication required by an attacker to have a chance of success.

Organizations can also, transparently, create many fake versions of every real document and use secret sharing to allow those who edit and read the documents to know which are the real ones. An attacker must then filter through a large number of fakes to try and find the real version. Fake documents can be built from real ones so that natural-language analysis techniques will not easily differentiate real documents from fakes[10].

Criminals can make money by using exfiltration to acquire valuable information. They may either be contracted to get particular data, or they may extract it and then try to find a buyer. Nations also have an interest in data theft for espionage. All nations use this to try and get insight into strategic thinking and even tactical planning of other nations, as well as to evaluate properties such as military strength. Some nations also combine espionage with industrial espionage, using their skills at data exfiltration to get data that can be used by state-supported businesses, as well as government.

3.2.5 Secondary markets

Some criminals make money by selling to other criminals. This is usually a great deal safer since selling in secondary criminal markets is hard to prosecute because the customers cannot complain. The dark web has been an enabler of this because it provides a way to handle sales and payment that decouples seller from buyer. Some platforms in the dark web even provide reputation management so that buyers can get some information about how reliable sellers have been in the past.

The three biggest products sold to other criminals are:

- Cyber tools (software) that can be used by others for cyber attacks. There is a considerable range of possibilities here, from zero-day attacks that require considerable sophistication to exploit, to attacks that are prepackaged so that they can be used by anyone, even with a low level of skill. For example prepackaged ransomware attacks or mass email spam tools can be purchased, as well as lists of email addresses against which they can be targeted.

  It is clear that some of the purchasers in such marketplaces lack even minimal skills to use black box products. Spam filters are full of completely misconfigured emails whose subject lines look like "[insert subject here]". One of the weaknesses of the global email framework is that it delivers emails even when they are clearly misconfigured, or when the From: addresses have clearly been spoofed.

  There are also users, presumably new to the Internet, who purchase email address lists, imagining that they can advertise legitimate products and services to large numbers of people and make their fortunes.

  In many jurisdictions, sending email spam is a criminal offence, but there is so much of it, and it comes from so many different jurisdictions that spam senders are hardly ever prosecuted.

  Much of the material for sale to other criminals amounts to preying on the purchasers who are too naïve to understand what they are buying and what its limitations are. But the pool of naïve would-be criminals is inexhaustible.

- Access to botnets for denial of service or extortion attacks. We have already described how botnets can be rented for DDoS attacks or other kinds of extortion. They are also sometimes used for email-based attacks, including phishing and spearphishing, against targets that might have blocked certain source addresses for emails. This provides a stable revenue stream for botnet owners, who often turn themselves into something resembling a conventional service business. For example, some have an open web presence, framing themselves as providing "load-testing services".

- *Personally identifiable information* (PII). Identity information can be used in multiple ways. The simplest is when names and associated credit card numbers are known, and this is perhaps the commonest PII that is sold online. It is doubtful how useful this information actually is. Using a credit card online requires knowing the CVV as well as the card number, and this is much harder to capture. For a long time, stolen credit card information was used to create fake physical credit cards because encoding information on a magnetic stripe could be done cheaply and easily – but the widespread use of chip cards has made this less viable. (However, there are some countries where swiping a credit card and signing a credit slip is still commonplace. This makes it easy to use a fake credit card since there is no real-time check on its legitimacy.)

  Lists of user names and passwords are also readily available, Buying these makes it possible to log into accounts and insert malware without the overheads of phishing or malware-insertion attacks. However, most purchasers probably want to use user name/password combinations to search accounts for directly valuable data such as bank account login details, Although all users should either not leave banking access details on a computer at all or protect them inside a password manager, many users still prefer the convenience of saving a step when banking, and may perceive their home computers as being quite safe (confusing physical security with cyberspace security).

  Many different kinds of web sites also require passwords for access. Users tend to use the same password on many different sites, or perhaps use a variant that can be easily inferred. Knowing any of a user's passwords may therefore enable access to many different sites using their identity.

  PII can also be used for identity theft, that is masquerading as someone else. Many of the ways we establish that we are who we claim to be do not actually require us to present much evidence for this – in some cases only a government identification number which may already be widely known, and a birthday which is also not much of a secret. Further background details can often also be purchased online.

  The simplest level of identity theft is to buy a user name and (usually hashed) password online, perhaps in a dark web marketplace. However, small pieces of an identity such as this are not very valuable. There is increasing growth in identity integrators, who act as wholesalers for identities, capturing different pieces of identity, packaging them, and selling a comprehensive identity package to other criminals. This may include name, address, social-media accounts, web site, credit card numbers, cell phone number, and any other aspects of both real-world and online identity. Because of the increasing use of risk-based authentication and multifactor authentication, such a package may also include the IP addresses of the computers that the person habitually uses, as well as configuration information (is their cell phone Android or iOS; which browser do they use?). This process of selling a complete online identity package been called *impersonation as a service*[11].

Identity theft enables a number of serious crimes. The most obvious one is financial. Assuming someone else's identity makes it possible to sell their house from under them, or to buy a house and get a mortgage under the false identity. Most financial resources can be accessed outside the normal mechanism ("I forgot my password") and this is easier if the criminal can provide personal details to convince someone that the resources belong to them. In the extreme, identify theft has been used to pose as the heir to a large fortune (for example, the Tichborne Claimant). Pretending to be the heir to a fortune is easier now than ever because so many personal details are public, especially for celebrities.

Identity theft may also be used by a criminal to avoid arrest by claiming not to be the wanted person, or to avoid other consequences of their criminality. This is partly a consequence of our identity-filled physical world (in contrast to cyberspace); criminals used to be able to disappear and reappear claiming to be someone else, but this is much more difficult without a determined effort to create or steal a new identity.

Identity theft is also sometimes used to get access to medical services. In countries with a large disparity in the quality or availability of health care, being able to masquerade as someone else can get access that is unavailable in a real identity.

This also applies to access to drugs. There are usually regulations about how much any one person is able to get access to a drug (even a legitimate medical drug) and being able to use multiple identities means that a single person can get access to much more than the regulated amount. This may be for their own use, but can also be used to get quantities for dealing.

Children are also often a target for identity theft because it is inherently easier. Children have left fewer footprints in the bureaucracies of most developed countries so there is less risk. These stolen identities can be used for trafficked children to conceal the fact that they have appeared in a new location. Many government programs provide financial aid to those who look after children, and so stolen identities can be used to create fake children to attract this kind of funding.

There is also the long-standing use of false identities used by spies and violent extremists who want to live in a country where they do not belong. A false identity from that country provides them cover.

Identity theft is, in a way, becoming more difficult. It relies on using identifiers from national bureaucracies or from large businesses, and the connections of the records of identity that these organizations create to other aspects of identity are inherently difficult to check.

However, anyone with a web presence leaves a permanent trail of identity that cannot be deleted, and which is easy to check. This could be a web page, which creates a historical record that is occasionally snapshotted by The Wayback Machine that preserves earlier versions of the Web. Social-media platforms keep a trail of posts by each individual, many of which provide contextual information about where they were when, with whom, and doing what. In 2021 slightly less than a half of the world's population has a web presence of some kind, the majority of these on a social-media platform, but also many with their own web sites or blogs.

To play the role of someone else, an impostor must not only know as much about this information as the real person might remember in case they are questioned, but must also be able to demonstrate that they were where their "history" says they were for the whole of their apparent recorded life.

An identity theft for a brief moment may still work, and crimes are possible when identities are only checked in bureaucratic ways, but trying to live someone else's life is increasingly unsustainable. Law enforcement have been slow to use the life record left by web presence as a source of data, but it is becoming increasingly powerful.

There have also been a number of cases of criminals exploiting dark-web marketplaces to collect resources, and then closing the marketplace and walking away with the resources. For example, many marketplaces keep payments in escrow until the purchaser has received the purchased goods. In a busy marketplace, the amount held in escrow can be large, and the marketplace's owners can make off with it[12]. This is called an *exit scam.*

A concerning development is *Crime-as-a-Service (CaaS).* This describes situations where criminals provide a complete turnkey crime to other criminals, either by renting or selling them the pieces needed to commit the crime. We have already discussed the early version of this: ransomware, and botnet rentals, but new prepackaged crimes of other kinds are being developed as well.

3.3 Crimes that rely on cyberspace

The second category of crimes are those that already existed but are done in a different way, and perhaps at a different scale, because of the existence of cyberspace. In other words, cyberspace enables these crimes to be done differently. The crimes themselves happen at the interfaces between cyberspace and the real world; it is the presence and properties of cyberspace as the connector for the real-world endpoints that changes the way these crimes take place.

3.3.1 Spam, scams, and cons

One capability that cyberspace provides is the ability to send an email to hundreds of thousands of recipients with a single click. This has enabled crimes that target the vulnerable or gullible with unprecedented ease because the victims self-select. While most people will easily detect that an email is suspicious ("too good to be true"), those most vulnerable to scams and cons are the least likely to have their suspicions triggered. Experience and education can help, but the evidence is that a small subset of people are trusting beyond all reason.

Mass emails have slightly different purposes, but they can be divided into:

- *Spam.* These are emails that are trying to achieve some quasi-legitimate purpose, usually to sell something. The problem is that they do it by mass emailing to people who have not given permission to be contacted. These mass emailings are the descendants of direct-mail marketing campaigns but, while direct marketing had costs for producing the material and posting it, email spam has extremely small costs. A traditional direct-marketing campaign requires a response rate of about 1% to be successful; an email spam campaign can survive with response rates 10,000 times smaller.

  Many countries make spam illegal in some form, but it is extremely difficult to prosecute because of attribution, and because it is usually cross-border.

  The top spam-generating countries contain some that might be expected, but some that might not. In early 2021, the top ten spam-generating countries in order were: China, the U.S., Russia, Japan, South Korea, India, Hong Kong, Turkey, Vietnam and the Dominican Republic[13]. Ukraine dropped off the list in the preceding year, and Brazil and the U.K. have also often figured on this list.

  Some of the senders of spam are simply naïve and delude themselves in two ways. First, they imagine that those who are not interested might still have their interest caught by, say, the subject line. They fail to realize that they are not the only sender who has discovered mass email, and that most people receive hundreds or thousands of such emails each day, and many are deleted automatically. Often the creators of mass emails are themselves new to the Internet and get little email themselves, so they make the wrong extrapolations about what the email environment is like. Their second delusion is that there is a natural and compelling market for whatever they are selling (a delusion common to many advertisers).

  Some senders are so incompetent that even if, on some rare occasion, a recipient might want to buy the advertised product, they cannot actually do so because the email has been so poorly configured. As long as Internet access continues to grow there will be a constant supply of these naïve would-be marketers. Large amounts of spam just induce head scratching about what the senders think they are doing.

These naïve marketers are also the victims of other criminals who sell them the email lists that they use for sending their spam, and charge them to use mass-mailing computer platforms. Some of the (few) successes with prosecuting have targeted these platforms and their owners, which has the added advantage that it stops spam from many different senders at once.

Some senders of spam have more malign purposes:

- to install malware using phishing, that is by including malware in an email that looks like it is advertising or selling something;
- to drive traffic to particular websites either to download malware, or to increase the number of advertisements seen at those websites; or
- simply to detect which email addresses are being read by actual humans (and perhaps especially gullible humans), so that they can create higher-value email lists for resale.

Spam is a perennial problem, partly because of its nuisance value, and partly because it consumes a huge amount of resources – by some estimates as much as 50% of Internet traffic. Spam is therefore both costly in dollar terms because network providers must over-provision their networks, and in ecological terms because of the amount of energy required to transport the messages, all to no purpose.

Many governments have put programs in place to try to combat spam, but it is difficult because spam tends not to originate in the countries to which it is sent, but is not considered serious enough for the sender's countries to take action, even if they wanted to. There have been some success stories but they are limited.

Large Internet Service Providers and telecommunications companies could remove a great deal of spam before it reaches recipients but do not do as much as they could, either because they have decided it would be illegal for them to do so, or because they are concerned about the possibility of mistakes (false positives, deleting legitimate messages thinking they are spam).

Most spam is dealt with by each user applying spam filtering products that they can train to differentiate between their legitimate email and the spam they get. While these tools can remove 90+% of incoming spam, it still requires some time by most users to deal with the edge cases. Those who use email provided by large Internet businesses are in a better position, since these businesses have the visibility to detect spam in a wholesale way. However, this does not yet seem to have had much effect in deterring senders or decreasing their motivation.

- *Scams and cons.* More serious are emails that target the vulnerable and gullible to try to induce them to part with their money. Some of these emails use the same strategy as conventional cons, working on the recipient's greed. The most well-known is the Nigerian Prince con and its variants. A typical email claims that the sender has a large sum of money that they want to get out of their country, but they need a bank account to transfer it to. If the recipient will collaborate on moving the money, they will be given a share. The target either reveals bank account credentials which are then used to remove money rather than deposit it, or the target is asked to pay various overheads up front. Needless to say, there is no money and the target ends up losing their own.

Another common con is based on supposed overpayment. The recipient is asked to help out someone from far away by, say, helping them do the administrative work to get them an apartment, and the sender apparently forwards a large sum of money to the target to pay for the costs of doing this, perhaps the first month's rent. Then the sender sends an email saying that they have sent too much, and they desperately need some of the money back to meet their remaining obligations where they are now. The target is asked to send a check for the (relatively small) repayment; but the large initial transfer turns out not to exist or the original check bounces, and the target is left with a net loss.

Often emails claim that the recipient has won a (usually foreign) lottery, miraculously even without entering. Fake surveys are another kind of con used to gather personal information.

Another important category of these email-based scams use emails that purport to come from government agencies in the target's country, have a threatening tone, and claim that the target owes money to the government, perhaps taxes. The target is asked to pay this money by buying negotiable objects, usually gift cards, and send them to a given address. (Having the target buy some cryptocurrency and send that would be better for the criminals, but the successful targets of these scams are unlikely to be able to manage such a step.)

Although it seems incredible that anyone would fall for many of these scams, especially after the publicity that many of the "traditional" versions have received, they still do. Part of the reason that these scams are worth doing is that the emails can reach huge numbers of recipients, and a success rate of one in five hundred thousand (which would succeed with 700 people in the U.S.) can still make money for the criminals because the upfront costs are so low.

The scam email contents are often deliberately made implausible (misspellings, poor formatting) so that only the most gullible respond. This limits the amount of the more-demanding work required to follow-up to those who are most likely to actually hand over money.

Some scams are intended to persuade the target to reveal personally identifiable information, perhaps bank account details, but also other details that could be used for identity fraud.

Individuals with control of business resources have also been persuaded to make fraudulent payments based on emails that purported to come from their bosses or even the business's CFO or CEO[14].

3.3.2 Financial crime

Another important category of crimes that has changed in the way it is done because of cyberspace is financial crime. This is because far more money moves through the financial system (that is, in cyberspace) than moves as physical cash. Robbing banks, armored cars, and even ATMS have become small-scale crimes because these mostly contain quite small amounts of cash, and quantities are getting ever smaller.

Some cyberspace financial crimes work by diverting money as it moves through the financial system, for example between banks using the SWIFT system. Financial system transfers are just data and flaws in the implementation of systems to handle such data can allow it to be intercepted and diverted. For example, in 2016 hackers, believed to be from North Korea, instructed the Swift network to transfer $1 billion dollars from the Bangladesh Bank to banks in Sri Lanka and the Philippines. Fortunately most of the transactions were flagged for human inspection, and subsequently blocked, but some of the money has yet to be recovered.

Other crimes work by stealing identities and credentials and using them to extract value from the places that hold it. This can range from thefts from individual bank accounts to thefts from business, or even sovereign, accounts. Frauds can also be used to persuade targets to transfer their own money to a criminal.

The difficulty with such financial crimes is that the stolen money must go somewhere, and so can be traced. Criminals must either extract the money into a bearer form as quickly as possible, or must have their own hook into the financial system so that the money can be made to disappear.

Most financial crimes use well-worn techniques such as invoice fraud but the speed with which they can be done is much greater in cyberspace, so there is less chance for second thoughts. It is also much harder to find out who committed a crime because money can be moved around the financial system rapidly and without leaving strong traces. It is also much harder to recoup money than when frauds occur in the physical world.

Transferring money across international borders has some potential risk (see the later discussion of money laundering) but this almost always breaks the trail for law enforcement. Especially when one of the countries is less developed, the ability and willingness to track financial transfers in cyberspace is small.

3.3.3 Online shopping

Online shopping is a blend of cyberspace and physical world actions and this has led to some novel crimes. The purchase happens in cyberspace, but the delivery in the real world. The process begins with a purchaser selecting what they want to buy at a seller's website, and paying for it using an online mechanism, usually a credit card for individuals but perhaps a purchase order or other mechanism for a business purchaser. However, after this the resulting actions – selecting the purchased product in a warehouse and sending it to a specified address happen in the physical world.

The opportunity for crime is created because sellers validate the purchaser's identity when the product is paid for, but do not match that identity to the delivery location. They could, because credit cards each have an address associated with them, but they do not want to because they want customers to be able to buy gifts for other people and have them delivered directly to those other's addresses. This decoupling of the identity at payment from the identity at delivery means that criminals can use stolen credentials to pay, but acquire the resulting mechanism without revealing that they are not the actual payer. (Compare this to use of a stolen credit card. The person with the stolen credit card is present both at the moment of authentication and of acquiring the purchased object because they are the same moment. If the fraud is detected, the person can be arrested on the spot and has, in any case, almost inevitably had their image captured by CCTV.)

This decoupling of purchase and delivery creates a hole that can be exploited by criminals. A criminal with a stolen credit card number and CVV can use it to buy things online and have them delivered to the address of their choice, rather than to the address of the card's owner. This provides a way to monetize ownership of stolen credit-card information which is otherwise difficult.

Of course, the criminals do not want to use their own address. There are two common options to avoid this. The first is to use an accommodation address, where someone holds packages until they are called for, for a fee. There is some risk in this process, but accommodation addresses can claim ignorance and pretend that they do not know why packages have been sent to them, so it is hard to prosecute except by arresting the criminal at the moment of pick up.

The other option is to use an empty house. Criminals look for houses that are for sale and whose owners have already moved out, and use them as delivery addresses. By tracking packages they can judge when each one is to be delivered, and come by and pick it up as soon as possible afterwards.

Even if the purchase is detected as fraudulent, say because the card is reported stolen, it is a lot of work to stake out the delivery address to arrest the person who picks up the delivered package, and they can claim that they know nothing about the fraudulent payment, so their crime is at worst some low-level misdemeanor.

Online shopping businesses try to fight back against this kind of crime, for example by sending an email to the account holder whenever a purchase is made. But there is little to prevent the person with the stolen credit card from opening a fresh account with a different email address so that the credit card's owner does not see the fraudulent purchases.

Online shopping businesses could withhold details of package delivery schedules, making it harder for the criminals to limit their exposure at the pickup location, but ordinary customers demand ever more detailed delivery schedule information,

These businesses could also develop models of the riskiness of each delivery address. For example, an apartment that gets deliveries for 80 different names (and these exist) is unlikely to be a genuine delivery point. Rudimentary modeling has been done along this line, but there are much greater opportunities here.

3.3.4 Crimes against children

There are three new affordances provided by cyberspace that have increased the levels of crimes based on images. First, the development of cheap cameras (mostly in phones) and the availability of enough bandwidth to move high-resolution images around have increased the generation and distribution of pornography (whose criminal status varies between countries), but especially child pornography. Networks of those who generate and consume child pornography can be much larger and more lucrative because of scale, and can remain better hidden because of encryption (to hide), the dark web (to find one another), and cryptocurrencies (to pay anonymously).

Second, social-media platforms provide a way to conceal any user's real identity, creating opportunities for pedophiles to act as children or teenagers, interact with targets, and groom them for meetings in the physical world. This is enhanced by the trends towards sexting in the target demographic. So many social-media environments contain both pedophiles intent on grooming children and law-enforcement officers pretending to be groomable children, both having to keep up with the culture of their target demographic.

Third, the ability of cyberspace to manage complex supply chains has enabled more sophisticated human trafficking networks, especially trafficking of children.

3.4 Crimes done differently because of cyberspace

The third category of crimes that have changed as a result of cyberspace are traditional crimes that have acquired a new lease of life or can be done in a novel way.

3.4.1 Disseminating hatred

The many ways in which cyberspace provides the ability to communicate, and mostly to communicate anonymously, has led to an increase in dissemination of hatred.

The legal status of spreading hatred is struggling to catch up with the ease and scale with which negative language of many kinds can be used against others. The picture in different countries is complex. The U.N. Universal Declaration of Human Rights[15] names a right to freedom of opinion and expression, but most countries limit this in some ways. The U.S. has few limits on expression, because of the First Amendment, but even they do not permit certain kinds of incitement. Many European countries do not permit speech that incites hatred, as well as speech denying the Holocaust. In Canada, speech may not incite hatred against certain protected groups: any section of the public distinguished by color, race, religion, national or ethnic origin, age, sex, sexual orientation, gender identity or expression, or mental or physical disability. Sometimes the target makes a difference; sometimes hate speech against minors is particularly forbidden. Some countries forbid certain kinds of speech against the government or religions. Like obscenity laws in some jurisdictions, it can be difficult to draw boundaries between what is and is not covered by laws.

At present, the issue of hate speech is being pushed to social-media businesses to control rather than to law enforcement. These businesses are being encouraged, or told, to filter out certain kinds of communication. This is mostly impractical given the wide variety of rules about what is and is not acceptable, and the technical difficulty of filtering in the first place. Social-media businesses are fighting back by claiming that they are information-delivery utilities and so have no responsibility for the information that is delivered.

It is not very long since negative language was not regarded as something of interest to law enforcement, an attitude captured by the adage "sticks and stones may break my bones but names will never hurt me". Hate speech (and related concepts) are now considered negative activities for two reasons. The first is that such speech does have a negative impact on the recipients, leading in some cases to suicide. This is especially true when the recipients are children or teenagers, which is why *cyberbullying* is often illegal when other kinds of similar hate speech targeting adults are not.

The second reason why hate speech is considered a societal negative is its effect on the authors. There seems to be a feedback effect when groups begin to use hate speech that leads to an intensification of opinion towards the target group. In other words, expression of negative language to others worsens the speaker's negative attitude to them, creating a vicious cycle. This process can ultimately lead to violence. Groups whose members are the targets of hate speech often react to it, creating a reciprocal intensification of opinion, potentially promoting reciprocal violence.

Scale also has an effect. Hate speech that might once have taken place on a school playground or at a demonstration can now happen at a global scale, where the negative impacts can be much larger.

3.4.2 Selling drugs

Drugs are an example, perhaps the best example, of how cyberspace is changing retail crime. Historically, those who wanted drugs bought them from someone very local, buying them in small amounts and paying cash. This retail mechanism generated a great deal of violence as competing gangs claimed the right to sell drugs in a particular area. There were also risks of arrest for purchasers, as well as sellers, made worse by the frequency with which they had make transactions. Because of the neighborhoods and times of day when drug purchases were possible, and the potential for violence among the sellers themselves, there was also physical risk for purchasers[16].

use the dark web to find drug sellers, buy drugs and pay for them using cryptocurrencies, and have them delivered using regular mail.

These online drug marketplaces are sophisticated. Sellers are rated by reputation (maintained by the marketplace whose interest is in making these ratings accurate), and will often guarantee replacement if shipments are interdicted by customs or law enforcement. Packaging is varied and professional looking, and the senders have considerable experience in making the letters or packets look ordinary, so that it is not easy to detect deliveries that contain drugs by looking at them[17].

This mechanism for selling drugs has started to consolidate drug sales in a few larger volume sellers. Rather than selling through unskilled local, street-corner dealers, sales are done through organizations with the skills to maintain a dark-web presence and deliver the product using professional-looking physical mail.

This does not mean that online selling requires a large organization – a German teenager was recently tried for running a drug-dealing operation out of his bedroom, selling more than 900 kilos of drugs worth 4.4 million Euros, using a dark-web marketplace and registered mail for delivery[18]. This case is far from unique.

This new mode of purchase and delivery is almost as easy across borders as within an individual country. Of course, international shipping of drugs faces the added inspection by customs at borders. This online drug traffic is retail rather than the wholesale mode that customs is used to, and intercepting and confiscating a single shipment makes a tiny difference to the amount of drugs entering each country. Yet a single retail shipment might require as much effort to discover as a much larger shipment. Also both drug-sniffing dogs and chemical sensors perform worse the smaller the quantity of drugs.

There are two opportunities for law enforcement to detect drug dealers operating in this new way, but both require the cooperation of postal authorities. The first is that such sellers necessarily produce physical mail in quantity. Even if they operate under the cover of some sort of innocuous mail-order style business, there may be patterns of mail use that are characteristic and so detectable. (So far, many of these businesses have been very small, and they do not seem to have been sophisticated enough to cover themselves this way.) The problem is that lots of businesses send a few hundred letters a week, so a drug supplier need not stand out; and the packages themselves can be dropped in mail boxes in a distributed way, so there is not necessarily much to see. Detection is further complicated by the growing number of other small-scale Internet businesses enabled by web sites such as Etsy. Such businesses have similar patterns of product distribution, although they probably do not make as much money doing so.

The second opportunity derives from the common pattern from seller to buyer, even though it is concealed. The suppliers tend to regularly change the look and feel of the packaging and the return addresses so that they do not create a signal around those receiving the shipments. Someone delivering the mail to the destination address at the local level might otherwise become suspicious of a stream of identical packages with no evident purpose.

This is all the more important for international mail, since it is important for the sender not to create a profile against which subsequent packages. even to other destinations, can be matched and intercepted by customs.

But this kind of delivery pattern has an unavoidable structure: it is a bipartite graph connecting potential sellers (defined by return address and look-and-feel) and recipients. Use this structure can be used to find both new recipients and rebranded senders. The key is that rebranded sellers will send to most of the same addresses as they did in their previous incarnation; and drug purchasers will buy from both the old and new versions (while nobody else buys from either). This approach was successfully used to detect stolen long-distance phone service, back when it mattered. Again this analysis is better done inside, or with the cooperation of, the post office.

The other way to detect this kind of drug distribution is to target the supply side – how do these distributors get their drugs? Some drugs can be manufactured by the seller, using chemical precursors that can themselves be purchased online, legally or illegally. Others are stolen from the health system of the seller's country. Plant-based drugs can be grown by sellers directly. And wholesalers also advertise and sell on the dark web, so some sellers are simply specializing in the retail distribution side, and taking a cut. All of these mechanisms are quite resistant to law-enforcement detection and prosecution.

The only drugs that have proved resistant to online selling are those that are grown far from where they are consumed, primarily heroin and cocaine. Long, organized, and sophisticated pipelines have been used to move and process such drugs from their initial forms to street sales. Organized crime investment in these pipelines is large, and they have so far resisted changing their basic form of operation. However, the pressure to change is real, so it is possible that we will begin to see mail-order drug sales from countries closer to where drug crops are grown, so that fewer profits will accrue to the later stages of the current pipelines. Sales directly from drug-source countries are unlikely to take off because of the suspicion already attached to mail from such countries, but their more innocent neighbors may become hubs of international mail-order drug sales. Of course, such a change will have an impact on criminal organizations in Western countries who rely on drug sales as one of their main forms of income.

Somewhat surprisingly, online sales of tobacco has not migrated to the dark web in a substantial way – total sales are estimated to be about 1% of drug sales[19]. This is perhaps because tobacco is relatively bulky for its value, because the profits to be had are smaller, or because tobacco smuggling has typically carried out by small-scale criminals, and often across national, rather than international, boundaries.

3.4.3 Stalking and crime preparation

The amount of information available in cyberspace has had an impact in two main areas. First, the availability of personally identifiable information, both illicit and public, means that it is possible to know a lot about any other person, especially with some skills in Web search. This means that any crime that is targeted at a specific individual can be based on rich information about location and travel patterns, tastes and preferences, and vulnerabilities, both online and offline. This, for example, enables spearphishing because criminals can find out enough about a target individual online to make the spearphishing email credible.

Second, rich detail is available for physical world crimes: details of particular locations, some of it implicit in photos taken for other reasons, technical specifications of technology such as burglar alarms and CCTV cameras, and ways to estimate traffic at different times of day, among many other possibilities. It is possible, for example, to infer the brands of locks from posed high-resolution photos of people standing in front of them, and discover how to pick them or otherwise get around them from online sources. Map apps with real-time traffic details can reveal both how busy particular locations are at particular times of day, but also the likely path a particular vehicle might take at a particular moment (to avoid delays).

All of these changes to the landscape of crime have developed over a few decades, and they continue to evolve rapidly. Criminal ingenuity is a plentiful resource; the challenge for law enforcement is to keep up (and even perhaps anticipate), especially as much of what happens in cyberspace is invisible.

3.4.4 Digital vigilantes

Vigilantes have always been an issue for law enforcement, and they tend to become more common when there is a widespread perception of the failure of law enforcement to keep public order. Cyberspace creates the opportunity for a new kind of *digital vigilante*, who can use the resources available in cyberspace to find perceived transgressors, and sometimes also to carry out non-violent forms of retribution.

Digital vigilantes may be responding to perceived violation of societal norms (although increasingly to violations of norms held by a small group who claim to represent society); to injustices; or to crimes. Loveluck[20] distinguishes four levels of digital vigilantism:

- Flagging or shaming a behavior or action without associating it with any particular individual – perhaps posting examples of "bad" behavior as a way of expressing outrage and encouraging a kind of general improvement (although it seems dubious that this has any effect on perpetrators). This kind of vigilantism need not concern law enforcement.

- Finding perpetrators and perhaps naming them publicly. This kind of vigilantism is the staple of many detective stories but is also a common community action when there is a perception that law enforcement is unable or unwilling to pursue the undesirable action. The existence of cyberspace has made this kind of investigation much easier, and also makes it possible for groups, whose members may not even know each other, to collaborate on an investigation. This kind of vigilantism is a potential nuisance for law enforcement, but could occasionally be useful.

- Hounding individuals or businesses, by taking retribution in some form (almost always non-violent). Again cyberspace makes low-level harassment possible, from defacing web sites to putting people on mailing lists for embarrassing magazines or annoying deliveries (from exotic sex toys to pizzas). This kind of digital vigilantism could be a target for law-enforcement action, but the identity problem means that it is hard to trace those carrying out the harassment.

The scale and speed of actions in cyberspace mean that digital vigilantism is likely to become a growing problem. Traditional vigilantism had the implicit support of the community, but digital vigilantism can be carried out by a small, like-minded group. The speed with which information can be discovered in cyberspace also encourages quick and intemperate responses, and perhaps conclusions too quickly drawn.

3.5 Money laundering

Money laundering is the process of turning the financial proceeds of crime into value that seems legitimate, either objects whose provenance seems innocent or money in the financial system that is similarly explainable. Money laundering is therefore the last stage of many crimes (except most crimes of violence). We treat the issue of money laundering separately because it is such a pervasive part of crime.

Money-laundering law is typically expressed in terms of "proceeds of crime" and the offence requires making the connection between the observed value of the proceeds and a crime or crimes. As we shall see, this connection is getting more and more difficult to make.

Financial proceeds of crime can exist as: cash (typically from drug dealing or crimes against the person such as mugging); money in the financial system (typically from frauds and thefts from bank accounts); and cryptocurrencies (typically from crimes of extortion). The proceeds of crime are often generated in countries where the criminals responsible do not live, so money laundering requires moving funds across international borders as well is concealing its origins. The goal for the criminal is to get these proceeds from wherever they were collected into the financial system of the country where the criminal lives, now looking completely innocent.

The essence of money laundering is to create a chain (or better still a network) of value movements, making the connection back to the original crime more and more difficult to make. There is a fundamental asymmetry in the process: it is relatively easy for a criminal to add one more link to the chain, but much harder for law enforcement to detect and follow it. Modern techniques for money laundering try to make the chain as complex as possible, to conceal some of the links, and to mix one chain with others.

Law enforcement has the power to examine bank accounts and transfers with a warrant and probable cause. Tax authorities have the power to track certain kinds of financial transfers. Customs authorities have the ability to see and investigate almost all cross-border financial transfers in any form. However, the exact details of these powers varies surprisingly much between countries and criminals are quick to exploit loopholes and variations. For example, a bearer instrument with a value of $1 million dollars must be declared when crossing some borders, will attract attention from customs if discovered when crossing other borders (but need not be declared), and is regarded as an innocent piece of paper when crossing still other borders.

Banks are able to see all non-cash movements but they are caught between the demands of governments that they prevent, or at least report, suspicious activities and the fact that they make large amounts of profit from these movements.

At present, prosecutions for money laundering are rare, and even then rarely successful.

3.5.1 Cash

Let us first consider the cash economy. There was a time when criminals made most of their money in the form of cash, inherently difficult to track, and then supported their lifestyle using the same cash. Law enforcement quickly learned to look suspiciously at people who seemed to spend more cash than they earned. As a detection method this worked reasonably well within a limited geographical scope and for criminals whose money burned a hole in their pocket. However, more self-controlled criminals could hold onto the proceeds and spend them a little at a time, or even move to a new location and reappear as someone with inherited wealth. This made them hard to detect.

However, living a cash lifestyle is risky, since in quantity the cash itself must be protected, and can become a target for other criminals. Moving cash is also difficult. It is physically heavy and voluminous, and in some cases (the U.S.) has a distinctive smell. One million U.S. dollars weighs 10kg and occupies a volume of slightly more than 10 liters, so it could be carried in a suitcase, but not an attache case. This amount is physically transportable with ordinary effort, but not in a concealed way.

The logistical difficulties increase when cash is to be moved across an international border since the volume required tends to be noticeable[21].

In most countries, it was always slightly difficult to spend cash in single large amounts, for example to buy a house or a car, although there seem always to have been sellers who were willing to operate this way. Many countries have cracked down on cash transactions, requiring an increasingly long list of businesses to report cash transactions above a certain amount (typically roughly $10,000 in the local currency). Many countries now require such reporting from lawyers, real estate agents, car dealers, and casinos. Australia tried to ban *all* cash transactions above $A10,000, but was defeated by lobbying that became increasingly implausible. Of course, transactions can always be divided into multiple purchases, each below the threshold, but doing this opens up the seller to charges of collusion; and many jurisdictions require "related" transactions (involving the same parties) to be reported if they total more than the threshold, regardless of how they were divided.

Some countries have explored doing away with cash altogether. For example, in Sweden less than 1% of transactions are in cash and they are planning to become cashless by 2025. Iceland was on a similar trajectory, but a financial crisis revived cash as a store of value – so day-to-day transactions are digital, but apparently many Icelanders have stashes of cash in large-denomination notes in their mattresses[22]. South Korea has eliminated coins, giving change as a top up to a common purchase card. The Covid-19 pandemic seems also to have encouraged increased use of debit or credit cards because it reduces the physical contact that cash requires.

Living in a cash-economy style, getting proceeds of crime as cash, and using it for day-to-day life is dying as a lifestyle because of the restrictions on what is possible, and because it draws attention in increasingly cashless societies.

Criminals also often live in a different country from the one where their crimes are committed, and they may need to pay suppliers of illicit products in yet another country. This creates further problems for trying to live a cash-based lifestyle.

Movement of cash across international borders can be done by *smurfing*. This mechanism uses travellers as carriers, each being careful to declare the cash being carried and staying just inside the (typically) $10,000 limit. The couriers are not doing anything illegal but, of course, there is the possibility that the pattern of their travels will attract attention possibly leading back to the senders and receivers.

Cash can also by physically moved across borders. It is alleged that containers full of U.S. dollars, mostly from drug sales, routinely cross from the U.S. to Mexico and they are not often detected. Interceptions run at roughly $40 million per year, but estimates of the actual cross-border cash movement, based on how many U.S. dollars are found in South America, suggest that it is at least several billion, so only a small fraction is ever detected.

Criminals whose proceeds are in cash but who do not want to live a cash-based lifestyle must find a way to convert the cash into value within the financial system. Value in the financial system can be spent with many fewer constraints, but it is much more traceable, and, of course, it almost inevitably gets taxed.

3.5.2 The financial system

Conventionally, cash was transformed to legitimated value in the financial system using a front business whose income was primarily in cash, but where there was little trace of how many customers were actually served. This stage of money laundering, moving cash into the financial system, is known as *placement*.

Pizza restaurants were a typical mechanism that illustrates the method. Suppose that a pizza restaurant served 1,000 customers each month. The restaurant bought supplies as if it served 10,000 customers per month, and flushed 90% of these supplies away. They could then claim as income the profit from the 1,000 regular pizza customers, plus the total income from the non-existent 9,000 other customers (less the cost of the materials they flushed away). Exposing this as fraudulent would require a careful count of the number of real customers over an extended period.

However, cash-based businesses that provide the opportunity for placement are dying out just because ordinary people are less and less likely to use cash now that credit and debit cards are easy to use by tapping, even for small amounts. This leaves a trail of the actual number of customers.

One of the remaining loopholes is that banks still allow cash deposits to bank accounts, often for reasonably large sums, This is an anachronistic mechanisms for allowing businesses that took in large amounts of cash to make deposits after hours where there could be little supervision.

For example, until recently Australian banks would allow deposits in cash up to $25,000 per day. Chinese tourists would open accounts with these banks, daily deposits would be made by criminals in Australia, and the balances in these accounts transferred via the financial system to China each day.

The art market was another avenue for turning cash into money in the financial system because the value of art is what a critic says it is. The discrepancy between the actual costs of producing an art work (canvas, paint) and its "value" when created provide opportunities for manipulating value. For example, a criminal can appear to pay $100,000 for a work of art, while actually paying the artist and the dealer $1,000 each. The $98,000 difference can be quietly repaid or passed on to someone further up the criminal organization, and is now legitimized because the connection to the crime that produced it has been broken. Jewelry is another commodity where the price and the cost of the raw materials can be of different magnitudes, creating similar opportunities.

Money laundering is also increasingly being offered as a service. Since the definition of the crime requires showing that the money is the proceeds of crime, passing it to an intermediary breaks the connection and makes it effectively impossible to demonstrate the connection required for the offence.

The money laundering service can mix money from varied sources to further muddle the chain of connections, can exploit economies of scale, and can develop the expertise to know the optimal ways to move money, and change these as they observe law-enforcement responses.

We now turn to money laundering within the financial system. The financial system moves money, but only abstractly as financial transactions carried out by financial-service organizations. So once cash has entered the financial system, or when it was obtained within the financial system in the first place, the processes of money laundering change,

The players in the financial system are of two kinds. The first are the overt financial organizations such as banks, building societies, and credit unions, as well as increasing number of quasi-banks set up by supermarkets and other non-financial organizations because they carry out many transactions and prefer to handle them in-house to save costs. These overt financial organizations are (in most countries) heavily regulated.

The second set of players are the informal organizations known as *hawalas*, *hundi*, or *remittance service providers*. These organizations developed to provide an alternative to banks for international transfers, especially transfers by guest workers sending money to their home countries. They are often orders of magnitude cheaper to use than conventional banks.

For remittance service providers, money transfers take place between known partners, usually in different countries. They are characterized by trust between the partners and the use of virtual transfers rather than actual ones. Suppose that A and B set themselves up in this business. Someone comes to A wanting to send money to someone in the country where B is located. This person pays A the money, and A instructs B to pay the money to the person in the destination country.

A is richer as the result of the transaction and B is poorer. If transfers between the two countries are roughly equivalent over time, then the transfers balance out, and there is no regular need for an actual reconciliation mechanism. However, if A is in a country with many guest workers, and B is in a poorer country, then there will be a net flow from A to B and eventually the imbalance must be corrected.

There are multiple ways in which this can happen. First, A may transfer money to B through the global financial system, but in one large amount which covers many individual transfers. This means that the banking costs are amortized and the exact structure of the component transfers concealed. Second, B may owe A a debt and these transfers are a way of paying off the debt. Third, A and B may have a shared business, often an import-export one, and the reverse transfer can be concealed in the underpricing of an export from A to B or the overpricing of an export in the reverse direction.

Remittance service providers are usually legitimate businesses, and must register with financial authorities in many countries. However, their opacity and freedom to move money invisibly have made them attractive to criminals and violent extremists. Each end of the channel between A and B must keep track of the balance between them, but there is no actual need to track each transaction once it is completed, and this provides the room to transfer money without leaving a trace.

Although remittance service providers have traditionally been used to move money internationally, there is no reason why they cannot be used within one country to break chains of financial movement.

Art and jewelry continue to be useful as ways to move value across borders since there is no easy way to match the claimed value with the (probably inflated) value that the transfer effects. For example, someone can declare the value of a painting to be \$1,000 as it crosses a border but then sell it to a confederate for \$1 million on the other side, and there is usually no plausible way for customs to argue for its greater value.

Banks, in many countries, are required to report transactions above a threshold, usually the ubiquitous $10,000 number in local currency. Criminals who are moving proceeds of crime are therefore wary of moving large sums unless there is an explanation or cover story for these movements. They therefore often use a process known as *layering*, that is organizing large transfers into smaller ones that do not invoke the reporting rule.

Banks are also supposed to report suspicious transactions to national financial intelligence units, but the decision about which transactions are suspicious is left to each bank. Layering is relatively easily detected by banks using data analytics, and they should generate suspicious transaction reports whenever they detect it. However, they have little incentive to do so. There is a mismatch between the interests of banks who make money by transfers of other people's money and the interests of law enforcement and financial regulators trying to prevent money-laundering transfers. The extent of the mismatch is revealed in the size of some of the recent fines levied against banks for being involved in money laundering, mostly failing to report manifestly suspicious transactions:

- JP Morgan Chase, more than $2 billion,
- HSBC, $1.9 billion,
- US Bancorp, $613 million,
- Commonwealth Bank of Australia, $A700 million,
- Rabobank, $369 million,
- UBS, $4.2 billion,
- DeutscheBank, $41 million,
- Danske Bank, still being decided but estimated between $2 and $8 billion, and
- Westpac, $A1.3 billion.

The magnitudes of these fines and the levels of management who were involved suggest that banks find money laundering profitable enough that they consider the fines just a cost of doing business, whatever they say in public.

Nevertheless there are some success stories of banks collaborating with law enforcement and financial regulators to look for the traces of layering. The difficulty is what to do when such traces are discovered. Money-laundering prosecutions are rare because they are often unsuccessful, and so layering is often prosecuted as a technical crime, with correspondingly small penalties. Even the huge fines listed above have usually been negotiated down from amounts ten or a hundred times greater.

Another way to break the chain of value movement is to step outside the conventional financial system, move value into a cryptocurrency, and then take it out again. We describe this technique in more detail in a later section.

The final stage of money laundering is called *integration*. Value is extracted from the financial system into accounts where the connection to crime has been completely broken and so the value appears innocent.

3.5.3 International money laundering

Moving proceeds of crime internationally is attractive as a means of breaking the chain of connections, even when the criminals are in the same country as the source of the illicit money. This is because the regulations about money laundering differ in different countries, because banks do not aggregate their data on an international basis so data analytics cannot find patterns, and because law enforcement and financial regulators in different countries do not necessarily have strong collaborative relationships or experience working together.

The process outlined above for remittance service providers provides the basic mechanism for transferring money internationally without leaving traces. This is not the only way; transfers may appear to be loans or even charitable donations to organizations in other countries and it may be difficult to decipher, at a distance, whether these are legitimate organizations or fronts.

Transfers are even more difficult to track if they involve three countries. Money is sent from country A to B, and then passed on to C. From C it is sent back to A, From A's perspective, these seem to be two unrelated transfers and so any connection the departing money had to crime does not apply to the returning money.

The fundamental problem with preventing money laundering is the legal framing that requires the connection of the money to the crime that produced it. In today's world, where it is so easy to move money around and where there are those who will do it for you, aggregating it and disaggregating it in many combinations, making the required connection is almost impossible.

A hopeful possibility is the development of *unexplained wealth orders* (UWOs). These target the back end of the money-laundering pipeline, integration and then spending the ill-gotten gains. The idea is simple: when someone is spending more than they can account for receiving then the difference is assumed to be illicit money.

This is a strong defence against criminality since it prevents criminals profiting from their crimes by improving their lifestyles. So far, it has been used in the U.K against those who have moved from other countries, typically Russia, bringing with them vastly more money than their positions in their country of origin can explain or justify.

There are ways to defend against Unexplained Wealth Orders, say inventing a back story that accounts for the money, but this is difficult in a connected world. A bequest from a distant relative, long the most popular explanation, is too easy to check today.

The challenge at the moment is to think through the extent to which UWOs infringe on civil liberties. Those who argue against them are concerned about the exact mechanisms that would invoke them, for example how much probable cause is needed. And of course they violate the principle of "innocent until proven guilty". The settings where these have been used so far have been for people who are egregiously wealthy despite having held mid-level jobs so there is plenty of low-hanging fruit, but the "thin end of the wedge" argument has some validity[23].

Another possibility is to target the enablers of money laundering rather than the criminals themselves. Many of the organizations along the chain of value movement are willing participants and each skim some value for themselves from the value that they transfer. These organizations are much easier to prosecute since only one link in the chain has to be discovered. However, this requires much stronger regulation of organizations who handle value than most countries have so far implemented: for example, real-estate agents, mortgage brokers, lawyers, and luxury goods dealers.

3.5.4 Cryptocurrencies

Cryptocurrencies are built on top of *blockchains*. Blockchains are chain-based records of actions that are designed to be tamper-resistant and tamper-revealing, so that they are reliable ways to record activities of all kinds where a permanent record is required. Most blockchains are open, so they are not owned by a particular organization and do not have gatekeepers to regulate access.

Blockchains are managed by a distributed set of computational nodes (from which nodes can come and go freely). Anyone who wishes to add a transaction to the chain sends it to these nodes. Once enough of these transaction have accumulated, these nodes compete to be allowed to add the next block to the chain. There are a number of mechanisms for this competition, but they are all designed to make it difficult for the same node to win the competition frequently, and for any significant fraction of the nodes to collude.

The winning node creates a new block which contains a digital hash of the preceding block, so that blocks cannot be inserted anywhere except at the end. The new block also contains all of the current set of transactions which are now "cast in stone" in the blockchain.

Users of the blockchain are identified using the public key encryption mechanism described in Section 2.4. Each user has a private key, which is used to encrypt transaction data. Their public key can be used by anyone to verify that a transaction indeed comes from this particular user. The private-public key pair are the identity of the user (and, of course, a single individual can have more than one). Thus transactions on the blockchain are effectively public; what is hidden is who is making them.

A financial transaction on a cryptocurrency blockchain begins by moving value from the financial system into the blockchain using a particular identity. This value can be moved around the blockchain, perhaps broken into pieces, and passed on to other identities. Eventually these others can take the value from the blockchain back into the financial system. The fact of each transaction is visible, but who made it is not. It is therefore a bit like the cash economy where, for example, ransom payments could be made by one person putting a suitcase of cash in a bin, and another person picking it up.

We have already mentioned that the anonymity associated with cryptocurrencies has enabled several crimes that were previously limited by the difficulty of extracting money without leaving broad traces for law enforcement to follow.

Cryptocurrencies also create new challenges for prosecuting money laundering. Putting money from the financial system into cryptocurrency and the removing it somewhere else breaks the connection between the crime and the benefit. If the crime itself acquired cryptocurrency, there may be little trace that a crime even happened. UWOs may be the only way to deal with money laundering that uses blockchains as intermediate stages in layering and integration.

Fortunately cryptocurrency systems have proven rather shaky financial vehicles, although we cannot rely on this to continue. First, the value of cryptocurrencies with respect to ordinary currencies has tended to oscillate wildly (after all, it took centuries for governments to learn how to stabilize their currencies). This impacts, for example, online drug dealers since the online markets may keep customer payments in escrow until successful delivery. The realizable value of the customer's payment may change markedly in the interval.

Second, many cryptocurrencies are slow to handle transactions – Bitcoin takes about ten minutes to create each block, and it is prudent to wait for several blocks to be successfully added to the chain to be sure that a transaction is irrevocable. Speeds will surely increase as newer blockchain technologies are deployed, but each blockchain defines a currency, and it is no easier to move value from one to another than moving value from one country to another. So penetration of new cryptocurrencies is almost certain to be slow, despite the hype.

Third, access to value in the blockchain depends on keeping the private key private. Criminals themselves can be hacked and their keys (and so the value they point to) stolen. Private keys are long strings of characters and so are rarely entered directly. Instead they are kept on their owner's computer where they may be exfiltrated or captured by malware that looks for long strings of nonsense characters appearing in the cut-and-paste buffer.

3.6 Overlap with violent extremism

The motivation for most criminals to carry out crimes is that they can reap rewards with less effort than working at a conventional job, although there are obviously other motivations such as a desire for excitement or pleasure in violence.

Violent extremists are motivated by a perception that there is something wrong with the environment in which they find themselves, and this wrongness is so substantial that violence is the only way to fix it. Different violent extremists diagnose problems in different domains. Broadly speaking, these domains are:

- The religious domain. Violent extremists perceive something wrong with the moral and spiritual life of their community. They commit violence against those who do not agree or behave as they ought: unbelievers, apostates, and heretics. Recent examples include the islamist movements Al Qaeda and ISIS, and some of the pro-life anti-abortion movements in the U.S.
- The political domain. Violent extremists perceive something wrong with the political environment, perhaps illegitimacy or injustice, and they see violence as the only way to change it. There are a wide variety of framings of motivations for anti-government violence:
  - Insurgencies, particularly in countries where the political system has no non-violent channel for dissent.
  - Anarchists, who see existing governments as beyond redemption, and believe that tearing down an entire political system will create space for a new, better one to arise. Anarchism is not common today but was a major issue for Western governments at the beginning of the 20th Century. However, there are some signs of a resurgence in such ideas, sometimes in groups called accelerationists whose fundamental posture is anti-government without necessarily have a clear idea of what to replace it with.
  - Left-wing movements, who wish political systems to be based in principles of common ownership and redistribution. Antifa is the most visible such movement at present.
  - Right-wing movements, who tend to see political systems as under the malign influence of some other group and want to fight back. Such movements range from fascism at its extreme to recent movements in support of Trump.

  Structurally, law-enforcement organizations are aligned with governments, so they are obliged to treat all anti-government action as a bad thing. However, this has always been a gray area since individual law-enforcement personnel may sympathize with politically motivated movements.
- The social domain. Violent extremists perceive something wrong with the social environment, especially as it impacts them as individuals, and want to use violence to change it. There are several varieties relevant at present:
  - White supremacists, who resemble and perhaps overlap right-wing movements. They tend to see their lifestyles and countries as being negatively impacted by people who are not like them (not white, whatever that means).
  - Incels (involuntary celibates), whose primary issue is that they are unable to attract sexual partners. This leads either to extreme misogyny or self-loathing that often leads to suicide, as well as outward directed nihilist violence.

Some of these groups carry out violence in groups, partly because their concerns attract others to address the same problems. However, both islamist extremists and incels have increasingly carried out so-called "lone wolf" attacks, which are therefore lower in impact because of scale, but correspondingly hard to detect in advance.

Cyberspace provides a natural place for propaganda and recruitment of new members, and for discussions about strategy and potential action. Several of these violent-extremist organizations, notably Al Qaeda and ISIS, have become skilled in using cyberspace for propaganda. They have produced magazines with high production values and in multiple language; and used social-media platforms to produce videos and messages explaining what they are doing and why. They also developed levels of discussion forums that could be used to move recruits from interest, to involvement, to recruitment for violence.

All of these groups have also created forums to discuss their ideology, both on the open Web and in the dark web. These serve as recruitment tools and ways to build group solidarity, as well as for the leadership to talent spot those who might be groomed to play a more significant role in the organization.

Whether this kind of activity is criminal depends on the laws in each country about hate speech, since many of these channels express negative attitudes to other groups and governments. However, the locations of the systems that host these channels is both difficult to discover and perhaps far from the countries that are the targets of the content, so in practice there is little that law enforcement can do about them. Intelligence organizations can watch the platforms that are public or semi-public, to get a sense of the topics of discussion, to judge whether activity is increasing, and perhaps to identify individuals, especially leaders.

Online platforms can also be used for planning violent action. This may happen in well-protected forums (in the dark web, with identified members, and strong access controls) and via email and text messaging. Law enforcement and intelligence access to this content cannot be done by infiltration (unless the group is extremely careless) but via interception. This content probably constitutes conspiracy in many jurisdictions, but conspiracy is notoriously difficult to prosecute, and so this data is typically used to provide warning about potential attacks.

Many of these groups also raise funds from sympathizers, those who support the group's aims but do not want to get directly involved. Supporting a violent extremist group financially is a crime in many jurisdictions. However, many violent extremist groups use something close to extortion to extract financial support from coreligionists (in the case of religiously motivated extremism) and ethnic groups (in the case of politically motivated extremism), so individuals and families may feel they have little choice but to support such groups.

There is significant overlap between crime and violent extremism, despite the supposedly more meaningful goals espoused by most violent extremist organizations. There are several reasons for this.

First, most violent extremists see crimes as destructive forces in the countries against which they are fighting, and so they see supporting crime as partially aligned with their own primary mission. They may see an active criminal landscape as an embarrassment to the countries' avowed principles, they may see it as a force destroying the countries from within, or they may pragmatically see it as a distraction for law enforcement so that they have less time and energy to look for the violent extremists.

Second, many violent extremists use crime as a way of raising money for their primary mission, using it so that they can afford to buy weapons, pay for travel, and pay for cyberinfrastructure for propaganda, recruiting, and as a vehicle for attacks. Crime supplements their fund raising.

Third, criminal groups and violent extremists have common interests in acquiring weapons and cyber-weapons, and need common skills in illicit activities such as breaking into buildings. Thus criminals and violent extremists may collaborate, even though their motivations are different.

Fourth, violent extremists can use the channels used for money laundering to transfer their own funds. When violent extremist groups raise money either by extortion or as "charity" contributions in countries other than their home bases, often from diaspora populations, this money needs to be brought back either to the home base country or to a target country to finance the group's activities. Money also needs to be moved to pay for materiel such as weapons, which are often available only in specific countries. Since they want all of these transfers to be undetected, the informal mechanisms of remittance service providers are often used; but the growth of money laundering as a service provides an alternative.

Notes

[1]Surprisingly, there is still a great deal of criminal activity that happens out in the open in cyberspace, despite the obvious vulnerabilities. This may be because those involved are not sophisticated enough to use the Dark Web. Although this may be temporary, it provides law enforcement with a source of useful information.

[2]It still seems to be the case that cyber criminals are relatively poorly skilled (unless they are state-sponsored). A recent examination of those convicted under the U.K.'s Computer Misuse Act concluded that the perpetrators had low skill levels (www.theregister.com/2021/04/13/uk_computer_misuse_act_conviction_analysis/). These, of course, were only the ones who were prosecuted.

[3]Recent analysis suggests that many malware attacks operate only for an hour or so. So by the time the signature of the malware reaches user devices, its moment has passed; many malware detection tools are looking for malware that is unlikely to be ever seen again.

[4]Browser developers are working hard to address these security issues but they are limited because (a) their browsers have to continue to work with every web site in every country, and (b) different browser developers have decided on different incompatible solutions.

[5]It is common to blame the recipient who was fooled by the spearphishing, and sometimes justifiably. But spearphishing can be so sophisticated that it could not reasonably detected

[6]cve.mitre.org/; attack.mitre.org/

[7]Microsoft used to send out their patches to Windows as plaintext, but they discovered that criminals were reverse engineering the problem that each patch was designed to fix, and designing an attack to exploit it. Those who did not apply the patch within about three days found themselves attacked courtesy of Microsoft telling criminals how to do it. Patches are now encrypted to avoid this problem.

[8]A firewall is a device that applies rules to traffic that passes through it. Typically these rules forbid certain kinds of traffic, and simply discard traffic that is forbidden.

[9]In their original design the blockchains that are the infrastructure for cryptocurrencies were visible, so that their behavior could always be publicly tested. New blockchains are experimenting with encrypting the content of the blockchain exactly to make transactions less public. However, this is a double-edged sword, and it is not clear whether this development will become mainstream.

[10]K. Chen, D. Skillicorn, X. Li, "Reversing the asymmetry in data exfiltration", *CoRR*, abs/1809.04648, 2018.

[11]M. Campobasso and L. Allodi, "Impersonation-as-a-service: Characterizing the emerging criminal infrastructure for user impersonation at scale", Technical report, arXiv:2009.04344v1, 2020.

[12]siliconangle.com/2019/04/23/30m-stolen-popular-dark-web-market-pulls-exit-scam/; www.theverge.com/2020/8/26/21403362/empire-market-dark-web-drug-marketplace-police-shutdown-silk-road-alphabay.

[13]www.spamhaus.org/statistics/countries/

[14]www.cbc.ca/news/canada/hamilton/employee-fooled-by-fake-invoice-pays-out-236k-in-ceo-scam-opp-1.5114951.

[15] www.un.org/en/universal-declaration-human-rights/index.html

[16]The need for anonymity for purchasers meant that purchases were made in cash, creating a major money-laundering problem for the dealers.

[17]J. Martin, *Drugs on the Dark Net: How Cryptomarkets are Transforming the Global Trade in Illicit Drugs*, Palgrave Macmillan, 2014.

[18]www.theguardian.com/world/2015/nov/03/german-teen-sold-one-tonne-of-drugs-from-his-mothers-flat.

[19]R. Munksgaard, D. Décary-Hétu, A. Malm and A. Nouvian, "Distributing tobacco in the dark: assessing the regional structure and shipping patterns of illicit tobacco in cryptomarkets", *Global Crime*, 22:1:1–21, 2021.

[20]B. Loveluck, "The many shades of digital vigilantism. A typology of online self-justice", *Global Crime*, 21(3–4):213–241, 2020.

[21]The need for a greater ratio of value to weight and volume is the reason why many criminals prefer high-denomination bank notes, which are often inconvenient for ordinary citizens to use. Some countries have reduced or eliminated these high-dimension banknotes exactly to make money laundering harder. Governments have also often demonetized existing high-denomination notes, that is made them no longer legal tender. Old notes can be exchanged for new at banks of course, but only in small quantities and visibly. Demonetizing was done in India in 2018; and in the run up to converting the lira to euro in Italy there was a spike in purchases of houses and boats in cash to avoid having to reveal the existence of large repositories of lira.

[22]www.bullionstar.com/blogs/jp-koning/the-future-of-cash-iceland-vs-sweden/.

[23]An alternative mechanism that has become popular is asset seizure, taking the assets of an arrested or convicted criminal as the *de facto* proceeds of crimes. The standard of proof is lower since this is treated as a civil procedure in many jurisdictions. Unfortunately, this process has been misused so that it is often perceived as corrupt – seizing assets is easy, but getting them back when justified is laborious.

Chapter 4
New ways for criminals to interact

Cyberspace is primarily a place for interaction, although it has a role as a repository of knowledge as well. Although many forms of interaction are synchronous, for example Skype and Facetime, many other forms are asynchronous, for example messaging and email. Asynchronous communication makes it possible for people who live in different time zones and with different schedules to interact in a way that was not conceivable in a pre-cyberspace world. We could add to scale and speed a third property: asynchronicity. Criminals have not been slow to exploit the interactions that cyberspace makes possible, although the role of communication is developing in its sophistication.

4.1 Criminal collaboration

Historically about half of criminals have acted alone in committing their crimes, at least most of the time, Most of the other half commit their crimes in pairs. Occasional larger groups exist, but they are rare. The exceptions are gangs, organized crime, and networks with a purpose that requires long-distance collaboration, for example drug- and human-trafficking networks.

Gangs are groups of moderate size. Their collaboration is not directly purposeful, but a side-effect of psychological needs and perhaps collective defence of territory. Gangs spend much of their time and energy in actions associated with internal dynamics and external respect, rather than in actions associated directly with their criminality.

Organized crime, on the other hand, developed as what might be called family businesses, with role differentiation and a management hierarchy. This enables organized crime to (mostly) avoid squabbles for dominance, and to make strategic decisions about what to do, but also what not to do.

DOI: 10.1201/9781003126225-4

Long-distance network criminal groups are structured because they run pipelines that span national borders, taking "products" that are cheap in one place to places where they are expensive (because illegal). Drug dealing, for example, has historically required a pipeline from the poor countries where drug precursors are grown to intermediate countries where precursors can be processed into usable drugs at low cost, and then to the rich countries where the drugs are consumed. When the product is sold in small quantities, an organized retail distribution and collection component is also required, especially when the sales team might be tempted to sample the product. Gun smuggling across the U.S.-Canadian border uses a different structure from drug smuggling across the same border. Drug smuggling uses mules to actually cross the border, while gun smuggling uses relatively high-ranking organization members[1]. This appears to be because it is a lot easier to sell on a gun than a packet of drugs, and so more trust is needed in someone who brings a drug across the border. Human trafficking networks have many of the same organizational structures for the same reasons; but they face the extra constraint that the people being trafficked may not be passive participants and so extra security measures are required.

There is considerable overlap among these different reasons to form large groups and so there are no clear boundaries between these group formats. Both gangs and traditional organized crime are involved in drug dealing because of the profits to be made. But large criminal groups carrying out other kinds of crime, such as widespread robberies, are mostly the province of fiction.

Criminals form themselves into groups mostly because of geographical proximity and ordinary social and familial relationships. Until recently, there was little alternative – advertising for criminal partners was not practical, so a criminal could only potentially collaborate with the people s/he encountered in ordinary life (although prison is famously a place for criminal community mixing).

Trust is also a critical issue that limits the potential for committing crimes with others. A criminal collaboration puts all participants at risk for one of the others deciding to inform or testify against them. As the group size increases, so does the risk unless careful compartmentalization is used. Collaborating with those who are already well-known, and who have common interests and shared social background increases trust, reduces risks, and provides mutual leverage to stay away from police. Not grassing to police works well as an abstract principle, but is much more compelling if the person informing to the police must then continue to live in the social environment of those arrested as a result.

Some crimes require a mixture of expertise, and here collaborations become more functional. The most common example is the role of a fence in the context of robberies and burglaries. This might not be thought of as a collaboration, but both sides are essential to the success of the criminal enterprise. The same is true of money launderers, who provide a service to criminals who acquire cash and want to legitimate it in the financial system.

Other kinds of specialist roles include: expertise with physical protection such as locks, expertise with electronic burglar alarms, expertise with surveillance equipment, familiarity with local geography and movement patterns, driving skills, access to weapons, and, increasingly, cyberspace expertise.

Finding collaborators traditionally happened by accident or because of the mixing that happens in prison. It is therefore a social-network phenomenon that is accessible to law enforcement in a limited way.

New ways to find collaborators are beginning to develop. It is now possible to advertise in, for example, the dark web to find needed expertise but trust issues make this problematic, and dark-web forums are not geographically limited, while most crimes are.

The existence of cyberspace has changed the way that criminals find each other to collaborate, but not yet in any fundamental way.

4.2 Planning together

Cyberspace also makes new forms of communication and planning possible but these are not easy for criminals to exploit. Traditionally, planning and communication happened in person or via phone calls. These are, of course, open to surveillance by law enforcement.

In-person communication may be difficult to separate from ordinary social interactions, for criminals who already know one another; and meetings can, of course, be held out of sight.

Phone call interception require warrants, which impose bureaucratic costs on law enforcement; and countries where cell phones can be bought without identification ("burner phones") make it hard for law enforcement to find the calls to intercept, and to know who is communicating using them.

The existence of *fake cell towers* (Stingray and its successors) have made surveillance easier in practice, although legally more murky. Such fake towers mimic standard cell towers and simply pass on all traffic to the nearest real towers. But, because phones connect to the tower near them with strongest signal, the fake tower can attract all of the traffic from a small area. Placing a fake cell tower near the location of a criminal is likely to capture all of the traffic from his/her phone without having to know which phone it is. (Of course, it will also attract the traffic of all other nearby phones.)

In cyberspace it is, in principle, easier to communicate without surveillance and interception. The practice is more difficult.

- Phone calls and text messages can be intercepted close to the device at one of the ends, using fake cell towers. However, once a text or a voice-over-IP phone call has entered the network it is difficult to know which paths it will follow, and so practically impossible to intercept it. Some providers may store text messages, retrievable after the fact but usually with some effort; but the volume of such messages will surely eventually discourage providers from continuing to store them all.

- It is possible in principle to encrypt emails, but there are few tidy ways to do this, and current techniques require considerable understanding and configuration. Emails are therefore easy channels for law-enforcement surveillance.

- There are many other systems that allow communication in cyberspace, for example Skype, Zoom, WhatsApp, Telegram, Facebook Messenger, and Instagram. These differ from text messaging because text messaging travels via the phone system's data connections, while these other tools mostly use the Internet, starting from each device's wifi connection.

  Some of these communication apps claim to provide end-to-end encryption. When this is true, there is no way to intercept the content, although the traffic patterns will still be visible, and may convey significant information. The devil is in the details for such systems: several claim encryption properties that they do not, in fact, have, and their properties are a moving target as systems are improved.

Cyberspace creates opportunities for concealed communication and planning, but exploiting these opportunities is, at present, limited to criminals with considerable expertise.

4.3 Information sharing

We now turn to how cyberspace enables criminals to share information among one another, and so improve their activities. This can happen by sharing techniques, so that criminals can learn how to commit crimes at global scale; by sharing resources that are tools for committing crimes; and by sharing opportunities and weaknesses so that each local criminal can get better at targeting in their own environments.

4.3.1 Sharing techniques

There has always been a concern in law enforcement that criminals improve their skills while incarcerated. There is no doubt other skill sharing among criminals in a kind of apprentice model, with an experienced criminal teaching a less-skilled one better ways to commit some kinds of crimes.

Cyberspace enables a much more distributed learning environment for criminals. A single description of how to commit a particular crime can be posted by one criminal with modest effort, and then viewed and tried by thousands of others, all over the globe.

Why would a criminal share knowledge that makes commission of a crime by someone else more effective? In the physical world, teaching someone else how to commit a crime creates a competitor; but in cyberspace the chances are that anyone who uses the shared knowledge is far away, and so is not competing. So the benefits to self esteem of being an acknowledged expert outweigh the disadvantages of increasing the potential competition. Specialized criminal knowledge is typically disseminated in the dark web, so that it can mostly be found by word of mouth.

Not all knowledge helpful to criminals is disseminated by criminals themselves. Law enforcement disseminate information amongst themselves. Decades ago this dissemination would have been on paper and sent through the mail; but increasingly this information is posted online. Obviously this makes it easier for other law-enforcement agencies to find out what is happening elsewhere, but this also makes it easier for criminals to discover more of what is being thought about by law enforcement. For example, many law-enforcement organizations issue annual reports where they describe the patterns of crime with which they have dealt in the previous year – including descriptions of novel crimes that were detected[2].

As another example, there is a great deal of information available in cyberspace about locks and alarms, how they work, and how they can be disabled. This ranges from data about the simple, ubiquitous locks that are used on post boxes or trains to sophisticated electronic systems. Some of these are posted by *penetration testers*, people who make a living stress-testing physical locations by trying to get into them. For example, someone carrying a clipboard and wearing a lanyard can roam unimpeded in many businesses, and can often talk employees into allowing access into sensitive areas just by asking. Knowing that this works can be helpful to criminals.

There are also always new kinds of frauds and cons being developed. For example, the Nigerian Prince scam ("I have millions of dollars to transfer from my country, but I need your bank details so I can deposit it in your account, or I need you to pay certain fees upfront") existed in the days of physical mail, moved to email seamlessly, and has spawned many variants, including cryptocurrency investment schemes.

Knowledge about developments in law-enforcement techniques and technologies are also useful to criminals. For example, the usefulness of fingerprints decreased quickly as criminals learned about them and started wearing gloves. There are constant developments in forensic analysis of trace evidence at crime scenes that is useful knowledge for those committing certain kinds of crimes. Developments in interception technology in cyberspace are also useful information for criminals. Fortunately television programs that emphasize the forensic side of law enforcement provide a constant stream of misinformation, and criminals are more likely to acquire their knowledge of forensics from these shows than from the academic literature. The other non-obvious fact is that most forensic techniques are expensive and often slow, and most police forces do not use them nearly as often as television programs would suggest.

4.3.2 Sharing resources

There is a considerable secondary market in criminality: criminals selling to other criminals. This secondary market is safer to participate in as a seller because it is hard for law enforcement to prosecute. The customers do not complain.

The sellers are also able to charge all the market will bear, since there is little useful information for buyers about appropriate pricing. In many cases, the buyers are less sophisticated than the sellers in every way, and so can easily be sold a defective "product".

The main product in these secondary markets is services. These range from the traditional activities of a fence, to the provision of money-laundering services, to the rental of botnets.

Secondary markets may also sell tools. These can, with caution, be physical tools, but they are more often cyber tools. Kits that can be used to send spam, insert malware, or exfiltrate data can be purchased and used (as we can all see) with little necessary skill.

Some of these tools and services can be advertised and sold openly because they are dual use – they can be used for criminal activities but also have a potential ordinary use. The ordinary use is often marketed as some kind of security testing tool. For example, some botnets are marketed openly as performance stress-testing tools. Spam tools are sold as marketing methods.

Other tools and services, more overtly criminal in nature, are sold from within the dark web. There is an active market in personal information, financial information, user names and passwords, cyber exploits, and email lists.

We have already seen some of the nascent crime-as-a-service organizations that are developing and seem likely to become an important part of the criminal landscape in the next few years.

4.3.3 Sharing vulnerabilities

Criminals may also share the vulnerabilities in certain kinds of systems or locations. For example, a vulnerability in a certain model of alarm system can be exploited at every site that has installed it. There may be little loss in one criminal making this information public to other criminals as long as they are far away.

For vulnerabilities in cyberspace, the incentives are more murky. On the one hand, knowing a vulnerability in a particular cyber mechanism means that it can be exploited from anywhere. There is an incentive to keep the vulnerability secret so that the criminal who knows it can slowly exploit it in many places. On the other hand, one criminal may not have the resources to exploit many targets and may judge it a better strategy to sell the knowledge rather than exploit it directly, or sell to those who are not likely to compete directly. The calculation is complicated by the fact that the vulnerability may be discovered and fixed at any moment. Indeed, the seller may know that the vulnerability has been fixed, but sell it anyway.

4.4 International interactions

Cyberspace does not have borders, so criminal collaborations and knowledge sharing can be international with very little effort. This makes it possible for a crime developed in one country to be exploited in other countries easily and quickly, by the same criminals or by others.

This creates difficulties for law enforcement who cannot necessarily see the spreading knowledge, and for whom the legal settings are often different. Something that might be criminal in one jurisdiction might be technically criminal but hard to prosecute in another, and completely legal in yet another. This is especially true of innovative crimes that exploit cyberspace, where the law has trouble keeping up with new opportunities.

Cyberspace also enables cooperation among criminals with greater simplicity. Drug-distribution organizations often involve those who deal with farmers in some countries, transport mechanisms to move the drugs to distant destinations, processing capacity which may be in intermediate countries, and a distribution network in rich countries. Before the Internet, managing these complex long chains required considerable trust within the criminal group, especially as there are incentives for everyone along the route to branch out into business for themselves. The ability to communicate quickly means that pure trust can be replaced by trust and verify, as well as the ability to interact "face to face" using video to make cheating more difficult. This in turn means that "vertical integration" along the supply chains becomes easier, and networks can become larger, with greater reach.

Rapid communication also enables rapid reaction to law-enforcement actions en route. For example, unusual police activity downstream can be quickly signaled back through the network to stop movement, or to change it to a different route.

Notes

[1]C. Leuprecht and A. Aulthouse, "Guns for hire: North America's intra-continental gun trafficking networks", *Criminology, Criminal Justice, Law & Society*, 15:57–74, 2014.

[2]For example, www.cyber.gov.au/threats/summary-of-tradecraft-trends-for-2019-20-tactics-techniques-and-procedures-used-to-target-australian-networks.

Chapter 5

Data analytics makes criminals easier to find

As we have seen, cyberspace creates many new opportunities for criminals to commit new crimes and old crimes in new ways. They can largely remain hidden as they do so for two reasons. First, identities are inherently difficult to associate to real people so it is hard to attribute criminal activities in cyberspace to the criminals who carried them out, certainly with the standard of "beyond reasonable doubt".

Second, there are a vast number of activities happening in cyberspace – much of the economic, governmental, and social life of the world – and it is difficult to pick out the criminal activities from the rest even though, from one perspective, they seem common. Indeed one of the successes of cyberspace is that it enables sophisticated actions without revealing the complex infrastructure behind the scenes that makes them possible. However, acting in cyberspace creates traces that are routinely captured and preserved, so although criminal activities are hidden they are not invisible.

Finding the traces of criminal activities is not an easy process for law enforcement for two reasons. First, it really is like looking for a needle in a haystack – the needle of criminals' activities in the haystack of the activities of the other three and a half billion people using cyberspace. Second, criminals, to the extent that they can, actively try to hide or disguise their traces. Fortunately, most criminals are not sophisticated enough to do a good job of this kind of concealment, although there is already a new kind of arms race between sophisticated criminals developing better ways to hide, and law enforcement developing better ways to find them.

The advantage for law enforcement is that *data analytics* can find traces of criminality even in large datasets. Data analytics is the computational process of building models of systems – in this case criminal activity – from data, inductively. Typically the data captures the superficial behavior of a system, and the goal is to understand what is really happening inside the system. A crime can be considered as such a system. A perpetrator carries out the crime (the system) but leaves evidence

DOI: 10.1201/9781003126225-5

(superficial traces of the system). To solve the crime an investigator examines the superficial traces of what happened, and infers from them who committed the crime. The process used in data analytics is one that is already well understood by investigators. Although investigation is often described as deduction, it is more naturally inductive: an investigator considers many possible mechanisms that could have produced the visible evidence and chooses the most plausible or likely. Data analytics automates this process. It is expensive, but the expense is in computational resources rather than in personnel time and cleverness.

Data analytics is a novel piece for law-enforcement investigation but it has the potential to change the calculus of cyberspace in favor of law and order.

5.1 Understanding by deduction

Using data to help detect crime is not a new idea. For more than a hundred years, law-enforcement organizations have collected data about criminal activities, stored it in carefully indexed file systems, and interrogated it to answer questions about what has happened in the past as a guide to what may be happening now. Law enforcement was probably the second user of the "big data" of the 19th and early 20th Centuries, after libraries, and some of the innovations in storing and interrogating complex data were developed by the law-enforcement community.

For example, matching *fingerprints* required an indexing system with an unusual set of descriptors, and a novel way of querying that was not required or developed in any other domain (initially the Henry system that classified fingerprints using 4 kinds of loops, 2 kinds of arches, whorls, and accidentals).

The kinds of repositories of data routinely collected and stored by law enforcement can be divided into several categories:

- *Records management systems* (RMS) data. These typically capture data about every interaction between police and citizens, and record attributes such as time and place, people present (perpetrators, victims, witnesses), crimes alleged, performance measures (how fast was the response?), and outcome measures (what was the result?).

  One of the early success stories using statistics derived from records management systems was CompStat[1]. This system, initially used by the New York Police Department was entirely passive; it collected aggregate statistics about categories of crimes, collected by type and precinct. Regular meetings were held to present and discuss these measures. Although by today's standards this is a very simple use of data, its effect was revolutionary. First, it changed the level of abstraction from an individual crime to collections of crimes in sensible groupings. Second, precinct commanders and senior police could see exactly how each unit was performing compared to others (and, as the saying goes, what gets measured gets done). Third, the grouped data naturally opened the way for techniques such as proactive policing, hot spot policing, and eventually intelligence-led policing. CompStat is widely credited with the reduction of crime in New York in the decade after it was introduced, although other factors, such as changing demographics and a changing drug landscape may have played more of a role. There have also been issues around police officers fudging the data, by making significant crimes into misdemeanors, to improve their apparent performance.

- *Large-case management systems.* These contain all of the data collected as part of the investigation of a complex crime, including people, places, evidence, and statements[2]. Such systems go beyond just data storage and querying, and are capable of developing task lists to collect data to fill in the holes in the current data. Their primary purpose is to collect and organize data in complex settings, but the data is also available for further analysis.

- Unstructured text. This is data such as witness statements or transcripts. Sometimes these are ingested into large-case management systems, but they are often not analyzed at all, except by a human reader.

- Databases of historical data related to crimes. These come in several forms:

  - *Modus operandi files* such as the Crime Index developed by Scotland Yard more than a century ago;
  - *Fingerprint collections*, dating back even further;
  - *DNA repositories*, usually only of convicted criminals;
  - *Rogues Galleries* of photos of known criminals (nowadays digitized and directly searchable);
  - *Bullet, gun, and weapons databases* containing descriptions and images of the weapons used in committing crimes;
  - *Digitally hashed cyber-artifacts*, especially images such as those containing child pornography, but also hashed versions of malware.

- The *World Wide Web* and other open-source repositories such as media sites. These are not explicitly collected and are not associated with crimes, but they can provide relevant information such as background on persons of interest. It is commonplace for investigators to look at the online footprint of individuals potentially involved in a crime. Because they capture almost all of world's information, they include data that might never have made it into law-enforcement records, even for professional criminals. (However, even though the World Wide Web contains a huge amount of information, there are still many areas where potentially useful information has either not been captured, or has not been well indexed by web search engines.)

- Systems that enable heterogeneous data to be organized and explored by an analyst. These often extract data from the databases above and use techniques such as visualization to make them more readily comprehensible. For example, tools such as Palantir Gotham and IBM i2 Coplink provide a single interface to multiple databases, so that an analyst can ask for, say, everything that is known about a particular person. This might include their demographics, arrest and conviction record, sentences served, and also connections to other people (family, cooffenders, cell mates).

We will discuss the issues around data collection in its many forms in the next chapter.

The common factor in the use of all of these systems is that they are *query driven*. An officer or analyst can interrogate the data by asking questions such as the following:

- "Have we seen something like this?" The main purpose of such queries is to see whether any previous crimes or perpetrators resemble those of a current crime. A positive response suggests either the same actors or copycats, and both suggest directions for investigation. In the case of fingerprints or DNA, matches from previous crimes provide strong evidence of who the perpetrators are.

- "What else do we know about this?" Queries like this find connections for people, places, events, and times based on historical information.

- "How many of these have we had?" Queries like this are useful from a management perspective. They are used for crime-reporting statistics, which may be actionable if they suggest that certain kinds of crimes in certain areas are increasing. They also enable performance measures to be calculated, both for internal management and to report to oversight bodies. They can also be used to plan staffing levels so that these are matched to expected levels of crime.

- "How many times has this officer seen one of these?" Queries like this are used to manage stress and PTSD for officers who may have encountered disturbing or violent crimes.

These data repositories and the interfaces that allow them to be interrogated are of high value, but they have some serious limitations.

First, repositories may have useful, even critical, data but they will only reveal it in response to the right query. In other words, only the right question will access some of the content of a repository. If person *a* has a connection to person *b* it may never be discovered unless someone thinks to ask.

Using repositories well requires the skill to construct clever queries and the experience to see how to modify the queries based on the responses from the repository. This is obvious when the repository is the World Wide Web – some people are much better at searching than others, even given the technology that search engines use to try and provide appropriate responses; and most people get better with practice. But skill is important when accessing more specific data repositories. This is one reason why many law-enforcement organizations separate the role of *analyst* from the role of investigator[3]. An analyst is responsible for accessing the data kept in repositories because of a perception that substantial skills are required to do so effectively. However, there are significant drawbacks to this separation of roles; for example, the time it takes an investigator to formulate a question, pass it to an analyst, have the analyst turn it into a query, obtain the results, and pass them back to the investigator.

Analysts may be good at formulating queries but may not have the context to say "That's strange" when they see a response to the query, and so realize that they should continue to investigate the data by generating follow-up queries. The need to pass queries one way and results the other also slows down the dissemination of useful information to the front line.

When queries are the only way to access the data, errors in the data remain hidden, possibly for a long time. Wrong data is very unlikely to match normal queries, so the records containing the error are rarely returned; and so analysts do not get to see that the errors exist. Queries are difficult to construct and even good ones do not necessarily find everything they intend to search for.

The second limitation of query-driven approaches is that it is very rare for repositories to implement *persistent queries*, queries that are automatically asked again whenever the data repository is updated. For example, if a repository is asked if there is a connection between person a and person b and there is not one, it will reply to the query saying so. If data about a connection between them arrives ten minutes later, the person who made the query will not typically find this out and is unlikely to (manually) ask the same query again.

Casinos have been quick to implement these kinds of persistent queries. For example, a croupier and a gambler who collaborate can cause payoffs that appear to have been the result of mistakes by the croupier. A pair attempting such a fraud will be careful to make sure that there is no obvious link between them at the time, so looking at their phone calls, addresses, travel patterns, and so on will show nothing suspicious.

A year later they may, say, move in together. Without a persistent query, this is unlikely to be noticed. There have been a number of success stories because of casino's incorporation of persistent queries in their normal operations[4].

Most car accidents happen between strangers. Insurance companies look for connections between the parties in case they are not strangers, which would be a strong signal for collusion. Again, a check at the time of the accident may indicate that the parties are strangers, but the same check a year later might paint a different picture.

However, neither insurance companies nor law enforcement have institutionalized the use of persistent queries in a substantial way despite their usefulness. One reason that cold cases are sometimes closed is that the same questions asked originally are asked again, and new data has become available in the meantime – criminal collaborators thought that it was safe to reveal their connections, or to spend the proceeds, or people who were on holidays during the original inquiry have returned and are finally questioned.

The third limitation to query-driven approach is that rare patterns or occurrences are especially likely to be missed because the queries that would elicit them seem inherently unlikely. Even if such queries are asked, it is difficult to judge if a response represents coincidence or a genuine pattern. The rule of thumb "Once is happenstance. Twice is coincidence. The third time it's enemy action"[5] encourages small responses to be ignored. Officers and analysts suffer from human blind spots, the so-called "failure of imagination"[6], that prevents certain queries from every being considered or made.

The development of new forms of discovery based on induction, which is the heart of data analytics, changes data from something passive that sits quietly until queried, into something that is active and, as it were, pushes itself forward whenever it contains something interesting. This is the message of the rest of the chapter.

5.2 Understanding by induction

A model is a representation (often a mental representation) of how a system works. We use models all the time: how our friends behave, how other vehicles on the road or pedestrians on the sidewalk will move, how the seasons will change through the year, and many more. We develop these models not by querying these systems but by observing them in operation and inferring underlying regularities. We do not represent these systems to ourselves as a large set of unrelated actions, but develop a representation at a deeper level. We replace collections of visible behaviors by models that at least implicitly provide explanations.

This process for us is mostly invisible. For example, English adjectives have a necessary ordering: opinion-size-age-shape-color-origin-material-purpose. All native speakers know this rule, but mostly do not know that they know it. Nevertheless they instantly realize when something is wrong ("an old big beautiful house" rather than "a beautiful big old house"). It is hard for additional-language learners to learn this rule when native speakers do not consciously know it. This adjective ordering is a model that we all induced from the examples we have seen and heard. It nicely illustrates the properties of inductive modeling: slightly mysterious but powerful.

In law enforcement, the models are of how crimes and criminals behave; in particular, who carried out the crime being investigated. When a perpetrator commits a crime, the actual "system" is invisible to us. The perpetrator carried out certain actions before, during, and after the crime, but we do not actually see these things happening in real time. An investigation tries to infer the structure of this hidden system from the traces that it leaves at the crime scene and elsewhere, including especially the part of the structure that delimits who committed it. Models at higher levels can also be inferred: what the common structure of crimes of this type is, including not only how they are done but perhaps where and when.

As we have seen, data repositories are conventionally used in a query-driven way that corresponds to asking queries like: "could it have been done this way", "could it have been done that way", "could it have been done by this person", or "could it have been done by that person", or "could this person have been at this place at this time". Many crimes are entirely routine and the method and perpetrators are obvious, so this approach is quite successful. But in complex crimes, the number of possible queries of the kind above can become impractically large, and ultimately unhelpful if the responses to many queries are "maybe". Also resource limits and imagination mean that some queries that might have been revealing never get asked. A good investigator might be one who can imagine better queries.

Inductive approaches reverse this querying process. Instead of data being queried explicitly by an analyst, the data is used to build models that might explain the crime. This process is computational and automatic, in the sense that models are not created in response to any particular question or issue; and many alternative models can be built.

The data about the system (crime or criminal) is superficial in the sense that it is only about what is observable about the crime setting, and what can be learned from physical evidence and witnesses (although it may not be possible to tell whether a witness is actually the perpetrator). The data does not contain the internal mental states or all of the actual actions of the perpetrator. All of the models that are built are consistent with the known data about the system, but may reach different conclusions about the "internal reality" that gave rise to this data.

A crime reconstruction helps to make the distinction. When a crime has taken place, those involved make statements about their actions during the time the crime took place. Apart from human fallibility, all but one of these is accurate; presumably the perpetrator does not mention the actions directly related to the crime. These statements describe the internal reality of the crime.

When a reconstruction takes place, the participants all repeat their actions, and the results are observed. These, together with the physical evidence, are the superficial reality – what is available to investigators after the fact of the crime. The purpose of a reconstruction is to evaluate whether the superficial reality agrees with the internal reality. If it does not, there must be issues in the (purported) internal reality, and these provide hints about who may have misrepresented it.

Data analytics provides a way to create representations of internal realities that are consistent with the superficial reality. Each such representation, a model, is automatically evaluated for internal plausibility and consistency with the available data, and the most plausible subset of models is presented to the analyst or investigator. The analyst's role is quite different from in a query-driven approach. Instead of having to generate and ask clever queries, the human assesses each presented model for its plausibility in terms of the environment of the system. This is a much easier cognitive task – we are much better at *recognizing* plausible explanations than *creating* plausible explanations[7].

The model-building system has already culled those models that seem implausible within the constraints of computational visibility, but the analyst can apply a much more subtle concept of plausibility, with an understanding of individual and social motivations and actions that are (for the present) inaccessible computationally. The model-building approach must be conservative, culling only substantially less plausible models so that it does not prevent the analyst from seeing a model that might be interesting. This is especially important in the context of criminal investigation since a perpetrator may have worked quite hard to make themselves seem implausible as the person responsible for a crime, for example by faking an alibi or obscuring a motive.

On the other hand, analysts have to be careful not to discard a model that seems, at first glance, implausible; they must be aware of their own cognitive biases.

The two main kinds of models (representations of systems) that are used in data analytics are *clustering* and *prediction*.

Clustering aggregates objects (crimes, perpetrators) based on concepts of what similarity means. In a query-driven approach, a user asks "which crimes are similar because of this property"; in an inductive, data-driven approach, a computational system reports "these crimes are similar because ...". The result of a clustering is a set of clusters; within each one are objects that are similar to one another, with each cluster containing objects that are different from those in other clusters.

There are many ways to be similar, so there is not *one* clustering for a given set of data, but *many* clusterings. Some will be of more interest and usefulness than others. A data-analytic system usually applies some internal criteria to filter out some of the less-plausible clusterings it has generated. The ultimate judge is the user, who is presented with possible clusterings and may consider some interesting and others not.

A clustering provides immediate information about the system being modeled. First, there are some number of clusters which implies how many ways in which objects can be placed in similar groups. Second, clusters have sizes – the number of objects that they contain – and this also provides information about the system. Third, for many kinds of clusterings clusters also have shapes (spherical, long and thin, spider-like) which also reveal something about mutual similarity.

For example, a data-analytic system might find a cluster and report "these crimes were all committed using a four-inch triangular blade" (probably interesting) or "these crimes all involved a blue car" (less interesting, but not necessarily useless). The advantage for the analyst is that there is no need to ask "how many crimes used a four-inch triangular blade", "how many crimes used a three-inch triangular blade", "how many crimes used a three-inch flat blade" , and so on.

Prediction models learn the relationship between inputs and outputs, that is what is it about a situation that led, or might lead, to a crime. They can be applied before a crime to predict what the risk of such a crime might be: given these circumstances (this time, this place, this weather) how likely is it that muggings will happen?[8] After a crime, a predictive model might predict how likely it is that this particular person committed it, or how likely it is that following this particular investigative direction will be productive.

There are many different ways to build predictive models, so some predictors might be more plausible than others in a particular situation. This can be assessed, to some extent, by seeing what the predictor would have predicted for past events, where the actual outcome is already known.

The high-level view of pipeline for data analytics is therefore:

- Build many models from the data (repeatedly if the data is changing);
- Evaluate the set of models produced using internal criteria (consistency, accuracy on historical data, plausibility, potential usefulness);
- Present the "best" models to analysts, who assess them, and then can use them to, for example, generate leads for investigation or prioritize actions.

The human user applies skills related to recognition and utility, rather than the more creative skills required to generate queries. Recognition skills are usually faster to apply and certainly require less cognitive effort. Creative skills are always in short supply and, as we have seen, can be limited by failures of imagination.

Many data-analytic techniques also allow the inclusion of prior knowledge, which may initially come from expert inputs. For example, a CCTV surveillance system that automatically generates alerts must be trained to know that it is unlikely for someone to put a box down and walk away but they might put a box down and wander around close to it. It is normal to throw something small into a trash container, but it is less normal to throw something large into a trash container[9].

Systems can allow users to score the models they are shown so that they can improve further. For example, a presented model could be labeled as "That's obvious" or "I already knew that" (although this latter should be integrated with care since something known by an experienced officer might be novel to a rookie). In a well-designed system, the most common response to a model might be "That's interesting".

The main advantages of using the data-analytic approach in contrast to query-based approaches are:

- It exposes information that is implicit in the data, often data that is difficult to find using or requiring an explicit search or query.
- It requires less user skill and creativity, and less training and experience, so it can be used more easily and widely. It provides a way to connect frontline officers directly with the data, rather than having to go via an analyst.

- It does not suffer from the biases and blindnesses that humans are prone to, so it will answer some questions that users are unlikely to ask[10]. Unfortunately, this can create countervailing *automation bias* in which humans take the results of models as absolute truth (partly because they do not understand inductive modeling).

- It can push model information without user action, for example, reporting to a patrol car that it is close to a location where a violent crime happened recently.

- It can help find errors in the data, because such data will produce unusual models, whose source can then be discovered. For example, a cluster of burglaries committed by individuals who are around 6 meters tall might reveal that someone has been entering heights that are supposed to be in meters in feet.

There are also some disadvantages, mostly because of the novelty of the data-analytic approach.

- The inductive nature of the data-analytic approach is not intuitive, and may seem slightly magical, producing something from nothing. This has sometimes had the contrary effects of either making users unwilling to trust its results, or alternatively putting too much trust in them.

- Because it is a new approach, it requires new kinds of training and experience, and retraining for some, and there can be resistance.

- Data analytics requires computing equipment and storage. This can seem expensive in organizations that have not previously needed large computational capacity. Senior management may see significant costs for the required computational infrastructure without appreciating the advantages.

Many businesses, and increasingly governments, use data analytics to improve their operations. When done well, there are significant success stories: Amazon recommending products to users; Spotify creating playlists for individuals automatically; Walmart filling shelves from a newly arrived delivery just as the last object is about to be sold; and Netflix deciding what new shows to make based on what they model that viewers will watch.

Using data analytics in *adversarial settings*, those where the interests of those being modeled and those doing the modeling are not aligned, require extra attention and caution. It is in the interest of criminals to spoil the modeling process in any way that they can. For this reason, law-enforcement organizations need to be extremely cautious about buying off-the-shelf tools that are designed for ordinary businesses. These tools may not be resistant enough to manipulation for use in adversarial settings.

What about *artificial intelligence (AI)*? It is often hard to know what is meant when the phrase “AI” is used. Often, especially in the media and business white papers, it simply means anything computational. Sometimes it is used as a trendy alternative to prediction. A better definition for AI would be "computationally mimicking human cognitive processes". As such, it overlaps with data analytics, but there are many substantial differences. At present the term has become so corrupted that it is better avoided altogether, and anyone who claims an "AI product or technique" should be regarded with some suspicion. Either they do not know what they are doing or they hope that you do not.

5.3 Subverting data analytics

There are three main avenues for subverting data-analytic modeling that are accessible to criminals, especially when they have both the incentive (always) and the resources (sometimes).

The first is to corrupt the data that is collected and on which the models are based. This is not a new problem in law enforcement – criminals have often deliberately provided false information to police to mislead investigations.

There are greater opportunities to corrupt the data when it is collected digitally. The data, as it is collected, does not receive the routine sanity checks for plausibility that humans apply without thinking. CCTV and licence plate data collection is particularly easy to deceive – a fake licence plate that would not deceive a human may seem completely plausible to a licence-plate camera[11].

Online activity creates an opportunity to seem to have been in one place while actually in another. An individual can seem to have been actively using their computer when in fact the actions are generated by a piece of software that simulates user activity.

On the other hand, some digital data is collected in unobtrusive ways, and criminals might not even realize that it has been collected – for example, explicit cell-phone location data which many users do not bother to turn off, or the implicit location that can be measured approximately from the direction and distance of a phone from the cell tower it is using.

Overall, though, law enforcement should stay alert to the possibility that they are being deliberately fed some of the data they are collecting. Collection paths that are least obvious will tend to be most reliable.

The second way to subvert data-analytic modeling is to use *social engineering*, manipulating people and social systems to get a desired effect based on the quirks of human behavior and cognition. Social engineering works on two areas of human behavior: perception and action. We as humans have blind spots which means there are aspects of the world that we not only do not perceive (ultraviolet radiation, say) but also do not realize that we do not perceive. We also require explanations to ourselves about why we should or should not act in each particular situation, and the evidence for these explanations can also be manipulated.

Social engineering leverages at least these two properties of humans and society:

1. *Truth bias* a strong cognitive property of our brains that leads us to believe others, even when the objective evidence should have made us at least extremely suspicious, Truth bias seems to have developed because of the risks of alienation in a tribal context that come from calling out lying and deceit (consequences that can still be seen in operation in villages and on islands today). Something that is functional in a tribal context is a disaster in the global context of cyberspace, but goes some way to explaining the high levels of observed gullibility in response to online scams and social-media discussions.

2. *Stereotypes*, which create blind spots, and which criminals can exploit if they are sufficiently aware of them. Stereotypes are shorthand ways in which we decide how to interact with someone by putting them into a category based on superficial data about them. Criminals use this by behaving in ways that suggest they are "too nice to ..."; neighbors and friends are often stunned when someone close to them is arrested. (Police officers also operate using stereotypes, for example "everyone lies".)

Social engineering is a special risk because, almost by definition, we are unaware of the implicit rules we use within a society and an organizational culture.

Social engineering is one of the common ways to break into a protected environment by pretending to the person who has the backup mechanism (spare key, password reset) to be the legitimate user who has somehow forgotten the authentication. Because of human fallibility there must always be these backup or recovery mechanisms, but they necessarily create security weaknesses. These techniques are often used by *penetration testers*, businesses that are paid to try and penetrate organizations, both digitally and physically, to assess how secure they really are[12].

Social engineering is also used to manipulate data analytics by trying to cause models to be built that seem implausible, so that those who might act on them ignore them. Since the role of a data-analytics user is exactly to judge model plausibility, this can be very successful. A clumsy form of social engineering can be seen in detective stories in which the master criminal is from a high class of society and so could not, from the perspective of the police, actually be a criminal.

The third opportunity to subvert data-analytic modeling is to use an insider who has the access to manipulate the data once it has been collected, to alter the way in which models are built, and/or to change the way in which results are presented. Insiders are an insidious threat for many organizations because they represent a particular kind of blind spot – nobody is willing to seriously consider that that nice person in IT has been bribed or suborned in other ways. Insider threat is a particular problem for law enforcement because those who manage the IT and data analytics are often not peace officers and have not had the organizational ethic inculcated to the same extent as frontline officers[13].

Data analytics is changing law enforcement, as it is changing many organizations. For this change to be effective, there needs to be a better understanding of what data analytics can do, what is required to make it work (ranging from data collection through computation to interfaces that can be used by officers), and the role it can play in policing and investigation. This is especially true because the background of senior law-enforcement or intelligence management is often in law or the social sciences, and the temptation is to see data analytics as something similar to forensic science, to be put into a specialty unit, rather than something that must be pervasive for maximal effectiveness.

5.4 Intelligence-led policing

Data analytics does not produce models that are true, but models that are plausible and are consistent with the available data. Their results, therefore, cannot be used directly to make consequential or forensic decisions. Decisions about arrests and prosecutions must be based on evidence, as they always have been.

However, the results of data analytics can be suggestive of what might happen, or have happened, in a particular crime setting, and so they can be used to direct investigations in what are likely to be the most productive directions.

This idea has come to be called *intelligence-led policing*. At its core it is an argument that tasks or actions should be chosen based on an analysis of (predicted) benefit.

Intelligence-led policing is a development of the concept of *problem-oriented policing*[14], which marked a change from policing as fundamentally reactive, to a more proactive view. In traditional policing, an officer walked a beat both as a generalized deterrent, and to be on hand to deal with any crimes that were committed within the fixed time and space of the beat. In problem-oriented policing, a particular set of crimes are examined as a set, with the goals of discovering their drivers, and then developing responses to deal with them more effectively. Responses can range from preemptive steps such as designs to reduce the opportunity for the particular kind of crime; to better training or patrols, to better investigation techniques.

In a prevention context, intelligence-led policing means deploying police resources to maximize the deterrence for certain crimes. This means using models of crime risk and then determining actions designed to reduce those risks: sending patrols to places (and times) where crimes are likeliest, hardening businesses that are most at risk of break-ins, educating citizens whose behaviors put them at greatest risk, and so on.

In an investigation context, the focus of intelligence-led policing is on choosing actions that are predicted to have the greatest benefit. For example, models can determine the ordering of tasks based on which are likely to be productive the soonest, rather than unthinkingly following an investigation routine.

Some investigations are less about finding the best order for investigative tasks, and more about finding any lead to investigate at all. These contexts are more of the "find the needle in the haystack" kind, and often arise when there are multiple apparently unconnected crimes, ranging from burglaries to murders; and also for many kinds of financial irregularities. Intelligence-led policing can find common factors that are difficult for humans to find either because the factors are non-obvious or because the size of the data involved is so large.

5.5 Hot spot policing

Hot spot policing can be thought of as a specialized form of intelligence-led policing based on the general observation that the distributions of crime are highly skewed with respect to almost any property. Hot spot policing assumes underlying models of why criminals commit the crimes they do, and when and where. These models are very general, and have been understood, at least broadly, for a long time. The surprising development that has come from collecting and analyzing data at scale is that the skews in the distribution of crime, and so risk, are much more extreme than intuition suggests.

The discussion of why a crime happens at a particular time and place, and with a particular perpetrator and victim has been a topic of research for a century. Obviously it must be a blend of geographical, physical, social, and mental factors but the exact blend has proved elusive.

The process was first framed using *rational choice theory*. This theory suggests that a perpetrator commits a crime by balancing the pleasure it provides (economic benefit, but also thrills or respect from fellow criminals) and the risk involved (violent response, prosecution, and incarceration). Rational choice has been a popular model in many social sciences but it has become less popular as the evidence mounts that human choices are mostly not completely rational (and perhaps this is even more true of habitual criminals). Rational choice theory is often the implicit model of those who call for more prisons or harsher sentencing since this is believed to increase the risk side of the potential perpetrator's calculus.

Routine activity theory is a specialized version of rational choice. It suggests that the occurrence of a crime is a result of the confluence of three elements (a) a perpetrator willing and able to commit a crime, (b) an available victim, and (c) the absence of a guardian who might prevent the crime[15]. At one level this is a truism. But this theory is explanatory of some of the properties of crime, for example the greater involvement of youth both as perpetrators and as victims.

Crimes are distributed in a skewed way with respect to at least the modalities of: place, time, weather, and people involved, and so there are hot spots of many kinds.

5.5.1 Place

The observation that crimes are more likely in some areas than in others goes back to the earliest days of policing. A number of different explanations have been suggested for this geographical skew in the occurrences of crime.

- The *ecological* explanation suggests that the explanation lies in differences in the socioeconomic status of neighborhoods. Some neighborhoods are high-crime areas because of characteristics such as high population density, poverty, mixed-use buildings, transience, and the presence of a high percentage of disadvantaged groups (immigrants, indigenous). Conversely, neighborhoods with low population density, single-family dwellings, and few pedestrians are more likely to be low-crime areas.

  While there must be some truth in this framing, it has fallen out of favor because of the discovery that even within a high-risk neighborhood, risk is still very unevenly distributed. Apparently identical micro-locations – much smaller in size than an neighborhood – still have characteristic and stable differences in their crime rates.

- The *semiotics* explanation suggest that signs of social disorder in a particular location convey a signal that other deviance, including crime, is acceptable there. This motivated the "broken windows" theory that was used to good effect in New York City – push back against minor crimes, especially those that create local signals, for examples petty vandalism, drug dealing, and panhandling, and more serious crimes will be reduced. Empirically, this seems to have worked[16].

Broader data collection has thrown doubt on the explanatory power of both of these theories.

Hot spot policing that considers much smaller areas than neighborhoods dates from a paper by Sherman[17] who showed that crime was strongly skewed even when the spatial unit considered was as small as a street segment, roughly a one-block unit. He showed that, when a location is considered to be either an address or an intersection, 50% of all calls to police came from 3% of locations. The skew of violent crimes is even stronger: all robberies were associated with 2.2% of locations, and all rapes with 1.2% of locations. Half of the locations that made a call to police made only one, but one location made 810 calls in the year of study. Vilalta *et al.*[18] showed that homicides occurred at much higher rates in what they called container blocks, areas that had been divided up into smaller pedestrianized areas containing small squares, access pathways, and dead ends. Considering crime rates and risks at the level of larger areas, such as suburbs or census tracts, clearly fails to capture important variations that exist within these areas.

Leveraging the skewed distribution of the locations of crime required thinking at a totally new scale, much finer than "neighborhood", and smaller even than the traditional concept of a beat. Neither the ecological nor the semiotic theories could explain this tight localization in the frequency of crimes.

Crimes are strongly local, even when the mechanics of the crime itself does not constrain location. For example, one might assume that the risk of burglary among the houses on a single street might be about the same, perhaps modulated by whether some had burglar alarms and some did not. Brantingham and Brantingham developed *crime pattern theory*[19] which suggests that locations of crimes are strongly driven by a need of criminals to operate in familiar territory, much more so than the opportunities available to them. The obvious meaning of familiar territory is spatial, but the other possible meanings are also included in this theory.

Crime pattern theory is based on the observations that most crimes are committed by criminals close to where they live, work, or along the path between them. For example, home burglaries are actually concentrated in houses that are on the edges of suburbs or subdivisions, perhaps only half a block or so in from larger streets. So on a particular street the houses at the ends are at higher risk than those in the middle, and the end that has the fastest access to larger streets has higher risk than the other end.

Crime pattern theory explains why locations in the same neighborhood (with the same ecology) or with the same semiotics have different crime rates – it depends on the nodes and pathways followed by the criminals local to the area. In other words, a particular location cannot be considered in isolation, but as part of a dynamic system of criminals on the move and at rest. Because criminals are not instantly detectable, and their paths to and from work even less so, identifying localized risk is difficult, and requires detailed data.

Habit seems to play a role as well. This is another kind of familiar territory, psychological familiarity. Criminals find ways to commit their crimes that work for them and then rarely change these ways, even though this makes them easier to identify, because their methods become associated with them. This explains why modus operandi repositories continue to be useful, even though criminals know that they exist.

In fact, locality seems to constrain criminals' actions beyond all reason. Criminals using stolen or fake credit cards or bank cards work their way down one side of the street, rarely crossing over even when there are businesses that they could target on the other side[20]. Drug dealers not only prefer particular intersections, but prefer a particular corner of those intersections (such as the North-East)[21]. Preferences such as these suggest that hot spot analysis should be considered at even smaller units than segments. In countries at higher latitudes, opposite sides of east-west streets receive different amounts of sun, and north-south streets offer different amounts of protection from ambient winds in many locales. This almost certainly has an effect on where criminals choose to act. Even locations as small and ill-defined as bus stops (which create impromptu gathering places) can have an impact on where crime occurs.

Many crimes are situationally driven, and often opportunistic. One response to the spatial skew in crime is to discover high-risk locations, and harden them, so that crimes at those locations become perceived as more difficult, and so rates of occurrence are depressed. For example, convenience stores, a common target for robbery when cash transactions were more frequent, are designed so that the service point is visible from outside, especially at night. Banks are carefully laid out to create an impression of openness, and have obtrusive security features. Public spaces can also be designed so that they are unwelcoming to crime, an approach known by the unfortunate name of *hostile architecture*.

Crime pattern theory suggests that focused hardening will be difficult because it requires an analysis of where criminals live and work, and these are necessarily hard to get. A more scattershot approach to hardening may be the best we can achieve.

An integrated approach to spatial modeling of crime is *risk terrain modeling*[22]. Risk terrain modeling ties together the physical properties of locations with their built-environment properties and demographic properties. It has been implemented in software called RTMDX[23].

5.5.2 Time

It is not surprising that the frequency of crimes varies with time, at all scales from the seasonal, the monthly, the weekly, to the daily and hourly. Most of the conceptual thinking about the dependence of crimes on time is framed in terms of opportunity. Predictably, violent crime patterns are more structured in time than property crime patterns. Targets of property crimes are available much of the time, but targets of violence are only sporadically available.

Seasons have an effect depending on climate. In countries far from the equator, more people are outside their homes in the warmer seasons. This has a marked effect in the Northern Hemisphere because many populous countries are relatively far north. Changes in the amount of time spent outside create differential opportunities for crimes against the person such as muggings, and also for property crimes against houses that are more likely to be empty. Conversely, in winter people stay inside, houses are more likely to be occupied, and snow shows tracks which decreases the number of burglaries.

Months have an effect because, for example, many people are paid at the beginning, midpoint, or end of the month, so crimes against the person cluster around the newly paid. The times just before pay dates may also represent the lowest financial ebb for some, who may turn to crime to make ends meet.

Weeks have an effect because both criminals and victims have different behavior patterns on work days and weekends. Part-time criminals have to be at their job locations or schools for a substantial fraction of each week.

Days have an effect because of the patterns of activities at different time. Times when people are commuting to and from work are busy in a focused way; many people are limited to a small range of locations during work hours; and evenings are busy in a different way because of visits to restaurants, bars, and entertainment venues. Afternoon and early evening are the commonest times for all crimes. There is a peak in minor property crimes around 3 p.m. presumably because the perpetrators are largely of school age and are not free until then. Moderately violent crimes are commonest on weekends, and around either the early evening or the very late evening/early morning.

Time also has an effect over longer time scales. The risk of a repeat residential burglary increases for more than two weeks after the initial burglary[24], and increases the risk for nearby locations for the same period as well. Many patterns of timing for crimes have been observed all over the world.

Study of temporal patterns of crime lags behind study of spatial patterns, partly because for some crimes the actual time that the crime took place is not known because the crime was only discovered much later. Also, in collected data, times tended to be aggregated at the level of days until recently. However, it is clear that the timing of crimes is skewed in the same way as we have seen that the locations of crime are skewed. However, although there are several competing criminological theories about the role of place in crimes, there is much less about the role of time.

A better analysis of temporal patterns of crime would help with hardening in a temporal sense – making sure that police are most present at times when crimes are most likely. Of course, many temporal patterns are well understood and police are familiar with the idea that there should be an increased presence when large sports events end, or bars close.

5.5.3 Weather

Weather also has an effect on the rates of crimes, perhaps motivated both by the effect it has on the movements of ordinary people, and the discomfort it imposes on criminals themselves. Both routine activity theory (an ecological theory) and internal state theory have been invoked as explanations[25]. Crimes that take place indoors are, unsurprisingly, affected by weather only weakly.

Studies have consistently shown that increasing temperature tends to increase crime rates (in a Finnish study, an increase of one degree Celsius produced an increase in crime of 1.7% and this was explained as mediated by measured changes in serotonin levels)[26]. However, studies in warmer places suggest that the response curve is actually an inverted U, so that at much hotter temperatures, the rates of crime decrease again[27]. This is usually explained as a change of focus by criminals from committing crimes to staying cool. Studies also suggest that really unpleasant weather (snow, extreme cold) decrease the rates of all crimes. There is not a consensus but there are some hints that rain has a negligible effect on crime rates.

The effect of weather on crime exhibits less skew than place or time, perhaps because, in most places, everyone is accustomed to the weather and just gets on with their lives. This "acclimatization" seems just as effective in places with extreme weather as in places where the weather is more temperate.

Obviously there are interactions between time, place, and weather, and these are beginning to be studied together.

5.5.4 People involved

There is also considerable skew in the way in which criminals work together, notably in the size of group involved in any particular crime. Some criminals act alone, but some crimes require, or involve, several people acting together. Sometimes the collaborators work together simply because they know each other; at other times, they work together because they have complementary skills.

Criminals also work together because some kinds of crimes involve supply chains. For example, a drug distributor at any level collaborates with a supplier upstream, and a set of lower-level dealers downstream. A thief often collaborates with a fence who is able to take stolen property and sell it on.

Criminals rarely collaborate with others they do not already know, so the discussion of skew in criminal group sizes requires us to consider social networks as the primary source of collaboration.

5.5.5 Social network position

Social networks are models of the way in which individuals or organizations connect or relate to one another. The nodes of the network represent the individuals or organizations; the edges represent the connections or relationships between the nodes. The edges are often weighted to represent the strength of the connections they represent.

A pair of nodes (individuals or organizations) initially forms a relationship, which will be encoded as a new edge, and goes on to maintain the connection, which may result in an increasing weight on the edge reflecting the continuing activity associated with the relationship.

From the perspective of the nodes involved, forming and developing the relationship feels like a purely local decision to connect and maintain. However, social networks develop macroscale structures that show that this is cannot be true – we make connections as a complex function of need, want, and human cognitive limits. Studying social networks as complete objects therefore reveals information about the participants and their mutual relationships that is not obvious in the pairwise relationships. In other words, social networks integrate local (pairwise) information into an emergent global structure that has consistent detectable properties. This global structure becomes, in turn, a background against which each local relationship can be re-evaluated.

Social networks, of course, pre-date computer systems. Societies have always had connections between individuals that form a rich structure: family members, tribal elders, friends, and possible partners. Many of the properties of these real-world social networks are also true of social networks in cyberspace because the same needs, wants, and cognitive limits apply.

For example, we appear to have between 125 and 150 mental "slots" that we can use to keep track of our relationships with other people. This quantity is called *Dunbar's number* and it seems relatively fixed, from prehistoric tribal societies to our current circles of online "friends"[28]. It has often been observed that when many kinds of organizations grow to the size of Dunbar's number they either disintegrate, or they split into two suborganizations, each of which begins to grow again.

This cognitive limitation that we each have impacts the structure of our social network in the following way. As we consider adding another person, and so another relationship, when all or most of our slots are already full, our brains either push back, making it harder to add that person; or we add the new person and relationship but downgrade an existing person to an acquaintance, and lose track of that person's detailed status. This is not a conscious process, but it operates in all of us nevertheless.

Within this set of roughly 125–150, there is finer structure, known as the "Rule of Almost Threes". Most people have about 3 really close connections (perhaps immediate family), about 9 slightly less close connections (close friends), about 27 even weaker connections (perhaps extended family and close colleagues), and about 81 connections that they still keep track of (perhaps colleagues we see every day but do not work with), but would perhaps not consider friends[29]. So even in normal social networks there is a skewed structure, in which a few people are tracked in detail, a slightly larger group in less detail, and so on.

Dunbar's number provides a baseline for "normal" connectedness in a social network. Someone with many fewer connections is unusually isolated; some with many more connections is unusually well-connected (but is more likely to be maintaining a number of superficial connections rather than real relationships).

Standing at a node in a social network we might each see a similar looking local environment of neighbors and connections, but each node's location in the larger social network can tell us more about the role of the person it belongs to. It is reasonable to define the center and the periphery of a social network by considering the paths that connect each node to every other node. A *central* node is one that has short paths to almost every other node, and such nodes are naturally considered to be powerful by virtue of their position in the network. Power can mean a variety of things but, from a command-and-control perspective, nodes in the center can communicate with everyone more quickly than anyone else. This property of having short paths to almost all other nodes is called *centrality*. A person with high centrality is therefore likely to be someone with power in a social network.

On the other hand, nodes on the periphery tend to have short paths to only a few nodes, and long paths to most. In an obvious way, their position makes them less powerful.

The number of *triangles*, triples of people who are mutually connected, is also a highly stable property of social networks. Triangles are the natural consequence of a person with two friends introducing them to one another, turning a V-shaped pattern into a triangle. Again a collection of purely local decisions creates a global property of the social network, the fraction of triangles as a function of the network size.

Social networks also give insight into how relationships work as carriers of influence among humans. People who are connected in a social network influence one another. The surprising thing is how far such influence flows. From the perspective of a node, there is a measurable effect from nodes that are three steps away in the social network, that is from friends of friends of friends. So members of a social network are measurably influenced by their direct connections, by the connections of those direct connections (who they may have heard of), but also by other people whom they probably do not even know.

Influence flows in this way for properties such as happiness, obesity, cigarette smoking, and generosity[30]. In other words, having a happy friend makes you measurably happier, but so does having a happy friend of a friend, and even a happy friend of a friend of a friend. This is also true of sadness but, fortunately, sadness flows with less intensity than happiness. There is no doubt some truth in the common statement that we are each are the average of the five people we spend the most time with, but the picture is actually considerably more subtle.

The social networks of criminals differ from ordinary social networks in a number of important ways that can be leveraged to understand criminal group dynamics.

First, the lack of trust between criminals means that their social networks are sparser (overall not as richly connected) and more likely to have well-defined subnetworks that do not have many connections to the rest of the social network. This is partly deliberate, for security, for example, keeping the networks of gang members with different roles or functions apart from one another to limit the effect of an arrest or a police informer. But trust issues also mean that social networks of criminals tend not to have as many connections as a conventional social network of the same size would have.

Second, triangles are much rarer in criminal social networks than they are in ordinary ones. This appears to be because criminals do not introduce their friends or contacts to one another, perhaps to preserve their access to them as a trusted resource.

However, those in command and control roles in criminal networks cannot help but form triangles with one another because of the need both to plan and to respond to difficulties quickly. Looking for those members of the network who are members of many triangles is an effective way to find the key players in a criminal network[31].

There are several kinds of special social networks that have been developed to describe the relationships and interactions among criminals. The first is called a *cooffender network*. The nodes of this network are criminals, and an edge is added whenever two criminals have collaborated in a crime. Edges can be weighted to count the number of times such collaborations have occurred.

Cooffending networks are straightforward to construct because the required information is captured in arrest records. In most countries about half of criminals commit their crimes individually, while about half are part of a cooffender network. These fractions depends on the time window being considered. More criminals would be part of the cooffender network if their entire careers were considered since youth criminals are more likely to cooffend.

Usually this cooffender network has a single large connected component, a subnetwork all of whose members are connected by paths, so that any node is, in principle, reachable from any other along relationship edges. There is also typically a set of components of decreasing size, with a substantial number of criminals committing their crimes in stable pairs. A co-offending network analysis therefore tells us that, roughly, half of all criminals commit crimes alone, another quarter or so commit their crimes in groups that overlap enough that they are all connected by paths of cooffending, and another quarter commit their crimes in small groups, mostly pairs, that remain stable over a long time.

Skew is a critical property of social networks too. The impact of crime and harm is strongly concentrated even within the cooffender network. In a Danish study, 3.6% of the cooffender network accounted for 50% of the harm caused by crime in the whole country[32].

Those who cooffend the most commit more crimes than those whose criminal activities involve fewer collaborators, and so those with many neighbors in a cooffender network are natural targets for law-enforcement attention. Bigger cooffender groups also cause more harm proportional to their size and should also be targeted.

The second kind of criminal social network is that formed by a criminal organization. This could be traditional organized crime (mafia, triads, yakuza), gangs, and drug-distribution networks. Here the connections are functional rather than relational – the social network resembles the organizational chart of a business, and for the same reasons. Understanding the structure of this kind of social network shows how the criminal organization works, and how it is managed. However, such social networks are more difficult to discover since the relationships are not obvious, and the members may actively conceal their interactions with other group members.

At one time it was widely believed that criminal networks were usually like business organizational charts, with criminal masterminds controlling large criminal groups. This view has been largely discounted as a result of gathering empirical data about actual criminal groups. While traditional organized crime groups have something resembling a management structure, most criminal groups have a much less organized structure, and even this structure is dynamic. Membership in the group may change (at least because some members are incarcerated), roles also change over time and, for some kinds of groups, issues with addictions among members cause them to fall in and out of active participation. Gangs are the least likely to have a detectable organizational structure, at least one that survives over time.

A particular problem for law enforcement trying to understand a criminal group is to discover its boundary. This is partly because the boundary is inherently poorly defined – some individuals are in, some are out, and some are weakly involved, rather like freelancers. It is also difficult because members of a criminal organization do not only associate with other members. It may be difficult, from observation, to decide if a meeting of a known member of the criminal organization is with another member, with a social contact, or with a non-criminal contact, such as a barber or tax adviser. This is one place where traffic analysis (knowing who met or communicated with whom, either by intercepting online activity or by surveillance) is much weaker as a tool for understanding group structure than interception that captures the content of conversations or communications.

5.6 Exploiting skewed distributions

If densities of crimes are skewed in time, space, weather, people involved, and social network position, how can law enforcement make use of these differentials?

The key property of skew is that it produces a few high-value opportunities, rather than a larger set of mediocre opportunities – but these few opportunities may be hard to see if they are not looked for carefully. In other words, skew leads to low-hanging fruit. Small amounts of effort, carefully applied, can lead to huge results. If, as we saw above, a few percent, not just of criminals but of criminals in a cooffender network, contribute to half the crimes, then focusing on this small set of criminals can produce crime reductions out of all proportion to the effort[33]. This is obviously attractive from a staffing and budget perspective. A focus on crime statistics, while superficially sensible, tends to drive activities towards averages, and can dissipate the advantages of exploiting skew.

Skew also means that, at the other end of the distribution, there are many, many low-impact activities by criminals. Citizens and government need to be educated about this means for their perception of risk. When a distribution is highly skewed, using a percentage or average measure of risk is meaningless. So it is useless (or worse) to talk about the average risk of being mugged, having your house broken into, having your bank account hacked, or being attacked in the street. The risk for individuals depends on how they interact with the skewing factors.

For example, if you stay at home between midnight and 6 a.m. your risk for being a victim of large classes of crimes becomes a tiny fraction of the "average". On the other hand, if you went to school with people who are now criminals, your risk for being a victim of large classes of crimes is higher than the average.

Although many people have some kind of intuition about skew, often embodied by the Pareto principle (also known as the 80:20 rule), they do not operationalize this in their perceptions of risk. In fact, for almost all crimes the skew ratio is much greater than 80:20. For example, for shooting deaths and injuries in the U.S. in 2013, the stray bullet rate was roughly 3 in a 1000 incidents, even though the U.S.

has one of the highest rates of gun violence in the world[34]. In other words, in 997 out of every thousand shooting incidents, deaths and injuries happened when there was already a connection between the shooter and the victim. Similarly, around 80% of murder victims knew their killer(s), so the chance of being murdered by a stranger is relatively low, especially as the murder rate in the U.S. is about 5 in 100,000[35].

Law enforcement (and the media) could make citizens feel safer if they communicated more clearly about the true risks of all sorts of crime, rather than talking, or allowing others to talk, about average risks.

Second, law enforcement must decide how to make use of information about skewed distributions. Skew represents an opportunity to make an impact on crime and criminals much greater than the effort expended, but it requires high levels of intentionality. When resources already seem slim, it can be a challenge to allocate some to high-value targeting based on what may seem to be unproven (and perhaps unlikely) distributional arguments.

In some ways, responding to hot spots is the most obvious way to leverage skew distributions. However, even this is not straightforward. There is much disagreement about whether hot spots are generators of high levels of crime – settings that provide opportunities for crime – or receptors of high levels of crime – settings that offenders seek out purposively to commit crimes.

A *generator location* is one where criminals happen to be because of other aspects of their lives. According to crime pattern theory, these are locations where criminals live, where they work, or the commute in between[36]. Criminals notice opportunities for crimes at these locations because they are already there, so the crimes are opportunistic in a targeting sense. That does not preclude a significant amount of planning for the crime before the crime is carried out, just that the possibility of the crime was noticed "by accident". So such crimes are not necessarily opportunistic in a smash-and-grab sense. The concept of generator locations explains why many kinds of crimes concentrate on and around arterial streets and along public transit routes.

A *receptor* or *attractor* location is one that criminals have to go outside their usual orbit to reach, that is which takes them out of their normal movement routine. Usually this is because something about the location is unusual or special, making it a target. Criminals who commit crimes at attractor locations are regarded as more highly motivated since they have to have conceived the possibility of the crime without seeing it in front of them.

For example, breaking in to a residence can be understood as the residence being a generator; while breaking in to a warehouse is much more likely to be understood as the warehouse being an attractor (unless one of the criminals involved works there).

A clear understanding of whether a location is considered a generator location or an attractor location will impact the steps taken to reduce crime there.

If hot spots are explained as generators, then there are properties of the hot spot that make it more likely that a crime will take place then, there, and/or in those conditions. Ecological theories will explain that the location is a generator because of the local demographics and physical geography. Semiotic theories will explain that the location is a generator because there are signals that social deviance is appropriate. Crime pattern theory will explain that the location is a generator because criminals live there, work there, or pass through it. Fortunately, regardless of which theory is believed, the actions to reduce crime are broadly similar: clean up the location. The exact form of cleaning will differ: for example, better social work for ecological generators, better maintenance for semiotic generators, and alterations to traffic patterns for crime pattern generators. There has been considerable research over quite a long time about how architecture can be used to reduce the incidence of crime[37] but successes seem to have been limited. For generator hot spots, the interventions are mostly not those available to law enforcement; rather they require action from (local) government[38].

If hot spots are explained as attractors, then crimes happen there because they, in a sense, must. As Willie Sutton is supposed to have said, he robbed banks because that's where the money was. If hot spots are attractors, there a fewer options for reducing crime and they all have the flavor of hardening locations. Some kinds of hardening can be done by local government (opening spaces, providing better lighting and sightlines) and by local businesses, who have the incentive to reduce their attractiveness to crime. But law enforcement can make a difference too by increasing police patrol presence, or providing more sensors (for example, CCTV cameras or gunshot detectors).

What happens when police forces begin to exploit their knowledge of hot spots? This depends to some extent on whether the hot spots are generators or attractors. Policing generator hot spots tends to have the effect of driving total crime levels down, since it reduces opportunities, and so crimes that would otherwise have happened do not.

When hot spot policing was first introduced, there were concerns that crimes reduced in the hot spots would simply be displaced to nearby locations. In fact, this tends not to happen – policing these kinds of hot spots produces a net reduction in crime and, when displacement occurs, it does so in a predictable way (along major streets, and towards downtown cores) so that compensating patrol patterns can be used. In other words, crime in generator hot spots really is opportunistic and, when depressed by law-enforcement action, disappears rather than moves.

There is one important exception – crimes that are detected only because of the presence of police. Public nuisance crimes and many drug crimes are not, on the whole, reported to police. Rather such crimes tend to be detected by police as a side-effect of their other activities. For these categories of crimes, the detected frequencies with which they are recorded is proportional to the amount of police attention to the area in which they take place. Unlike other generator locations, increasing police presence will increase the (apparent) occurrences of crime. This creates a feedback loop that can make a hot spot seem increasingly hotter, and lead to a poor deployment of resources, as well perhaps as a sense of victimization in the citizens present at the location. This is a difficult issue because, of course, such low-level crimes also happen in a skewed way, and so there will always be hot spots for their occurrence[39].

The effect of policing attractor hot spots is less clear. In these settings there is a kind of arms race between police and criminals, with criminals trying to guess where/when there are opportunities to commit a crime in the hot spot, and police trying to ensure that there are as few opportunities as possible.

There are two important considerations that improve attractor hot spot policing. First, police activity at each hot spot should have a large element of randomization in it. If it is a physical location, for example, police patrols should visit at random intervals. Some care is needed here to make the timing truly random, because human ideas of randomness tend not be very random at all.

Second, what happens when the police start thinking "if I do this, then the criminal will do that to avoid me, so I should do something else instead"? This problem has been addressed using game theory (the theory of Stackelberg games) which provides an optimal solution for how to reach a conclusion for settings where this kind of reasoning is natural. An implementation of this approach has been used, for example, for the timing and routing of security patrols at Los Angeles International Airport, where potential terrorists might use exactly this kind of recursive reasoning[40].

Other ways to exploit skew at smaller scale are being developed, but there is little experience with their use. For example, several police forces are developing *mission sheets* which describe high-profile locations and individuals, and can be taken on patrol by frontline officers. These partly replace daily briefings, with the advantage that an officer who briefly loses concentration during a briefing can still receive the most critical information for the day. A mission sheet focuses on the most significant content that an officer should have top of mind, and so is a natural way to exploit skew. Mission sheets can even be generated automatically or partly automatically based on data from a record management system[41].

There are also downsides to exploiting skew, especially when the public's perception of the distribution is different from that of officers. Consider one example, the practice of police officers having a conversation with someone on the street. Such discussions can occur at a number of levels. The simplest is when the officers are not pursuing any particular investigation, the person is free to leave at any time, and the person need not reveal their identity. Such discussions are not usually problematic, although they may become so if the police offers create a record of the interaction. Interactions like this have happened since the beginning of beat policing, and both police and citizens have benefited from the broad community knowledge that officers gather in this way. Some of the benefits have been lost with the change from officers walking to a beat to patrolling in a vehicle; and from a tendency to make all interactions with the public adversarial in flavor.

The level above this kind of informal encounter is called, in the U.S., a Terry stop (Terry v. Ohio (1968)), or sometimes "stop and frisk". In these interactions, officers stop someone, ask for, and record, their identity, but require some reasonable and articulable suspicion that the person has or is about to commit a crime (although the details vary state by state). In Canada, a similar process is called carding, but can be done without any focused suspicion (although it has now been banned across most police forces).

It is often argued that the intelligence gathered by these kinds of interactions with the public is of limited value, and that may well be true (although the risk of such an encounter with police by a criminal surely has a damping effect on his activities). However, the biggest criticism of these techniques arises exactly because of a lack of understanding of skew. It is claimed, for example, that the people stopped using these mechanisms are disproportionately from particular communities. But the right question to ask is not "do police interact with members of some communities more than others?" but rather "do police interact with members of some communities in proportion to the rates at which those communities commit crimes?". In other words, in the name of fairness, police are expected to sample uniformly from the available population even when crime is extremely disproportionately caused by some subgroups. The same underappreciation of skew happened with airport security in the wake of the 9/11 attacks, where women over 85 were receiving enhanced screening at the same rate as everyone else, despite the extreme unlikelihood that they were terrorists. This issue is politically sensitive at present, and police forces need to both understand why they act as they do, and be able to articulate it. (If they cannot do either, then perhaps they have a problem and should be actively considering how to remediate it.)

Other ways that skew can be exploited are:

- Send patrols to locations with high rates of visible crime (much) more often than to other locations;
- Match staffing levels to the times of day (and months) when crimes are expected to peak;
- Use weather forecasts to adjust staffing levels;
- Pay attention to cooffending patterns during arrest and processing (rather than just as an offline intelligence function);
- Collect and record social network data from anyone arrested, data about their families and friends to the extent possible, as well as cooffenders.

We have seen that skew is present in almost every aspect of crime. Its existence is a great benefit to law enforcement because it means that there are always areas where effort will produce enormously disproportionate positive results. However, skew is a counter-intuitive property and law enforcement is still struggling to leverage it to the full.

Notes

[1]CompStat won an Innovation in Government Award in 1996 (https://www.innovations.harvard.edu/compstat-crime-reduction-management-tool). More details about its design and use can be found here: https://bja.ojp.gov/sites/g/files/xyckuh186/files/Publications/PERF-Compstat.pdf.

[2]The HOLMES (and now HOLMES2) systems were built for the U.K. police, initially to help senior officers manage complex cases and to make sure that important facts and issues did not slip through the cracks. It is now a fully functional case-management system that can be used both for police investigations and natural disaster management (https://www.holmes2.com/holmes2/index.php).

[3]At present, analysts often serve as intermediaries between frontline officers and data. We will argue that this is an artifact of the way that data is managed and leveraged today, and that there is much to be gained by allowing frontline officers direct access to data; or better still to models built from the data.

[4]www.popularmechanics.com/technology/security/how-to/a5226/4341499/.

[5]Ian Fleming, Goldfinger, Ch. 14.

[6]Report of the 9/11 Commission, Ch. 11.

[7]This process is used in traditional "fair play" detective stories, where the reader induces the models about who might have committed the crime, and so tries to guess the ending. Particularly skilled authors, for example Agatha Christie, make it possible to infer many possible models that are consistent with the superficial data presented, with different levels of sophistication. Constructing these models is part of the enjoyment of reading such books. On the other hand, when the detective presents the solution, there is often a sense of letdown because, in retrospect it seems so obvious. In that sense, recognizing solutions is less difficult than constructing hypothetical solutions.

[8]Note especially that such models cannot predict that an individual will commit a crime with enough reliability to have forensic value, although such a prediction might have intelligence value.

[9]A system that does this kind of detection automatically from CCTV video was developed for the New York Transit system. There are also systems that detect anomalies in video feeds, particularly unusual vehicle or person movements.

[10]There remain some biases which arise from biases in the data that is used, and potentially in some of the modeling techniques.

[11]In one particularly striking example, a licence plate was replaced by a database command. The collection system captured the string and, because of a security flaw in the design of the system, passed it to the database as if it were a command. This had the effect of deleting the entire database. This technique is known as an *sql injection attack*.

[12]Penetration testers discussing the ways in which they get access to buildings can be found here: https://www.youtube.com/watch?v=rnmcRTnTNC8, and https://www.youtube.com/watch?v=edLXMm7m4bM. Their success stories are both amusing and concerning.

[13]A common challenge today is whether data analysts should be trained peace officers. There are good reasons to want this, including a deeper understanding of the challenges of frontline policing. However, as the demand for data analytics explodes, not only in law enforcement, it is increasingly hard to find qualified personnel, let alone insist that they go through peace-officer training and spend some time on the front line.

[14]H. Goldstein, *Problem-Oriented Policing*, Temple University Press, 1990.

[15]L.E. Cohen and M. Felson, "Social change and crime rate trends: A routine activity approach", *American Sociological Review*, 44(4):588–608, August 1979.

[16]Although whether this works in general is still considered contentious.

[17]L.W. Sherman, "Repeat calls to police in Minneapolis", Technical Report 4, Crime Control Reports, Crime Control Institute, Washington D.C., 1987.

[18]C.J. Vilalta, R. Muggah and G. Fondevila, "Homicide as a function of city block layout: Mexico City as case study", *Global Crime*, 21:2:111–129, 2020.

[19]P.L. Brantingham and P.J. Brantingham, *Environment, Routine, and Situation: Toward a Pattern Theory of Crime*, in: *From Routine Activity and Rational Choice: Advances in Criminological Theory*, volume 5, pp. 259–294. Routledge, 1993.

[20]Told to me by the fraud unit of a major bank.

[21]A.A. Braga, A.V. Papachristos and D.M. Hureau, "The concentration and stability of gun violence at micro places in Boston, 1980–2008", *Journal of Quantitative Criminology*, 26:33–53, 2010.

[22]www.riskterrainmodeling.com/.

[23]https://www.rutgerscps.org/software.html.

[24]Partly because the homeowner has just purchased new objects to replace those stolen in the first burglary.

[25]S. Towers, S. Chen, A. Malik and D. Ebert, "Factors influencing temporal patterns in crime in a large American city: A predictive analytics perspective", *PLOS One*, 13(10), 2018; M. Reichhoff, "The effect of weather on crime: An investigation of weather and annual crime rates", Speciale, University of Wisconsin Whitewater, 2017.

[26]J. Tiihonen, P. Halonen, L. Tiihonen, H. Kautiainen, M. Storvik and J. Callaway, "The association of ambient temperature and violent crime", *Nature Scientific Reports*, 7:6543, 2017.

[27]R. Murataya and D.R. Gutiérrez, "Effects of weather on crime", *International Journal of Humanities and Social Science*, 3:71–75, 2013.

[28]Of course, many people have many more people they label as friends, followers, and so on, but sociologists would argue that, beyond Dunbar's number, these are acquaintances at best.

[29]And if about 3 is actually 3.2, then the sum of these numbers is close to 150, so Dunbar's Number agrees quite well with the Rule of Almost Threes.

[30]N.A. Christakis and J.H. Fowler, "The spread of obesity in a large social network over 32 years", *New England Journal of Medicine*, 357:370–379, 2007; K.P. Smith and N.A. Christakis, "Social networks and health", *Annual Review of Sociology*, 34:402–429, 2008.

[31]D.B. Skillicorn and F. Calderoni, "Inductive discovery of criminal group structure using spectral embedding", *Information and Security*, 31:49–66, 2015; D.B. Skillicorn, F. Spezzano, V.S. Subrahmanian and M. Garber, *Understanding South Asian Violent Extremist Group-Group Interactions*, in: *FOSINT 2014 at ASONAM 2014*, August 2014.

[32]C. Frydensberg, B. Arial and M. Bland, "Targeting the most harmful co-offenders in Denmark: a social network analysis approach", *Cambridge Journal of Evidence-Based Policing*, 3:21–36, 2019.

[33]However, this does not mean that other crimes can be ignored. Citizens get upset if "minor" crimes are effectively ignored by police. For example, in many countries, burglaries are never realistically investigated. This frustrates ordinary citizens and their tolerance may eventually be reached.

[34]The rate of shootings of any kind is 1 in a million in Singapore, and 1 in 2 million in Japan.

[35]Another misleading average since this rate is much higher in, say Chicago than in, say, Irvine.

[36]Note that different kinds of commutes create qualitatively different opportunities. On foot, there is time to notice details; on public transit, these times are reduced; and driving is a kind of tunnel, with very limited observation opportunities because of the amount of attention that must be paid to the road ahead and other traffic.

[37]N.K. Katyal, "Architecture as crime control", *Yale Law Journal*, pp. 1046–1149, 2002; O. Newman, "Architectural design for crime prevention", Institute of Planning and Housing, New York University, 1973; "Designing out crime", Design & Technology Alliance against Crime, 2015.

[38]With the exception of vigorous prosecution of low-level crimes that leave visible traces, such as vandalism (from a semiotic perspective) or arresting panhandlers (from an ecological perspective).

[39]This is further complicated by the attitudes of many ordinary people towards activities that are crimes, but which they somehow feel should not be. A good example is speeding: many people regard speeding as a kind of game where police should be strongly limited in how they are allowed to detect it. Minor tax evasion falls into the same category: people feel aggrieved if their attempts to pay less tax are detected.

Minor crimes such as panhandling may be regarded as acceptable because of a feeling that those who do it have few other opportunities. There is a tension between the legal system and cultural feelings about what the legal system should be that play out in the arena of minor crimes. Note that, although the tension is often framed as a moral one ("this law is oppressive"), it is different in different countries, even those with similar moral standards. Hence it must be culturally, not morally, mediated.

[40]M. Jain, J. Tsai, J. Pita, C. Kiekintveld, S. Rathi, M. Tambe and F. Ordò nez, "Software assistants for randomized patrol planning for the LAX Airport Police and the Federal Air Marshal Service", *Interfaces*, 40:267–290, July–August 2010.

[41]An important added advantage is that the mission sheet is electronic and can be updated during a shift if something new and important comes up. The mission sheet can also be pushed to officers' mobile devices so that they always have it with them.

Chapter 6
Data collection

6.1 Ways to collect data

Data analytics relies on the ability to collect data easily and cheaply. Some forms of data about crimes and criminals have always been collected by police forces. What has changed is that data about crimes and criminals can now be collected easily and often automatically; data such as locations and travel can be collected at scale; and some brand new forms of data (DNA) have come into use. Issues of ease, scale, and the existence of new forms of data undoubtedly make some aspects of law enforcement easier, but they bring their own problems.

The first issue that has to be considered is that citizens are broadly concerned about collection of their personal data. Attitudes to data collection by law enforcement are part of the larger picture of data collection by governments. Citizens will not trust law enforcement more than they trust their governments, and may well trust them much less. Public perceptions of the downsides of data collection are often ill-formed and inchoate, but that does not prevent them from motivating resistance. Law-enforcement organizations must always articulate, initially to themselves, why they are collecting any form of data, and the cost-benefit analysis that goes with it. Unhelpfully, many law-enforcement organizations have been at least slightly reticent about new data-collection practices, when perhaps it would have been better to be open about them, and encourage a full discussion of the issues. For example, facial recognition systems have been trialled, and purchased, by several police forces, only to face a backlash from citizens about the perceived privacy violations. As a result, such systems are being banned in some places[1].

Open-source data is data that is in the public domain. This includes news stories, blogs, and personal and professional web pages. This data is visible to everyone connected to the Internet, and so to law enforcement. It might seem strange that citizens would be concerned with law-enforcement collection, or examination, of such

DOI: 10.1201/9781003126225-6

data – after all, it is all publicly visible. Nevertheless, collecting such data may raise concerns among some people even though they might find it hard to articulate their concern.

At the next level is data that is public on social-media platforms, that is data that is visible to members but not to just anyone on the Internet. It is relatively common for law enforcement to have a presence on these social-media platforms, not even necessarily for the purpose of data collection. Looking at social-media data as part of an investigation, for example looking at the profiles of suspects, is routinely done, but could be considered problematic by some members of the public. There is at least implicit consent by users, since those who post about themselves have a choice, within the platform, about whether their profile and posts are public or private. However, the extent to which consent in a social-media platform context should be considered informed is far from clear; it is well-known that users tend to ignore privacy until a particular incident impacts them.

Collecting social-media data for downstream analytics, that is capturing the data from the social-media site using a crawler and putting it into storage controlled by law enforcement, is even more problematic. In principle, nothing is different – data that was considered public at a small scale is still public when collected as part of a larger scale collection. Furthermore, many different individuals and organizations collect data from social-media sites to analyze it, with many different motives. Nevertheless, there might well be resistance from members of the public to wholesale data collection of this kind, particularly because of some high-profile cases of use for modeling that were considered egregious by almost everyone.

Collecting data from the dark web is a different issue. There is certainly the expectation of a certain kind of privacy by those who use it – that is why they use the cumbersome mechanisms required in the dark web. On the other hand, the dark web is an open system and must be so to be accessible to those who want to use it in dubious ways. Pragmatically, those who use the dark web are unlikely to complain since to do so draws attention to activities that they are already trying to conceal.

The second category of data is that collected in government-mandated ways without any association with particular individuals. Some of this data is explicitly collected for law-enforcement reasons, for example CCTV or licence-plate cameras that look for stolen cars.

However, ordinary citizens are often ambivalent about data like this for reasons that are often difficult to understand. For example, consider speeding. In some countries, fixed-location speed cameras are not allowed, and a police officer must stand or sit and use a radar speed gun. In other countries, fixed locations are acceptable but mobile locations are unacceptable. In some countries, speeding inference based on the time the vehicle took to travel between two geographical locations is acceptable, but in others completely unacceptable. These different perceptions seem to be based on a feeling that speeding is more like a game than a crime, and drivers should have a "fair" chance of getting away with it. In some societies, other officially criminal actions are regarded as of little consequence, and the same mindset kicks in. For example, minor tax evasion, tagging, and minor bar fights are often regarded as innocuous. There is little rationality to public perceptions of what kind of data collection with the potential to reduce crime or improve detection is acceptable.

A third form of data collection is that permitted by warrants and directed at particular individuals. These require specific, motivated reasons why data should be collected. Traditionally, a major class of data collection is the result of search warrants, which allowed data to be collected about particular locations. Interception warrants allowed physical mail to be intercepted, and both real-world and telephonic communications.

Increasingly communication takes place in cyberspace, so that interception includes all of the data channels that can be used there: email, chat, instant messages, voice over IP, and social-media messaging subsystems.

One of the challenges of warranted interception in cyberspace is *finding* the endpoints and channels that are being used by particular individuals. The match between an endpoint and person who uses it is weak at best. In many jurisdictions, "burner" phones can be bought and used without their owners being identified. Accounts for social media can be created without any validation of identity. Many connection points to the Internet perform only minimal validation of the device, let alone its owner. Once on the Internet, the particular path followed by a communication may be hard to discover, and indeed may change dynamically during the interaction. It is therefore relatively easy for criminals to communicate in ways whose existence even may be hard to discover.

This muddles the distinction between wide data collection (without a specific targeted individual) and narrow data collection. It may be impossible to find the communications of an individual without collecting the data of innocent citizens that "surrounds" it.

The whole area of what data collection is acceptable is a fast-moving one, but one where neither side has come up with clear, compelling arguments for their position. Law enforcement often comes across as arguing on a purely operational basis ("collecting this data will reduce crime so of course it is the right thing to do") while citizens tend to act as if data collection is inherently evil, although they often cannot explain why.

When data is collected from this large range of sources, there is a further challenge – to integrate it into a meaningful whole. While warranted interception requires careful identification of the target, matching an individual of interest to an online persona is much more difficult. Even quite uncommon name combinations can appear multiple times among the 3 billion people online. The problem is made worse by the use of screen names for posting in certain contexts such as forums. So, while collecting data has its challenges, integrating data from multiple sources has even greater challenges.

Progress has been made here in the past two decades. Many of the analysis tools available to law-enforcement analysts make serious effort to disambiguate names based on a wide range of data about them. This is important, because it has become a common strategy for arrestees to use name and address variants, small enough to pass as genuine mistakes but with the goal of breaking query-driven systems. For example, "John Arthur Smith" may claim to be "Johnny Smith", "Arthur Smith", "J.A. Smith", "Artie Smith", and "Art Smith" for different arrests. It is only recently that such obfuscation techniques have been defeated by smarter indexing techniques.

These analysis tools also allow data from different backends to be integrated into a single response. They make it possible to query RMS data, criminal record information, drivers' licences, and gun licences at the same time.

The ability to store data digitally and index it cleverly has made a difference, since a piece of information can be found in seconds when it might once have take hours or days. For example, a comprehensive but routine background check that might once have taken a week can be completed in a few minutes.

6.2 Types of data collected

There are several qualitatively different kinds of data, based on size and complexity, and also on the legal basis by which they can be collected. We now consider them in greater detail.

6.2.1 Focused data

The first category of data is *focused* data, data about a particular crime, person, or group.

For example, data about a straightforward incident such as a traffic accident generates a record in a Records Management System with perhaps 50 attributes (time, place, driver details). As the crime increases in complexity, more data is collected. For a burglary, a list of the stolen property becomes a further part of the record. For a major crime, even more data is collected, including witness statements, and alibis. This data is a mixture of forensic data (evidence that might eventually be used in a prosecution) and intelligence data ("this person should be questioned"). Data like this is collected under investigative powers that give police the power to ask questions (with statutory protections in place), to enter and protect scenes of crime, and so on.

Focused data can also be collected about an individual for an intelligence purpose without being tied to a particular crime. This kind of collection of data might most often be from open sources or from human sources; but there might be grounds for warrant-based data collection (tapping phones, for example) if there were some evidence of involvement in a crime.

Similarly, focused data can be collected about an organization such as a drug-smuggling group. Again there are multiple sources of data, from open-source to warrant-based.

One area of focused data collection is the cyberspace footprint of an individual. This can be divided into two kinds of data: data that can be acquired remotely, because of the traces it leaves in cyberspace, and data that can be acquired from a particular device itself.

Data that can be acquired remotely includes: phone calls made (numbers and timing), texts sent (both using a phone company's tools and wifi-based tools such as Signal or Telegram), apps downloaded, web sites visited, and data downloaded. In most jurisdictions, these data require a warrant for collection, although some online businesses seem willing to provide such data more informally. Of course, the content of phone calls and messages requires more complex interception, since the platforms that provides such tools for communication do not necessarily capture or retain the content. Encryption also makes the content inaccessible. One of the issues, though, is that even criminals do ordinary things in cyberspace and it may be difficult to find the activities of interest in the midst of a great deal of ordinary, and so irrelevant, activity.

When a device has been obtained by law enforcement, the data described in the previous paragraph can potentially also be captured from the traces it leaves on the device itself. However, this may be a fleeting possibility as criminals learn to wipe the traces of their communication and web traffic from each device routinely. Sometimes the content of a device may provide a shortcut to understanding its owner's intent because it contains files, for example plans, that have been built from their cyberspace accesses. This avoids the need to pick through large volumes of data to find the traces of relevant activities.

Criminals can protect their devices by good security management, practices such as using strong passwords, using browsers that routinely delete browsing traces, and deleting traces of other activities such as messaging regularly. Some phones and computers encrypt the entire contents of the device, so that it cannot be extracted by taking out the memory chips or SD cards and putting them into another system. Nevertheless, law enforcement's record of extracting useful data from devices has been quite good, partly because the implementations of security on them are frequently poorly done. This is definitely an area where there is an arms race going on.

6.2.2 Large volume data

Another kind of data collection collects large amounts of data, with the expectation that criminal activity is hidden within it, but rare, probably concealed, and so hard to find.

For example, CCTV and video surveillance is collected routinely based on the (political) judgment that it both dampens the activities of criminals who have to be careful that their illicit activities are not captured, and it can be used after a criminal incident to discover aspects of what happened, including who and which vehicles were present.

The presence of CCTV certainly makes criminal activity more difficult, but it has not been the panacea that it was claimed to be. Coverage is often spotty, and one figure wearing a hoody looks much like any other figure wearing a hoody. The problem is made worse because cameras are usually mounted high, and so have a view that obscures facial features. The camera angle may also make it difficult to estimate body heights and properties such as gait. Although the U.K. has many more CCTV cameras per person than comparable countries like Canada, this has not translated into markedly different arrest or crime rates.

The use of CCTV surveillance after a crime has been committed has been more successful but is limited because of the expense of analyzing it. It is almost inevitable that it has to be scanned by humans and, although it can sometimes be sped up, this risks missing activity[2]. When a crime occurred in a limited time and space window, CCTV video is straightforward to analyze.

A newer area for video data collection is police *body cameras*. These are widely supported by citizens because of the perception that they keep officers honest; that is, any other reporting of an incident or interaction must agree with the captured video. Because of the sheer volume of data that body cameras generate, and the particular viewpoint, there is little to be gained from analyzing the footage from a data-analytic point of view, and analysis is almost entirely restricted to post-event analysis with a particular time and location focus.

One other post-crime use is to track individuals from one camera's view to another, and so create a trajectory. Again this is much easier if the individual can be localized in space and time at some point in the trajectory.

Licence-plate cameras are more useful because the images of the plates themselves are heavily constrained by licence-plate regulations, and so it is easier to process them automatically. As a result, licence-plate detection is more reliable than person detection. This enables trajectories to be determined automatically, at least after the fact. Such systems can also be queried ("where is the vehicle with this licence plate") whereas it is effectively impossible to query a CCTV system and ask "where is this person"?

Citizens seem reasonably comfortable with systems that track vehicles, and with basic CCTV. As data-analytic functionality is applied more extensively to CCTV video, it is far from clear that this comfort will continue.

For example, if a licence-plate camera system began to push alerts to operators instead of responding to queries, there might be concerns ("this car is going somewhere it has never been before"). But alerts of the form "this car was parked two minutes ago and someone else has now entered it and driven it away" might be useful to detect car theft. So technology developments here create another two-edged sword, and it is unclear how this area will develop.

Systems that observe people directly and push alerts are also problematic. For example, there have been research projects trying to detect unusual gait patterns ("this person is loitering") with the intent of flagging potential problems to police in real time. There are issues about the accuracy of such systems, but even if they worked, ordinary citizens might find them repugnant.

At present, most large-scale surveillance systems are query based – they can be searched by time and location but not content. As a result, data-analytic approaches have hardly been used on such data. When they are, the benefit of these systems will increase, but this may raise difficult privacy trade-offs.

A special case of surveillance systems are those for facial recognition. Although these look as if they might make general CCTV systems become more like licence-plate systems because they could be queried along the lines of "when was this person last seen and where?" or "who is this person?", their effectiveness is much lower than marketing literature and media would suggest. A moderately large number of police forces have trialled facial recognition systems at scale and they have almost universally concluded that they are useless[3]. This is not surprising as even humans have trouble detecting when two faces are the same person unless the face is distinctive and the images clear.

There are multiple problems:

- The reference images that are robustly connected with an identity tend to have been taken under controlled conditions and especially at the same level as the face, whereas almost all CCTV footage is taken from above and under much poorer lighting conditions.
- As the number of images in the system increases, the number of near-matches to any particular face increases and the accuracy tends to go down. So a system that performs well in a small trial sees its performance drop as soon as it is used in a more realistic setting.
- Minority faces are usually under-represented in the data used to train such systems, so these systems perform much worse than expected for such faces[4].
- There is a great deal of potential for misuse for stalking – a photo can be taken on the street using a phone and the system used to find out who that person is. This is not a theoretical concern – officers have done this repeatedly in trial environments.
- Since the match between faces and identities is often pulled from the Web and social-media sites, criminals can create fake profiles using their faces but other identities, making the matching difficult, and perhaps useless[5].

There is, at present, a backlash against facial recognition systems, with legislation banning their use in some places. Since they are relatively ineffective, this does little harm at present. There may come a time when law enforcement may want, once again, to make the case for their usefulness.

There are other kinds of large data that are collected and potentially analyzed by law enforcement. One of these is financial data, often produced by banks and then handed over to financial regulators, and then sometimes on to law enforcement. Most of this data concerns ordinary financial transactions, but some may represent payments for crimes or criminal products, and some money laundering.

More informal data is collected by street intelligence (the informal interviews described earlier), which may be supported by tools; and by observations that are communicated informally among officers in a certain area, or working on a certain category of crime.

As well as data explicitly collected to help with crime detection, open-source data can also be used. This includes news sources of all kinds, personal and organizational web sites, and social media presence. For some people and some kinds of crimes, posts on forums may also be relevant.

There is no need for explicit storage of truly open-source data since it can be searched for as needed using a Web search engine. However, it is important to realize that web search will dramatically improve with training. The fact that there are highly regarded multi-day courses on open-source search (arnoreuser.com) shows how much developing skills can help users to be more effective.

Social-media systems and forums are more difficult since they normally require membership and so there must be an organizational access point, Social-media platforms like LinkedIn and Facebook are straightforward to access with some care in usage, but more sensitive platforms may be suspicious of a law-enforcement presence and may have to be used with increased care. For example, discussion groups and forums used by those holding views that are far from mainstream may be open in principle, but law-enforcement interactions have to be carefully done so that moderators do not block the account used for access. Other web platforms require active participation to really be able to collect data so there are specially trained officers who can simulate young teenagers, for example to have a presence on sites where sexual grooming may happen.

There may be some advantages to extracting data from online platforms on a wholesale basis, and then storing it in a law-enforcement repository. This protects against the online site being taken down, either by suspicious organizers or by the site's host because of public disapproval.

Taking a copy of an entire site requires a crawler which visits all of the accessible pages of the site, and takes copies of their content, preserving the structure. There are several advantages to doing this: it may be faster to access direct from the repository than from the original platform; and the content can be analyzed using data-analytic tools, for example looking at the natural-language patterns used. However, many platforms, even innocent ones, do not like to allow crawlers to visit their site since it puts extra load on their servers; and those with less innocent content may be suspicious about who is collecting their content.

This is especially true of dark web forums and platforms. They camp in the dark web in order to be hard to find, and a crawler is, by definition, an attempt to use the content for an unintended purpose. Dark-web crawlers must use sophisticated techniques to vary their apparent origin and behavior, and may use timing to simulate a human-driven interaction (rather than collecting documents as quickly as possible). Considerable expertise is needed to build crawlers like this.

Not all dark-web forums are in English, posing one barrier to law-enforcement participation in them. Some are also developing distinctive culture and language patterns (argot), creating another difficulty.

6.2.3 Incident data

All police forces collect data about all incidents, whether responses to calls for service, or people who appear at front desks. Data about these interactions includes what happened, who was involved, how the interaction was resolved (including whether arrests were made), as well as locations (street addresses and usually GPS coordinates) and times.

This records management system (RMS) data is often used only for statistical analysis, calculating rates of various crimes in various areas to enable month-on-month and across year comparisons. However, they contain a wealth of information that can be used to understand patterns of crime and almost all police forces could use this data more extensively than they do.

6.2.4 Spatial data

Records management data typically captures spatial data about interactions between police and others. The patterns in this data can be used to understand spatial hot spots.

Locations are often expressed in GPS coordinates, although systems that have been collecting such data for longer often use archaic and arcane positional information. There are several issues with recording locations. First, it is not always clear what position is being recorded: the position of the incident or the position of the responding unit when the record is entered. Second, such coordinates make incidents similar based on direct distance between them, rather than a distance based on geography. In urban settings, locations that are physically close may be well separated in reality because of having to go around large buildings, and this may even be time-dependent. For example, the two sides of a shopping center are reasonably close when the center is open, but may be quite distant when it is closed. In rural settings, locations that are physically close may be separated by rivers or by impenetrable foliage. Analyzing such data using physical-distance (as the crow flies) similarity for clustering may produce misleading results. Although GPS coordinates are nominally 3-dimensional, it is non-trivial to get accurate GPS coordinates underground in, say, a subway station because devices rely on satellite visibility. So the depth/height dimension may be completely missed by data collection, and yet is often critical in urban areas[6].

Location data is also much more useful if it can be mapped to human structures such as street corners, sides of streets, and particular buildings. We have seen that the locations of crimes are not simply at particular spots on the surface of the earth, but occur in relation to human structures.

RMS systems often have ways to add more relevant information, but it is typically freeform text, untethered to the GPS coordinates, and so subject to variation based on the officers' knowledge of the local environment. The information entered in this way tends to be unfindable on a map because, for example, locally used names are not those that are captured in the map[7].

Street addresses are also routinely captured, but these are not necessarily accurate ways to locate an incident. Some street addresses are for a building, such as a shopping center or a major office building, that covers a whole block. Incidents that happen in the open (in parks, on sidewalks) are also a problem for officers entering data into an RMS record that requires an address. Often they use a nearby address, which can be misleading especially about the environment where the incident happened, and sometimes such fields are filled with some kind of null value, chosen more or less at random. Large open areas also often tend to have names for different subareas that blend into one another. In one well-known example, Central Park in New York contains areas known as North Woods, Great Hill, North Meadows, Sheep Meadow, and The Ramble, but the boundaries between such regions are not well defined.

Refinements of RMS systems and training about the importance of specificity in locating incidents would open up significant new possibilities for data analytics, but describing locations accurately is inherently difficult.

6.2.5 Temporal data

There is a considerable amount of anecdotal evidence about temporal patterns of crime, most of it readily explainable. For example, violence is associated with the times when bars and clubs are open, and just after they close. Burglaries tend to happen when householders are at work, and suburbs are quiet, with an extra peak when high schools end for the day. Most crimes are more common when it is dark than in daylight, and so tend to increase in locations where winter hours of darkness are long but it is not too cold. Many crimes are more common on weekends, and others cluster around days when welfare payments are delivered.

Although time stamps for crimes are routinely captured, there has not been much analysis of these patterns in a detailed way. In particular, there are probably stronger patterns that have not been noticed, and settings where the anecdotal rules do not apply. Partly this is because data about timing can be captured accurately for the events of a call to police or the arrival of a unit on the scene, but timings before that rely on witness statements and are much less accurate, and perhaps reliable. The use of phones by bystanders as cameras to record incidents and to post about them to social media may help to tie down incident timing more tightly but, so far, this has been done routinely only for major incidents.

6.2.6 Non-crime data

It seems obvious that weather has an influence on patterns of crime. Again there is anecdotal evidence: outdoor crime may be depressed by rain, snow, or cold. More attention to this aspect, which is not usually captured in Records Management Systems, might elicit interesting and useful relationships.

When studies have been done, they have relied on weather data captured in large regions – it is difficult to get weather data at the level of, say, a suburb long after the fact. And weather in much smaller microregions might turn out to be significant, for example the way in which wind direction creates sheltered regions where potential victims tend to be funneled.

Ordinary events also have an impact on crime. For example, it is well-known that pickpockets take advantage of large gatherings of any kind, and other crimes also become easier to carry out when there are large, distracted crowds. Law enforcement is used to leveraging this kind of knowledge for large, and typically regular, events such as sporting events, parades, street parties, and political rallies. Similarly, the effect of early evening crowds of people going out to restaurants and shows is also well understood. Less attention has been paid to the effect of events at other scales. In particular, the use of social media to create pop up events, some of which turn violent, is fairly new and most police forces have not yet become used to looking for such events before they develop. This is especially challenging as social-media platforms proliferate, and those intent on violence gravitate to the more obscure platforms.

There are also a few forms of data that are captured and used in real time, but have not yet been used as inputs to a data-analytic process. For example, several cities have installed gun shot detection systems. These consist of a number of towers, each of which is capable of detecting the sound of a gun shot and its direction from the tower. Multiple towers that detect the same gun shot can determine where it came from, and this can be fed to dispatchers, who can send a patrol to the location immediately. Gun shot detection can also be installed inside buildings, although sound reflection inevitably weakens location prediction.

Some systems can also estimate the kind of gun that fired the shot; some can also detect explosions. Gun shot detection systems are also being installed in locations such as schools, universities, and industrial plants, especially in the U.S. where guns are prevalent. Each detector has to be able to communicate with others, and with a central hub from which notifications are sent. These network connections, either wifi or cell-phone based, are a potential weakness since destroying the network neuters the gun shot detection system.

Gun shot detection systems have substantial error rates, missing actual gun shots and confusing other noises (popping balloons) with them. There does not seem to be any data about the spatial resolution that such systems achieve, that is how close the location they predict is to the actual point of the gun shot.

The effect of such systems is partly deterrent: criminals are reluctant to shoot in the open since they know that this will produce a rapid response. In the U.S. a large fraction of gun shots are never reported to police, so data collected by gun shot detection systems provides a more accurate picture of gun violence. The data collected from gun shot detection systems could be integrated with RMS systems to improve the representation of criminal activity, in particular to refine the concept of hot spots. Unsurprisingly, a gun shot at a particular location means that another gun shot at a close location is likely in the immediate future.

6.2.7 Data fusion

Although we have categorized data into different modalities – spatial, temporal, extrinsic – it is obvious that these modalities interact with one another. A time of day that is usually high-crime will be less so if it is raining, and perhaps not at all in heavy snow. Ordinary Mondays and Public Holiday Mondays will seem very different.

There is a need to be able to integrate these disparate modalities into a single framework so that it is available for analysis in an integrated way. For example, Records Management Systems capture details of each police-involved incident, with spatial and temporal information. As we have seen, both the spatial and temporal information attached to an incident are fuzzy. But RMS systems do not normally allow weather to be captured, except as an informal note, as is sometimes done for a traffic accident. Other data about what else is going on in the immediate neighborhood is also not typically captured as part of an RMS record. This can sometimes be inferred later but only with great effort.

The problem of merging or fusing heterogeneous data becomes even more complex if other sources are considered. Several of the systems we have discussed are able to produce responses to queries whose data comes from multiple sources. For example, it is possible to ask "tell me everything we know about this person". Various analyst intelligence tools exist (for example, i2 Analyst Notebook, or Palantir Gotham). These have interfaces that present multifaceted data in useful ways – but they are heavily query driven, so that they rely for their effectiveness on clever analyst exploration. The integration of such interfaces with data analytics is developing, but still weak.

There are very few ways to have data repositories push information appropriate to a particular moment and context. It would be helpful to have a data-fusion system say "did you realize that the person who answered the door during your door-to-door has outstanding warrants". Interfacing datasets with frontline policing is in its infancy[8] with tools that alert officers when they encounter a person of particular interest, or when they are at a location of particular interest. However, the interface between RMS systems and intelligence systems does not routinely provide a heads-up that, for example, richer data should be collected about a particular incident.

There is also considerable difficulty on the output side of systems that integrate heterogeneous data. It is difficult to tell a meaningful story that integrates many different kinds of data, especially when a part of it is speculative. Finding ways to present such data in a way that can be readily understood is a difficult, and so far understudied, problem.

A good example of the problems with data fusion is the so-called Yorkshire Ripper case, where Peter Sutcliffe was interviewed by police 9 times before finally confessing. An extensive investigation afterwards laid the blame at the inability of the incident room to fuse data adequately, so that multiple inconsistencies were not noticed.

The Los Angeles Police Department's use of Palantir is another example of the problems of data fusion. Their system ingests data about criminal activity: dispatch data, warrants, arrests, and convictions. It also ingests data about individuals: whether they are suspected gang members, their friendships and romances, their addresses, their phone numbers (once public information but much harder to obtain now), and the licence plates of the cars they drive. The system also collects image data such as mug shots, and traffic light and toll-booth camera images. At present, the main use of the system is via queries, but these queries can return a large amount of heterogeneous data, providing a rich picture of whatever was asked about. For example, individuals can be searched for by race, gender, gang, tattoos, scars, or via their friends or family. As we have discussed, queries have limitations; the advantage of the system is that one identifier is enough to find out much more about an individual, and it is easier to reduce a pool of people to a smaller set because the extra information tends to eliminate some. Palantir also allows any of its data that is geotagged to be overlaid on maps (for example, arrests), and can present trends in data.

The use of the Palantir software has been contentious. One system product that has now been abandoned is *chronic offender bulletins*. Each individual whose information was held in the system was given a score, focused towards their propensity for and previous use of violence. The top 10 such offenders were published each day, so that officers would be able to report sightings, and perhaps to be aware of the risk of interacting with them. It is not clear what went wrong, but either data corruption or misconfiguration of the algorithm led to persistently inappropriate rankings. For example, individuals with no violent record (and sometimes no convictions) would appear on the list. An earlier system assigned individuals a risk score: green, yellow, or red using data-analytic models. However, the company that built the models claimed that its algorithms must be kept secret, so the labels produced by the system could not be explained to officers. Some embarrassment followed when the mayor was labeled as yellow, and nobody could explain why.

A similar system has been developed in the U.K., the National Data Analytics Solution[9]. Its initial use case is to address the problem of modern slavery, with potential applications to serious violence or domestic abuse. The uses of data and privacy concerns were quite carefully considered in its design[10], but there has still be considerable pushback from concerned citizen organizations.

The difficulty of the problem of fusing data from multiple sources is partly concealed because experienced officers are able to carry out such fusion within their own heads, relying on a wealth of knowledge of neighborhoods and their histories, and local criminals and their habits.

6.2.8 Protecting data collected by law enforcement

Law enforcement has not yet faced up to the issue that the data they collect is itself a high-value target for criminals: those who want to know what is known about them, and those who want to find out about other criminals, perhaps for extortion. Apart from data exfiltration of police data, the ability to corrupt data held by police would be a huge advantage for criminals. So far, there do not seem to have been major cyber attacks aimed at either exfiltration or corruption (but perhaps they have not been made public) but it is unlikely that police data is protected substantially better than business data – and we see cyber attacks against them every day.

6.3 Issues around data collection

We have discussed the kinds of data that should be collected to enhance crime detection, and now we turn to some of the issues that surround this kind of collection.

Citizens' attitudes to data collection are visceral rather than cognitive, and so it is not easy to make arguments about what is acceptable and what is not acceptable. For example, in Europe citizens trust their governments and are comfortable allowing them to collect personal data, but they are strongly averse to businesses collecting personal data. In the U.S. it is almost exactly the opposite – citizens are comfortable with businesses collecting their personal data, but strongly averse to governments collecting it. On both continents, people will advance carefully reasoned, impassioned arguments why they are right[11],

This makes it difficult to collect data in the intersection between data about crimes and criminal activities and personal data, since it is completely unpredictable what kinds of data collection will trigger a reaction from the media or general public. Law enforcement need to have carefully thought out their motivations, and arguments that support them, before collecting any new kinds of data, collecting data automatically that was previously collected manually, or even scaling up the amount of data they already collect.

6.3.1 Suspicion

Many of the concerns of ordinary people about data collection can be understood by looking at these concerns through the lens of *suspicion*.

There is a widely held view that suspicion, in and of itself, is tainting. This is captured in the folk saying "there's no smoke without fire". In other words, to have even been suspected of involvement in some crime is taken to be a slur on one's character. To make things worse, the media often actually does take this position: that suspicion equals accusation equals conviction.

Of course, most people understand that, with respect to a particular crime, all of those who could have committed the crime must face some level of suspicion. But most people feel that it should be obvious that the suspicion directed against them individually is *a priori* unjustified. This is a good example of Stephen Covey's maxim: "we judge ourselves by our intentions, but others by their actions"[12]. Nevertheless suspicion has a tendency to stick once created so these concerns are, to some extent, justified.

The problem for law enforcement is that many people take the position, perhaps in an unexamined way, that data collection is itself a form of suspicion[13]. This is especially true if the data collection is large-scale, and unrelated to any particular crime. "After all", they say, "why would you think I could be guilty of this particular kind of crime and, if I'm not, why are you collecting data about me?" If suspicion is tainting and data collection is a form of suspicion, then data collection is tainting, and many people react to it in exactly that way.

There is a revealing contrast to data collection by businesses. In most cases, having a business collect data about you is not to your advantage, but it raises many fewer issues for ordinary people. The implications of large-scale data collection by businesses do not have the same negative associations[14].

From the perspective of suspicion, an investigation is about redistributing suspicion, increasing it for the perpetrators (until it reaches the level of "beyond reasonable doubt"), but simultaneously reducing it, ideally to zero, for everyone else. When an investigation begins, suspicion should ideally be distributed uniformly. Of course, all investigating officers bring with them to each investigation a prior probability distribution of suspicion based on all of their experience. Problems arise when this prior drives the investigation at the expense of evidence.

There are two dangers. Taking the prior too seriously in the early stages of an investigation creates an opportunity for criminals to mislead by creating an obvious investigative path and scapegoat. When the prior is itself biased, then it may drive the investigation down the wrong path, and it may be hard to recover and find a better path. All humans have perceptual filters that are applied based on our preconceptions, and we can be blind to certain kinds of evidence without realizing that we are.

A failed investigation leaves suspicion distributed across everyone involved, and this *is* tainting. Even in situations where the investigators are sure who the perpetrator is but cannot prove it, they have no reliable way to announce that others are free of suspicion. To announce that someone is no longer a person of interest may be a relief to them, but they are still likely to be regarded with suspicion by those around them.

6.3.2 Wholesale data collection

How much data should be collected? Here we can distinguish between what could be called specific data, about a defined set of people and/or incidents, and wholesale data, about a large set of people or incidents, not all of which are relevant from a law-enforcement perspective.

Of course, if the data is about crimes and criminals, then it is unproblematic that data should be collected about those specific incidents and people. But there is already a subtle issue: what about victim data? Although it is useful from a law enforcement perspective to collect data about victims, for example because it can help to detect when the same person (or same type of person) is the victim of multiple independent crimes, victims may not always want this. Witnesses are in a similar ambiguous position – details about them may be needed for a resulting criminal case, but the witnesses themselves may not want data collected and recorded about them. However, we are used, as a society, to the idea that investigating a crime requires intrusion into the personal lives of all of those involved or potentially involved[15]. For complex crimes, this may involve data about hundreds of people, and so becomes quite intrusive.

The issue of scale seems to become a concern as data about individual crimes is aggregated and analyzed. Generally speaking, data analytics improves as the available data becomes larger. There are two reasons for this. First, as the number of records increases it becomes more obvious how records are similar to one another. The confidence that a set of rather similar records really do form a cluster is reinforced as the number of records increases, and the "gaps" are filled in. Second, the status of a record that does not seem to fit into any cluster, and so seems unusual, becomes more obvious and convincing against the background of a larger number of records. There is an incentive to collect large amounts of data, not to become more intrusive, but because more data makes it easier to see the structures that are present. This case is rarely made in response to concerns about data collection.

The second kind of data is collected without any presumption that it is about criminals, although data about criminals could be contained within it. In other words, this kind of data is usually large, is collected for some other reason, but it contains information that could be useful for law enforcement. National intelligence units often collect this kind of data to look for, for example, potential violent extremist activity, but there are typically strong constraints on such collection that prevents data on each nation's own citizens from being collected.

Some examples are: social-media profiles and posts, forum posts. and DNA databases collected so that people can find their ancestry. Governments also collect data such as emails, phone call metadata, financial transactions, and travel patterns, although the extent to which this happens varies hugely by country. Increasingly law enforcement are buying large datasets just like any other business (although, curiously, citizens sometimes seem more concerned about this than the fact that such datasets are for sale at all, or that other businesses are buying them).

Law enforcement's interest in these large, general datasets is focused on the traces of criminal activities that may be hidden within them. There are two distinct approaches to such datasets. The first is obvious – law enforcement is looking for traces of particular individuals and their activities. When the individuals concerned are already known then the large dataset can be queried to return the records relating to these people of interest.

However, often the keys needed for a query may not be known, but it is known that the data of interest is present in the large dataset. For example, in banking data there are traces of layering transactions from money laundering. When the relevant records are not known, they may still be found by a winnowing process: finding a subset of the records that match some known criteria, and then going through the resulting list by hand. For example, a witness might have identified a car involved in a robbery by its color and the first two characters of the licence plate. A list of cars that match these criteria can be generated, and their other attributes checked to see which belong to local owners.

Data analytics can also be used inductively in this situation, to look for anything that is unusual and interesting in the data. For example, a data-analytic system might find a cluster of cars that always travel at exactly the speed limit. This is not a behavior exhibited by ordinary people, but might well be by drivers who are anxious not to attract a traffic stop.

A second approach to large data is the converse: use the data about ordinary activity to build a model of normal behavior, and then use this to help understand, and perhaps detect, criminal behaviors as deviations from normality. Here the data about ordinary activities is the target of attention. A model of normality throws the activities of criminals into greater relief.

These two approaches are the two sides of a coin. In the first, the goal is to build a model of abnormality, and use that to find criminal traces. In the second, the goal is to build a model of normality and use that to find traces of anything that is not normal.

The set of non-normal activities typically contains two kinds of activities, the criminal and the weird. There is therefore a secondary problem, separating these two kinds of activities. Fortunately, the weird is often carried out by individuals, whereas criminal activity tends to involve more than one person.

As an example, we might consider that criminals involved in large criminal organizations are likely to own more cell phones than usual because they want to muddy their communication activity to make it harder to trace and intercept. People or households that own many cell phones might be potential targets for investigation. But how many cell phones should be considered unusual and so suspicious? This can only really be determined by collecting data on the number of cell phones owned by ordinary people, and how much this varies. If normal individuals have only one cell phone, then an individual who has five stands out as worth some attention.

The collection and analysis of large-scale data raises issues with ordinary citizens and again a careful argument needs to be made about exactly how such data is used by law enforcement, and how that use is constrained. Conspicuously, such arguments have often not been made, especially in the aftermath of the 9/11 terrorist attacks when wholesale data collection was rapidly expanded.

6.3.3 Privacy

Many of the arguments against collecting data (at any scale) are based on *privacy*. Privacy is a slippery concept, and arguments involving its role are often not very clear. Opinions about the relative importance of privacy range from claims that privacy is non-existent in our world today ("You have zero privacy anyway; get over it" – Scott McNealy, of Sun Microsystems) to claims that privacy is a human right (Navi Pillay, UN Commissioner for Human Rights, 2008–2014).

The basis for discussions of the importance of privacy is shaky, and that is why much of the debate is inconclusive. Until perhaps a hundred years ago, nobody was ever alone because, if poor they lived at close quarters with many people, and if rich they had ubiquitous servants. To the extent that anyone had privacy it was a social construct – everyone knew everything, but pretended that they did not to make social interactions possible. So it is hard to see where the idea of privacy as a human right came from.

Moral and religious codes have nothing to say about privacy as a virtue or a moral good. Indeed, in the context of an all-seeing deity, it is hard to see how privacy could ever have been a significant issue in religions.

The only well-motivated argument for privacy comes in democracies, where the idea of a secret ballot has prerequisites such as information dissemination and discussion without state interference. This argument tends to become broadened to argue that any kind of widespread data collection and analysis has a "chilling effect", although it is often not clear on what.

6.3.4 Racism and other -isms

Particular groups have particular concerns with data collection. Sometimes this concern is that data about the group is over-collected, and that this is unfair. Often this is the result of the "data collection = suspicion" issue discussed previously.

Equally a concern might be that data about the group is under-collected, although this is less often enunciated. The problem with under-collection is that members of the group are underrepresented in the data used to make models; and so these models will tend to perform poorly in modeling members of the group. Mostly this is detrimental to group members.

The solution, although it is an idealistic one, is to collect data proportional to the membership of each group in the larger population from which the data is being collected.

The particular problem for law enforcement is how the larger population is defined. Suppose that half of all convicted criminals are from group A, but group A makes up only 10% of the population at large. It is no surprise that, in law-enforcement datasets, half of the records about individuals are about members of group A. However, they are often accused of anti-Aism because the fraction of records about individuals from group A is 50%, not 10%.

Law enforcement can expect to have to justify collection and use of data to many different audiences, and to be blindsided by unusual arguments coming from many different directions. They should pay considerable attention to the arguments they want to make (and there are many good ones) before data collection, rather than afterwards in response to media questioning.

6.3.5 Errors

Attention must be paid whenever data is being collected to avoiding errors. Whenever data is collected by a process that requires humans to input it, there is the possibility of errors during the process, especially when the input is done under stress. One thing that should be done routinely is to validate the input as it is entered, for example by checking that locations are actually within the region that they should be. Unfortunately, the most common approach to input validation is to force each entry to be filled in from a dropdown menu[16]. This is annoying and extremely slow to use. Better user interface design is a priority for all such systems, but those who purchase such systems are almost never those who use them, so there are few incentives for improvement. It is also difficult for a designer to capture all of the possibilities for the menu in the open-ended environment of law enforcement, so data is inevitably lost.

Some data can be entered automatically. For example, times can be entered automatically, but some care is needed to ensure that the systems from which the time is taken are themselves correct; and the windows around changing time for daylight saving create their own problems (especially as 1 a.m. to 2 a.m. is a time window when law enforcement is often active).

Locations are also potentially problematic as we have discussed. The GPS location of an incident may be captured automatically (but note that it is therefore based on the position of the vehicle rather than the position of the crime). Street addresses are typically entered manually; the building number may be accidentally transposed; and the building may not be on the street it appears to be on, especially on corners. Addresses in green spaces can be problematic and vague. None of these errors is deliberately introduced, but they all create uncertainties for the modeling downstream.

When data is collected directly from sensors, errors can be introduced even though the process seems entirely digital and so inherently reliable. Sensor data may be affected by power fluctuations, or by unfortunate placement of the sensor. For example, a temperature sensor may be carefully placed out of direct sunlight but sunlight is reflected on to it at certain times of day creating incorrect readings. A licence plate reader may incorrectly read the symbols on a passing vehicle, or on clothing and interpret it as a licence plate[17].

When data is moved within digital systems, it is tempting to think that this must also be error free. This is far from the truth. For example, tools such as Excel treat fields as having meanings, even when they do not. A ten-digit identification number is likely to be converted into scientific notation, losing content and making it impossible to process downstream. Fields that contain hyphens may be interpreted as dates, and silently reformatted[18].

Database administrators define what size and shape of data can be held in each database field, based on what it is supposed to contain. It is challenging for a database administrator to conceive of the entire range of data that a field might be called upon to hold, especially for systems that might be used for decades. It is relatively common for data stored in a database to be silently truncated or "corrected". For example, telephone numbers in North America are usually 10 digits long, but not always because, for example, they might contain extension numbers. Some phone numbers used by phone scammers show up as 15 digit strings with a "V" in front of them. Telephone numbers for the phones carried by travellers from other countries may be of a different lengths but still need to be included in North American databases. In general, there is little control on what a phone number can look like, so systems that capture them cannot assume a standard pattern or length. Often these issues go unnoticed until data analytics begins to be used, because previous query-driven uses of the data either did not access the problematic records, the corrupted data was not selected as a possible response to the query, or the human users compensated for the errors using their common sense.

There will necessarily be errors in collected data, no matter how well the collection process is designed. Data analytics must always be designed with some awareness of the presence and effect of errors.

6.3.6 Bias

Another serious problem with data collection is the introduction of *bias*. Bias means that there is a systematic mismatch between reality and its representation. Of course, there will always be a gap between representation and reality (Korzybski – "the map is not the territory"), not least because all representations are finite and must omit something. The problem arises when the gap has structure to it; it is systematically different in some parts of reality than in others.

Some forms of bias arise in the data-analytic process itself, but it is important to take into account that bias also exists in the minds of the humans involved in the process: those who collect the data, those who do the analysis, and those who act on what the models reveal.

Bias arises in three different parts of the data-analytic process:

- Bias in data collection;
- Bias in the data-analytic modeling itself;
- Bias in applying the results of the modeling.

The biggest source of bias in data collection is that almost all data is what is called a *convenience sample* – the data that is collected is the data that is easiest to collect. In the context of crime, for example, this means that more data is collected about the stupidest criminals. Smarter criminals are more aware of data collection, are better at avoiding it, and are arrested less, so less data about them is ever captured. Some crimes leave more obtrusive traces than others, and so it will always seem that there are more of these.

Some data will be missed entirely because there is no straightforward way to collect it. The truism that "what gets measured gets managed" points to the risk of uncollected data.

The second kind of bias in data collection is when data about certain subgroups are collected at rates than are not commensurate with the actual frequencies for those subgroups, as we discussed earlier. Often this is the result of a feedback loop. For example, if group *A* commit a particular crime at twice the rate that group *B* does, officers may start to assume, and act as if, the ratio is much larger than two. This assumption colors their activities to the extent that they notice crimes involving group *A* where there were none, and perhaps miss or discount crimes involving group *B*.

An obvious case of this kind of data collection bias is the disastrous performance of election polls in recent years. The reason is, at least partly, that pollsters cannot get access to people who only have cell phones because it is not easy to get the numbers and because, increasingly, people do not answer calls from numbers they do not know. It is often younger voters who have only cell phones, and do not use them for calling, so they are underrepresented in the samples that pollsters use.

Some data-collection biases can be reduced by using a second-order strategy that looks explicitly for those exploiting bias in data collection. For example, an obtrusive data-collection method can be deployed, but with a secondary data-collection method that looks specifically for those who try to evade the obtrusive one. This strategy has been used with some success for checkpoints for impaired driving – watching for those who turn off suddenly just as they come within sight of the checkpoint[19].

Humans are also biased in their data collection. The well-known phenomenon of planning to buy a certain brand of car, and suddenly noticing them everywhere shows that we have filters on our perception that help us see some things and ignore others, both unconsciously. Psychologists call this *set*.

It is inevitable that data collection will be less than perfect because of the forces that act to select some data rather than others, not necessarily with any intent.

There are two ways in which models can be biased. The first is that the decision boundary that separates one outcome from another is in "the wrong place", so that some records that should be predicted to have one outcome are predicted to have the other. For example, an online insurance site may compute premiums by calculating the risk of each potential purchaser based on their demographics, location, and the object being insured. If their model is biased it may reject applicants who are good risks or give insurance to applicants who are poor risks.

The second way in which a model can be biased is that the decision boundary it uses to separate the outcomes is too simple to reflect the actual complexity of the decision. The boundary is, informally, not wiggly enough to allow records to be placed on the correct sides. This is usually because they are not powerful enough to represent the full richness of the system that are supposed to be modeling, and so ignore some of the structure.

As humans we often build and use biased mental models because they fit most of the data reasonably well, and because they let us make quick decisions when it is not worth taking more time and effort to make better ones. For example, a model that predicts that seeing a sunny day out of the window indicates that the day is warm works reasonably well in many parts of the world, but not in Canada in winter, where the opposite is true.

Many examples of human prejudice are the result of using too simple a model: "all people of X have property Y", when only some do. The word "prejudice" has its origins in the idea of pre-judging, that is judging without considering all of the available information.

It is often difficult to detect and deal with bias in models because some of the incorrect predictions that a biased model produces are not noticed. For example, a person using a dating app such as Tinder might discount many candidates who might actually be good matches because of biases, but they will never detect the negative effects of their biases because they never meet the good matches they discounted. Google produces ranked search results, but we never really know how good the results are because we do not see results that did not appear in the list of results, and these might have been better than the ones we were not shown.

Police officers build mental models that can be biased. Two especially common ones are "Everyone is lying" and "The person who finds the body is probably the murderer". Models like this are too simple to represent reality, but they developed because they were often accurate. It takes some skill to know when a simple model is too biased to be useful. In particular, the more consequential the setting, the more care must be taken not to overrely on biased models[20].

The same issues arise in building models computationally. A model that does not have the flexibility to represent the system well will not be able to perform adequately. It may, of course, seem to perform well in settings that are close to those from which it was built, but this is misleading. This is why model building involves a testing or validation phase where a model is applied to previously unseen data to make sure that it continues to perform well.

There can also be bias in interpreting models, and taking action based on them. This takes two opposite forms. The first is captured in the saying "the computer is always right", a belief that a model must be right because it was produced as the result of a computation, and perhaps because its results support what the user already believes. The second is to ignore a model because its results contradict the user's intuition. For example, a security screener may not take action based on an alert because the person who triggered the alert seems too nice to be a threat.

Both biases are dangerous. The challenge is to stay in the middle ground of using models, with the awareness that all models are approximations of reality, and are only as good as the assumptions they embody and the data they are given; but also that models can see structures and patterns to which we humans are blind.

6.3.7 Sabotaging data collection

Because the models built using data analytics are used as a tool against crime and criminals, it is also critical to keep in mind that criminals have an interest in sabotaging the modeling. The easiest way for them to do this is to insert data into the data-collection and modeling system to cause the model to make mistakes. There is a long tradition of this in law enforcement: criminals giving false names, or creating fake alibis. There is still the obvious interest in doing this in a data-analytic world, and it provides one of the motivations for identity theft, since this allows a criminal to masquerade as someone else, even under robust scrutiny.

When the data-analytics process itself is the target, criminals have new disruption strategies at their disposal. This applies particularly when large amounts of data is collected, and the criminal activity is a small fraction within it.

For example, they can use the following strategies:

- Avoid data collection. When data collection is automated, say using CCTV cameras, those who want to avoid collection can plan their routes away from coverage, or spray paint over camera lenses[21].

- Passively change the data that is collected. Continuing the example of CCTV cameras, criminals may allow their images to be captured, but disguised in such a way that the resulting data is useless for police purposes. For example, facial hair, sunglasses, and a hat can make one person look much like anyone else of similar build. The kind of disguise necessary to fool CCTV surveillance can be much simpler than that required to fool a human.

- Actively corrupt the data that is collected. Automated data collection is cost-efficient but it lacks the implicit sanity check of human data collection, and so creates opportunities for criminals not just to conceal themselves but to actively insert misleading data. Recent CCTV back-end systems can (to some extent) do facial recognition and object identification. The deep-learning data-analytic tools that do this are susceptible to being spoofed, not by concealing the features of interest or camouflage, but by presenting at the same time a carefully constructed patch visible somewhere else in the camera's view. The analytic tool, as it were, finds the pattern of the patch more interesting than the face or object, and reports the presence of something encoded in the patch rather than the more obvious aspect of the image. Thus these systems can be subverted by wearing an appropriate t-shirt with the patch on the front; and the patch does not necessarily look like anything other than a typical t-shirt design[22].

A false licence plate may be good enough to fool a licence-plate camera system, even though it would not fool a human observer. Licence plate covers exist that, to a human, look like a transparent cover, but which are difficult for CCTV systems to read through, especially when they use infrared or the angle between camera and plate is large. Paint can also be applied to a licence plate which is invisible to the naked eye but makes the plate highly reflective so that cameras, especially speed cameras that flash, get overexposed images. Those who sell these tools claim that they work well, but it is not clear if this is true in practice.

- Insert records designed to alter the modeling. Systems that collect large amounts of data do not usually use all of it to build models, purely because of cost and complexity. Some selection process is used, and this often focuses on the most interesting records. A criminal can therefore manipulate the modeling by creating records that seem particularly interesting but are actually misleading. For example, a drug dealer might recruit some lower-level sellers from a particular demographic and then make anonymous calls reporting them. Before long, officers start to assume that low-level dealers are most likely to be from that demographic, leading them to ignore others who are not, and so the others become partially protected.

Building and using models that have as little bias as possible requires constant attention to all three stages of the process.

6.3.8 Getting better data by sharing

Models built using data analytics are most useful when they are built from the richest possible data. Unfortunately, this is often difficult because of jurisdiction issues, some legal and some perceptual.

For example, it is often difficult for police forces operating at different scales (national, state or province, county or city) to share data because they do not use the same infrastructure. Data sharing is conceptually simple, but practically can be extremely difficult.

There are other cases where it would be in the long-term interests of both parties to share data, but one or other side is unwilling. For example, banks can often detect what must be criminal activities within the financial transactions that they manage, but they often do not share this information with law enforcement claiming privacy, legal restrictions, or simply a desire not to look foolish. Banks tend not to share information about ways they themselves have been defrauded with other banks, even though this would obviously be a common good.

Intelligence organizations and police forces often do not share information well either. This is partly because of incompatible systems, partly because one side or the other has no natural way to incorporate external data into their processes, and partly because the differences in mission alignment make the shared data seem irrelevant to the other side. A special case is the sharing of information between tax authorities and police forces. Here many countries explicitly created a wall to prevent information sharing. The idea was that criminals would at least pay tax on their ill-gotten gains if they knew that this would not lead law enforcement to them. It is dubious that this every worked well; recall that Al Capone was prosecuted for tax crimes but this seems hardly ever to have been the case. It may be time to remove this barrier since tax returns reveal a great deal about the way money flows around the activities of individuals and corporations.

Notes

[1]Fortunately, the performance of facial recognition systems is limited, so this is not hugely consequential at present, but it is an object lesson in not getting ahead of public opinion.

[2]Automatic analysis of video is an area of active research, but it is limited to recognizing particular objects, detecting unusual actions, and measuring (human and vehicle) traffic flow.

[3]www.theguardian.com/world/2019/aug/17/police-halt-trials-face-recognition-systems-surveillance-technology for Kent and Midlands police in the U.K.; www.forbes.com/sites/thomasbrewster/2019/07/04/london-police-facial-recognition-fails-80-of-the-time-and-must-stop-now/\#2457acc4bf95; www.fastcompany.com/90440198/san-diegos-massive-7-year-experiment-with-facial-recognition-technology-appears-to-be-a-flop; www.wired.co.uk/article/met-police-london-facial-recognition-test.

[4]In one of Apple's early use of faces to unlock cell phones, a significant number of Chinese faces were able to unlock the same phone, that is the facial recognition software could not tell them apart. Obviously not enough Chinese faces had been used in the training.

[5]Several journalists have accessed the set of images that purport to be them in facial recognition systems in use. It is instructive to try and decide which of these is actually the intended person.

[6]Famously, Monaco has traffic circles (roundabouts, rotaries) *inside* the cliff face, creating challenges even for ordinary traffic apps.

[7]In my own city, long time residents still describe locations in relation to a traffic circle that disappeared forty years ago. I recently worked with RMS data where an incident was described as occurring "in the lane behind X", but no map showed a lane at that location. Perhaps it was a large driveway. There are many jokes about rurals giving directions of the form "turn right by the barn that burned down last year". These jokes contain a grain of truth about how humans represent the geography around them.

[8]For example, J.W. Streefkerk, M.P. Esch-Bussmakers and M.A. Neerinc, *Field evaluation of a mobile location-based notification system for police officers*, in: *MobileHCI '08: Proceedings of the 10th International Conference on Human-Computer Interaction with Mobile Devices and Services*, pp. 101–108, September 2008.

[9]https://west-midlands.police.uk/about-us/privacy-notice/national-data-analytics-solution.

[10]Requiring consideration of the General Data Protection Regulations (GDPR), the Data Protection Act 2018, the Crime and Disorder Act 1998, the Human Rights Act 1998, the Serious Crime Act 2015, the Home Office's Management of Police Information Code of Practice 2005, the Rehabilitation of Offenders Act 1974, the Freedom of Information Act 2000 and Common Law. This illustrates the complexities of data collection and use, just within a single nation.

[11]In North America, the argument goes like this: should governments misuse the data they have about you the consequences are limitations on your freedom of action, up to and including incarceration. If businesses misuse the data about you, the consequences are only economic. At present, there is some sense to this: a business that creates a poor model of you may serve you inappropriate advertisements. However, the goal of many businesses is to establish your price sensitivity (although they cannot quite do this yet). So the economic consequences could be substantial; your favorite online shopping site might present you with top prices for everything if it established that were relatively insensitive to price.

[12]In his book *The Seven Habits of Highly Effective People*, 1989.

[13]Indeed there is subgroup in academia that conflates the chain: data collection – suspicion – taint and assumes that all surveillance is tainting.

[14]Although they should perhaps have other negative associations.

[15]Although issues remain about whether and how long such data should be retained.

[16]As an example of the difficulty of clean data collection the Violent Crime Linkage Analysis database system was developed by the Royal Canadian Mounted Police, and is used by many police forces. It captures detailed information about certain categories of violent crime. There are 263 possible inputs for each crime, and the training course in its use runs for 15 days. Officers enter data into a booklet. This data is then entered into the system by analysts. Despite this careful process, the inter-rater agreement showed only 31% agreement over 106 attributes: B. Snook, K. Luther,

J.C. House, C. Bennell and P.J. Taylor, "The violent crime linkage analysis system: A test of interrater reliability", *Criminal Justice and Behavior*, 39(5):607–619, 2012. The system does not detect linkages automatically; this must be done by analysts, which is challenging given the data issues.

[17]Clothing that confuses licence plate cameras is available (https://www.vice.com/en/article/qvgpvv/adversarial-fashion-clothes-that-confuse-automatic-license-plate-readers. Licence plate cameras do not routinely check that licence plates are attached to vehicles either.

[18]Biologists have had the change the names that they give to some genes because Excel was silently reinterpreting them as dates. Microsoft was either unable or refused to fix this issue, but Excel is too popular to discard as a standard platform.

[19]This strategy has also been used by criminals. Pickpockets used to call out "beware of pickpockets" in crowds, and many people would instinctively reach for the pocket containing their wallets. Confederates would then know exactly where to look for them.

[20] Quite apart from data analytics, it is clear that some police officers are biased against certain groups. For example, according to the Washington Post's police shootings database, in the U.S. whites are 60.1% of the population but are killed in 45.4% of police shootings, while African-Americans are 13.4% of the population, but are killed in 23.8% of police shootings. Of course, there are many issues that these simple figures ignore, but it is hard to ignore the size of the disparity. Similarly, arrests of African-Americans for drug possession take place at twice the rate of arrests of whites, although the rates of possession are about the same between the two groups. This bias seems to be worse in the U.S., perhaps because of their particular history and the militarization of U.S. police since the 9/11 attacks, but no country is immune.

[21]Law enforcement have sometimes tried to collect data covertly to make it harder to avoid data collection, but this almost always lead to a backlash from ordinary citizens when the collection is eventually discovered.

[22]www.theverge.com/2019/4/23/18512472/fool-ai-surveillance-adversarial-example-yolov2-person-detection; syncedreview.com/2019/08/29/adversarial-patch-on-hat-fools-sota-facial-recognition/.

Chapter 7
Techniques for data analytics

We now consider the techniques that can be used to build the models that we have discussed so far in abstract terms. Although all models are representations of a system of interest, the kind of representation differs. There are two major kinds of models: clusterings, which show the macroscopic *structure* of a system; and predictors, which show the *behavior* of a system. There are some smaller special cases that we will also consider: *anomaly detection* which focuses on finding the most unusual parts of the system being studied, and *ranking* which is a special form of prediction that orders elements of the system according to the magnitude of some property of interest, in our case usually risk.

7.1 Clustering

The first kind of data-analytic models are *clusterings*, and their purpose is primarily to understand the structure of the system being studied, based on similarities among the observables or behaviors. For example, businesses cluster their customers so that they can respond to each group of customers in a custom or specialized way, providing all customers with service they will consider to be better.

Most often data analytics begins from a set of records that describe events, incidents, individuals, or groups. Each record contains the values of a (usually fixed) set of attributes. For example, an RMS record typically contains attributes describing times and places of actions relevant to an incident, people involved, codes for what took place, and flags for particular properties of the incident. These records might be collected for a week, a month, or a year and then the resulting dataset clustered.

Clustering is based on similarity (and dissimilarity) among records. In other words, clustering algorithms try to find ways to aggregate the records into groups, called clusters, which have the property that the records in a cluster are similar to one another, and the clusters are different from one another.

DOI: 10.1201/9781003126225-7

Clusters represent the different possibilities in a system, and so give us insight into how the system, as a whole or in its parts, is structured. For example, clustering RMS records shows ways in which crime occurrences are similar because of the times, locations, and kinds of crime that occur. There might be a cluster of incident records for traffic accidents that happened in a narrow time window (late Friday and Saturday nights) at a small set of intersections. There might be a cluster of breakins that happen in the middle of the day on Wednesdays and in a particular suburb.

Clustering enables the following kinds of questions to be answered:

- Are there clusters at all in the data about the system? There is no necessary reason why the records should form clusters, rather than being, as it were, evenly distributed; but most data about humans does contain clusters. For example, the set of lottery numbers drawn each week should not form clusters (because they are supposed to be completely random). However, the sets of lottery numbers chosen by players each week is very much not random – nobody chooses 1, 2, 3, 4, 5, 6 even though that combination is as likely to occur as any other[1].

  Humans vary infinitely in physiology, but we find it natural to talk about, say, tall versus short people; and we vary infinitely in our tastes, but we find the concept of culture a useful way of grouping common taste differences.

- If there are clusters, how many are there? The number of clusters reveals how many qualitatively different kinds of actions or objects there are in the system. This is often revealing of different kinds of behaviors, or different kinds of individuals.

- What are the sizes and shapes of the clusters? A cluster is a set of records that are similar enough to be counted as belonging together, but the number of records that comprise each cluster reveals how important or popular each one is.

  Shape is a bit more difficult concept, but intuitively the records making up a cluster can be extremely similar (and so form a tight cluster) or much less similar (and so form a looser cluster). The cluster may be shaped like a sphere, so there are some records that are "central" in a meaningful sense, while others are peripheral. It may also be shaped more like a cigar, or even an octopus, so that there are still some central points, but the peripheral records are qualitatively different both from these central points and from one another.

  These shapes provide information about how similarity works in the system: how much variability is present in each cluster either because of freedom within the system, or the choices of the participants. When clustering is applied to systems of human activity, the sizes and shapes of clusters is affected by social processes as well as individual behavior.

It is useful (even necessary) to consider why clusters exist, if they do. The most intuitive reason is that the records in a cluster are mutually reasonably similar to one

Figure 7.1: Three different kinds of similarity that could be understood as clusters

another because they represent something that people (or criminals) do in a standard or typical way, each with a slight differentiation. So groups of rather similar records result. Intuitively, such clusters can be imagined to be roughly spherical – the records are not all exactly the same, but the variation among them is relatively small.

Not all clusters need to have this spherical shape. Imagine a set of records with a spherical core, but then a set of "arms", groups of records that have some members who are close to the core, then other members that are similar to these others (but not as similar to those in the core), and then other members that are similar to the previous group (but quite different to the core). The core plus these arms certainly seems plausible as a kind of cluster, but one that is quite different to the spherical kind.

Another kind of cluster arises because there is a reason for the cluster's existence, but there is some other process that causes the actual records to diverge predictably from this reason. For example, the amount of cash carried by cross-border mules (smurfing) will be no greater than $10,000 to avoid having to make a declaration, so the actual amounts might all be $9,999. Some may decide that this is too obvious and so choose random amounts slightly smaller than the $10,000 amount. If the cash is carried in some other currency, the amount will be slightly smaller than $10,000 because it will be carried in (large denomination) bank notes. If we consider all the amounts carried by mules, they will tend to be close to $10,000, but will vary slightly in one direction.

These three different kinds of clusters are illustrated in Figure 7.1.

The greatest payoff from clustering is when it is possible to come up with a reason or explanation for each cluster, in other words its meaning. Such a meaning cannot be inferred automatically from the data itself. It can potentially be inferred by an analyst, by considering what makes the records in each cluster seem the same, and perhaps using some knowledge about the domain from which the data comes. Considerable skill is required, but the computational process at least reduces the skill required from understanding the entire set of records to understanding a (smaller) set of clusters.

When an analyst thinks s/he understands the meaning of a cluster, this insight can be checked by creating artificial records that embody the potential meaning of the clusters, adding these records to the dataset, repeating the clustering algorithm, and making sure that the algorithm places the artificial records in the expected cluster(s).

Clusters that do not seem to have an obvious explanation for their existence can be the most valuable because they can lead to new insights. If any explanation can be found, there are almost certainly intelligence benefits. It is also important to remember that algorithms can find clusters that no human would have constructed naturally, but these can often be understood afterwards, and may be valuable exactly because they are so unexpected.

The result of a clustering depends on the assumption of similarity that is used to build it, and so there is not *the* clustering of a dataset, but *a* clustering for each choice of similarity (and other algorithm parameters).

The choice of similarity has to be made beforehand, at a time when the appropriate choice might not be obvious. This is an example of a circularity or chicken-and-egg problem that is common in data analytics, having to choose the parameters of a model before knowing which choices are best. The circularity is resolved by iteration – choose a measure of similarity, see what the resulting clustering is and what it reveals, and then repeat with a different, more appropriate measure of similarity as necessary.

The obvious choice for similarity is based on comparing two records based on the values of the same attributes in each one. For example, suppose we wanted to cluster people by their height and weight. Most people could probably do a reasonable job, especially if there were "natural" clusters in the people.

But even this simple task shows some of the subtleties. First, if the clustering was done with the people in front of us, then the ways that height and weight were measured would not matter; we would judge them by eye. But if we were asked to cluster them based only on their data, that is given heights and weights but without seeing the people, then it becomes more challenging.

Second, we need to consider the relative importance of height versus weight. Should they be counted equally in comparing people? Should one be more important? We might not consider this explicitly, but it is one important reason why two people asked to do the same task might come up with different clusterings – without necessarily even realizing that there could be different answers.

Third, this relative importance requires us to consider the magnitude of the units in which the heights and weights are given to us. If they were given in units familiar to us (probably feet and inches, plus pounds; or meters plus kilograms) our intuition might allow us to understand how to consider relative differences in heights and weights. But in unfamiliar units, it is not so easy. For example, if heights were given in miles and weights in stones (commonly used in the U.K.) the problem seems much harder.

So if we ask how similar two records are we need to assume something about the meaning of the units in which each attribute is given and, more difficult, how differences involving different attributes should be weighted relative to one another. Consider grouping some people based on age. If we treat ages as numbers, then two people who are 36 and 38 would be considered quite similar, but so would two people who are 1 and 3. The numerical difference is the same, but the significance is very different. We might automatically take that into account if we were asked a clustering question, but an algorithm can only use the numbers, or have them recoded to represent the significant similarity (perhaps: baby, child, teenager, young adult, middle aged, retiree, elderly). For most datasets, there are no obvious units that both accurately represent what each attribute is measuring *and* allow different attributes to be compared fairly.

This is further complicated by the fact that many attributes are not numeric, and so it is not even obvious how to compare different records with respect to such an attribute. For example, the FBI created Universal Crime Codes in an effort to regularize the way in which crimes were recorded, so that statistics and patterns could be seen. Although these values are numeric in form, they are not numbers and so the difference between them is not directly meaningful (for example, 04.01: aggravated assault on a peace officer and 060.01: larceny/pocket picking look just as different from one another as 05.01: burglary with forced entry and 07.01: motor vehicle theft do).

So the intuitively appealing idea of clustering based on attribute similarity turns out to be much more difficult than it seems. The usual solution is to:

- Map non-numeric attribute values to numeric ones in ways that preserve their meaning (not so easy, as the UCR code example shows), and
- Convert the numeric values to *z-scores* (for all of the values of a particular attribute, subtracting the mean and dividing by the standard deviation). This has the effect of expressing the range of values taken by each attribute in terms of the standard deviation for that attribute across the whole dataset. Since all attributes are coded in the same units (standard deviations) their similarity can be compared plausibly (although the validity of the conversion to z-scores is always at least questionable and often dubious).

The approach of measuring similarity based on the sum of the similarities between values of the corresponding attributes is known as *distance-based clustering*. It is simple to understand and efficient to compute (using an algorithm known as *k means*). It embodies the intuition that a cluster consists of records that are mutually similar (close in the space spanned by the attributes once these have been converted to comparable values).

The drawback of distance-based clustering algorithms is that they must be told, in advance, how many clusters to expect. This is another example of having to specify something about the dataset that is not yet known, and therefore usually requires trying different numbers of potential clusters to see which produces the most plausible or useful result. This cannot be made systematic, because increasing the number of clusters will always produce a "better" clustering since it provides more ways for records to be close to one another.

What happens to records that are far from all of the clusters, so that they have no natural membership in any cluster? Distance-based clustering allocates them to whichever cluster they are closest to, regardless of how different they might be to the other members of that cluster. Worse still, this is typically done silently, so the user gets no feedback that a cluster contains records that do not fit it well (that are not close to the other records of that cluster).

Density-based clustering weakens the spherical or blob idea of a cluster to allow it to include records that are similar to "enough" other records (while distance-based clustering requires records to be close to *all* other records). This allows clusters that have a core of mutually similar records (as in distance-based clustering), but then other records that are similar to only some of the core records; and then other records that are similar to some of these records, and so on. This allows clusters to have arms, like a spider or octopus, as long as these arms continue to be dense enough that all records have enough close neighbors.

Algorithms to construct density-based clustering do not have to be told how many clusters to expect, but instead must be told what "similar enough to still be in the same cluster" means, and how many records there must be for a group to be big enough to be considered a cluster.

Density-based clustering algorithms work by selecting a random record, and trying to use it to nucleate a cluster. Given a record, first, build a protocluster by including its neighboring records, those close enough to qualify as core points. Then extend this set outwards to include peripheral points that are close enough to *some* records in the protocluster being grown. This can happen for several rounds, as farther records are close enough to the cluster members so far. Eventually no further records are close enough to qualify to be added to the protocluster, and its growth is complete. If the protocluster is big enough, the records in it are removed from further consideration and the protocluster becomes a cluster and is added to the list of clusters. If the cluster is too small, all of the records considered are returned to the dataset, and another random starting record is chosen. The process ends when no remaining record can successfully nucleate a cluster.

These algorithms therefore produce clusterings which contain a set of clusters *and* a set of leftover records. Unlike distance-based clustering, the clusters contain only records that plausibly belong to them, and leftover records can be thought of as anomalies.

An alternate view of clustering is that clusters are not derived from the similarity among the particular records that happen to be present in a dataset, but that clusters exist because of, and reflect, real-world processes. Observed similar records are the way they are because of these processes, with some superimposed more or less random variation. In other words, a cluster has a center, although this may not actually be a record in the dataset, and the other members of the cluster are similar to the center, but with some variation because of other factors. Most of the records will be very similar to the center; records slightly less similar will be rarer; and records that are very dissimilar will be extremely rare.

Algorithms for this kind of *distribution-based clustering* look for sets of records that look like random variation around a center. The most common way of thinking about random variation is as a Gaussian or normal distribution, the bell-shaped curve of probability moving away from a center, represented by the peak. The distribution of all of the records that belong to a cluster must fit such a distribution, so being a member of a cluster is a collective, not an individual, property.

Once again algorithms must be told the number of clusters to expect in the data. They then try to find the required number of Gaussian distributions that best fit the data, where the fit can depend on the height, the width, and the orientation of the bell shape.

Unlike the previous clusterings, distribution-based clustering produces a *soft clustering*. Every record is associated with every cluster, but with a probability that will be small when a record is far from that cluster's center.

A soft clustering can always be converted into a hard clustering by allocating each record to the cluster for which its membership probability is greatest. But knowing the probabilities provides extra useful information. A record that is associated with cluster 1 with probability 0.95 and with cluster 2 with probability 0.05 is firmly a member of cluster 1. A record that is associated with cluster 1 with probability 0.52 and with cluster 2 with probability 0.48 should be counted as a member of cluster 1 if absolutely necessary, but there is clearly great uncertainty about this allocation.

The challenge of any clustering is to understand the meaning of the clusters – what is it about the system that makes each set of records similar. One good reason to use distribution-based clustering is that each resulting cluster comes with an explanation. The center is a kind of "reason" for the cluster's existence, and the orientation and extent of the distribution explains the subsidiary reasons for variation around the center. This does not make a cluster instantly interpretable but it provides a solid starting point for trying to understand it. The starting point for understanding is a higher level abstraction, the distribution, rather than just a set of points which is all that other clustering algorithms provide.

Datasets that contain many attributes are difficult to cluster because there are many dimensions in which each pair of records can be similar. There is a meta-approach to clustering which reduces the difficulty of clustering in many dimensions by projecting from the original high-dimensional space into a much lower-dimensional one. All of the clustering algorithms we have discussed could then be applied in the lower-dimensional space; and if the lower dimension is two or three, the records can be directly visualized. Visualization means that we can apply human pattern-recognition skills to understand the numbers, sizes, and shapes of the clusters in the data, and perhaps some aspects of their meanings.

The question then becomes how to project from a high-dimensional space to a low-dimensional one in such a way that the similarity structure among the records, especially the clusters, is preserved. It turns out that even a random projection works reasonably well (because high-dimensional spaces are non-intuitive places) but it is more usual to chose the directions for projection so that as much variation as possible is preserved.

A standard way to do this is using two related algorithms: *Principal Component Analysis* (PCA), and *Singular Value Decomposition* (SVD). These clusterings consider the records as a cloud of points in high-dimensional space, and recursively re-orients the view so that the maximum amount of variation is preserved. Then the dimensions that have the least variation can be removed by projection, leaving a lower-dimensional representation that preserves as much as possible of the structure.

These projections have the useful property that it is possible to estimate how much structure is being lost by deciding to project to k dimensions, rather than $k+1$, and they provide a mathematical guarantee that they preserve as much of the structure as possible in the remaining dimensionality.

Clustering algorithms do not have natural and accurate metrics for measuring how well any particular clustering captures the actual structures in a dataset. Clustering is therefore an exploratory process at the algorithm level. It is usual to experiment with multiple families of algorithms, and also to try various parameters. The resulting clusters do not announce themselves as good; they can only be assessed by their usefulness in helping understand the system being examined.

Typical law-enforcement payoffs from clustering can be divided into clusters that are expected, and clusters than are unexpected. Expected clusters provide reassurance and demonstration that police forces understand the crime and criminal landscape for which they are responsible. For example, clustering RMS records can show that response times are homogeneous for different regions, so that some citizens are not being penalized for where they live[2]. Results of clustering can be reported to oversight committees to show that forces are being effective, or perhaps that citizen perceptions and complaints are not supported by the analysis. Used in this way, no surprises is good news.

Unexpected clusters suggest directions for further investigation that might not have been obvious. For example, they might suggest an activity that has been hidden inside the data from which the clustering was derived, but reveals itself as a surprising cluster.

Repeating clusterings at intervals can also provide the information that something is changing, since the natural expectation is that a new clustering of data from the same environment ought to produce similar clusters of similar sizes and shapes to previous ones.

There is a specialized form of near-neighbor similarity calculation that is useful in law-enforcement contexts, but not much in more mainstream data analytics. A query-driven approach can be used to find other crimes that are similar to a particular index crime: "have there been other crimes like this?". However, getting a useful response depends on describing the index crime carefully, without omitting properties that might make it similar to other crimes, and without including properties that might have been accidental. The similarity techniques that are used for clustering can be used to find such sets of related crimes automatically, that is without the need for a query to start the process.

Such a set of related crimes is, of course, a kind of cluster but may not be detected by conventional clustering algorithms because it is small, and because its members are also similar, perhaps more weakly, to other crimes. However, techniques that focus on finding such small sets explicitly can be successful, and have proven useful. For example, the New York Police Department developed a tool called *Patternizr* that looks for such sets of closely related crimes. At present, it is still query-driven: officers can enter details of a seed crime, and the Patternizr system returns a list of the most similar crimes. A few success stories have been made public. The underlying technology, however, uses data-analytic techniques to decide what similarity between crimes means.

7.2 Prediction

The second kind of data-analytic models are built for *prediction*, and their purpose is to predict the behavior of a system into the future based on its behavior in the past. A predictor increases the understanding of a system by indicating how it is likely to react to particular situations. In other words, predictors indicate outcomes given the current state of a system.

When the outcomes are chosen from a small set of possibilities, prediction is called *classification*. When the outcomes are chosen from a set of numerical values with a large range, prediction is called *regression* (an unfortunately overloaded term).

The overall goal of prediction is to learn how some property of a system – the outcome – depends on all of the other properties of the system. For example, weather prediction learns how the temperature in this square mile or square kilometer depends on the temperatures, humidities, wind speeds, and cloud cover of this location, and other nearby locations in previous time periods. Given values for those other attributes, a weather predictor predicts the temperature in the next time frame.

When prediction intersects with law enforcement, many misconceptions arise about what kind of property can be predicted. Many people have seen the film *Minority Report*. The premise of this film is that a data-analytic system was able to predict when someone was about to commit a crime so that police could be dispatched to arrest the perpetrator and prevent the crime from ever happening. A similar premise was used in the long-running television show *Person of Interest* ("The Machine is never wrong, Mr. Reese").

Such systems suffers from the problem that there is no way to tell if it is working. All of those arrested claimed that they were not about to commit a crime, and there was no way to tell if their claims were true. These scenarios are fictional, but they illustrate one of the issues of predicting properties such as risk. If the predictions are accurate, and law enforcement respond to them appropriately, then the bad events associated with the high prediction of risk do not happen, or happen less. As a result, it is hard to show that the prediction system is actually achieving something; after all, the bad events that did not happen might never have happened even without the law-enforcement response. This is common to all systems whose goal is prevention; it is hard to justify the costs when the benefits seem hypothetical. Those designing risk prediction systems should be aware of this issue, and consider carefully how success will be measured.

Even approximating a system such as that described in *Minority Report* is infeasible: humans are erratic at the scale of deciding to take a particular action at a particular time, so it is intrinsically unlikely that a model of this kind could actually work. Even in long-term relationships, where the people involved might claim that they can accurately predict other's responses, this claim is not rigorously tested because they notice when they predict correctly but not when they predict wrongly. Games such as *The Newlywed Game* are predicated on the fact that even people deeply in love do not know as much about their partners as they think they do.

The power of prediction is limited both practically and fundamentally, so that algorithmic predictions should be used for forensic purposes only with great care, and with extensive safeguards. However, predictions can be very useful for intelligence purposes.

The best use of prediction techniques is to predict *risk*. In other words, it is useful (and possible) to build models based on past data that will predict, for this situation now, how great the risk of certain bad events happening is. Such a prediction is probabilistic, and it is the nature of crime and criminal settings that these probabilities will never be 0 or 1. So the output of a predictor will almost always be given to a human user who must make the actual consequential decision if one is required.

There are four natural ways in which predictions of risks can be made actionable.

- The first is when the action based on the prediction is relatively minor. For example, allowing or declining credit card purchases is an entirely automated process based on a predictive model. This model uses information about the credit card's owner and recent history, the products being bought, and the sales location to decide whether to approve each new purchase. One easy way to get a credit card purchase declined is to use it to buy gas (petrol) at a location you have never used before, and then immediately use it to buy electronics at a big box store. This is because that pattern of purchases is often used when a credit card is stolen – the gas purchase to check if the card has been cancelled, and then the electronics purchase to acquire something valuable that is easy to sell on.

  In such settings, there is always a fallback mechanism so, although the decision is consequential in the short term, it need not be in the longer term. If the predictor made a mistake, there is a mechanism to undo it.

- The second kind of action based on prediction is one that provides deterrence. For example, suppose that, in a close approximation to *Minority Report* a prediction system predicted that a certain individual had an 80% chance of committing a particular crime. Then it would not be altogether unreasonable to keep a watch on that person to make sure that they did not go near the place where the crime would be committed. (In fact, police officers have always done this kind of prediction informally.)

- The third kind of action based on prediction is to harden the potential targets. For example, if the model predicts high risks for certain locations, or times, or kinds of businesses then it is natural to take steps to make crimes of those kinds more difficult to carry out. (Again, police officers have always taken steps to warn those they perceive to be at special risk so that they can change their structures or behaviors to make it less likely that the potential crime will actually happen.)

- The fourth kind of action based on prediction is when the prediction model predicts likelihood (which is just another framing of risk). For example, such predictions can suggest which directions for investigation are likely to be the most useful. Informal models like this drive murder enquiries to look first and most closely at immediate family members as potential perpetrators. *Psychological profiling* can also be viewed as a kind of predictive model of the characteristics of a potential perpetrator based on the facts of the crime.

These last two are the key to using prediction for hot spot and intelligence-led policing.

It is instructive to ask why a predictive model of crime should work at all, given that criminals know that law enforcement are searching for their actions, even their potential actions. There are a number of reasons why prediction of risk still works. First, criminals, like the rest of us, are creatures of habit and so tend to do things in the same way they always have even, sometimes, when that way has not worked very well. This is why it is worth collecting modus operandi data.

Second, criminals are already doing things that are risky, and trying to do them in novel ways is perceived as, and probably is, riskier than sticking to how it has always been done.

Third, many criminals have limited skills and may not be able to do tasks required for their crimes in more sophisticated ways, even when there would be obvious benefits to doing so. Together, these make criminal activities far more predictable than they would be if criminals were, say, using game theory to make detection more difficult. And there are always a few sophisticated criminals who do indeed vary the ways in which they commit crimes to make attribution harder.

Predictions are built from datasets where the right answers for the outcomes are already known, usually because these outcomes had already happened. Prediction algorithms use this data to learn how the known answer or outcome depended on the values of the attributes of each record in the given dataset. All algorithms have some kind of constraint to force them to learn a generalized dependency of outcomes on attributes, rather than just memorizing the right answers for the particular records it has seen (called *overfitting*).

When a prediction model is applied, it is given a new record with values for the attributes but, of course, without the outcome. The model then indicates what it thinks the correct or most likely value of the outcome would be, based on the relationship of attribute values to outcome that it has learned from the dataset it was given.

7.3 Meta issues in prediction

Law enforcement use of data analytics is more challenging than more conventional uses such as in business. We now consider some of the specialized issues that must be considered.

7.3.1 Classification versus regression

Most uses of prediction for law enforcement are based on regression rather than classification, because the outcome that is being predicted is most often a risk. In fact, many uses will actually be predicting probabilities, a special case of regression.

Regression is inherently more difficult than classification. Consider, for example, the case of the decision to give someone a mortgage. Such decisions are often made using predictors, which enables them to be made online and in a few minutes. The classification version of this problem is simply whether or not to give each applicant a mortgage of the amount they ask for. The regression version of the problem is to predict how large a mortgage to give each applicant (with $0 corresponding to refusing them a mortgage at all). The regression prediction provides more information about an applicant: if they ask for a $100,000 mortgage and the predictor predicts they should be given a $10,000 mortgage, then this implies that they are a poor risk. This level of detail is not available if the prediction is either yes or (in this case presumably) no. The extra information in the regression prediction requires the algorithm building the predictor to work harder.

Because of these factors, many applications of prediction use classification (even if they have to convert a natural regression problem into classification by binning the possible outputs). Algorithms for building regression predictors, unfortunately, lag behind algorithms for building classification predictors.

7.3.2 Problems with the data

We discussed in the previous chapter some of the ways in which data can be corrupted during the collection process, either accidentally because of the technology, or deliberately by criminals keen to hide themselves from the data-analytic process. Further corruption can happen after the data is collected but before it reaches the data-analytics stage because of storage and data-transfer issues.

The best approach to such corruption is to work to mitigate it, as much as possible, during the collection and transfer stages. However, it is common that the result of the first round of data-analytic modeling reveals errors in the data rather than interesting properties of the system being studied. As mentioned earlier, this is sometimes because errors have accumulated over time but are never exposed because the corrupted records are rarely sensible responses to queries. The expectation that early modeling will reveal problems with the data rather than usable models should be built into planning for using data analytics for the first time

It is also important to work out ways to deal with values that are missing from the data. Some records will have attribute fields for which no attribute value is present. For example, in RMS systems an officer may fail to enter an address or a UCR code. It is difficult to prevent this; designing systems so that they force data entry into every field makes them tedious to use. When there is no sensible entry for a field, officers are forced to invent one, which may be worse than leaving it empty because it is harder to detect and compensate for later.

It is also common to find that fields that are logically empty are filled with some special value that is intended to convey that "this field is deliberately empty" or "not applicable". However, the values chosen for this purpose often cause havoc in downstream data analytics. In some disciplines, the value "99" is used, even for fields that are not naturally numeric. This breaks the processes of conversions and normalizations to a common scale. Sometimes the string "NULL" is used, even for fields that are naturally numeric, with the same issues. These methods for signaling deliberately missing values are holdovers from times when tables of data were small enough to be looked at by humans, but they do not scale to large datasets, and they can be extremely difficult and time-consuming to find and fix[3].

When values in records are genuinely missing it is important to consider why this is so. The easy case is when the missing "slots" are distributed at random throughout the data, in which case there are workarounds. For example, it is common (although rather dubious) to replace such attribute values with the median of the values in the column in which it appears. When there are many missing values in a record it may be safer to delete it from the data altogether but that, of course, is not without consequences.

When the pattern of missing slots has structure, then the issue must be considered more carefully, and there are fewer potential workarounds. For example, if it is the values of one particular attribute that are missing in many records, then perhaps it is not clear what value is supposed to be entered there and staff training or interface redesign can help. Or it could be that it is not obvious what a meaningful value for the entry is. In some rural locations, street numbers are not widely used, for example, so this field may often be left empty in RMS records. It can also happen that some values of some attributes are considered sensitive, and so individuals refuse to reveal them.

When values are missing in a structured way it is much more difficult to compensate for them because the "missingness" is a property of the system being modeled. Some algorithms will continue to work well even when there are missing values, so relatively low frequencies of missing values can be ignored. Other algorithms require a value for every attribute in every record. In this case, it is common to fill the holes with surrogate values, perhaps the mean or median values of the relevant attribute, but there is little justification for this.

7.3.3 Why did the model make this prediction?

Predictive models all make predictions, but they can be divided into two categories:

- Opaque models. These predictive models do not provide any indication of why they predict the outcome they do for each new record. They behave like black boxes – they produce a prediction of outcome but nothing else.
- Transparent models. These predictive models produce a predicted outcome, but also provide an indication of *why* they have made this prediction. Each prediction comes with a reason that explains it. This explanation comes only from the processes that the predictor used internally, so it is not a real-world explanation, but it is still helpful.

Sadly, for all of the predictive techniques currently known, opaque approaches typically produce more accurate predictions than transparent ones do.

There are many good reasons to prefer transparent predictors, all of them based around issues of trust in the modeling by those who must act on the prediction:

- Humans prefer an explanation whenever a prediction is consequential; and this preference increases with the severity of the consequence.
- Some kinds of predictions are legally mandated to give reasons that explain them, so that it is clear that forbidden criteria were not used. For example, the decision to give a mortgage or not is often made using a predictive system, but certain criteria cannot be used as the basis for such a decision, for example race. Forcing the system to explain why it made each decision makes it possible to verify that it is not using forbidden criteria.
- Many countries require those affected by predictive systems to be provided with an explanation for their decisions. The concern here is not the use of forbidden criteria, but biases built into the entire algorithmic process itself.

  The most prominent example is the European Union's *General Data Protection Regulation* (GDPR), whose effect is widespread because multinational businesses find it easier to apply it across their entire organizations rather than treat the EU as a special case. Citizens have a right to an explanation[4] which essentially compels the use of transparent predictions.

The presence of an explanation also helps the data modeling itself, since it provides a sanity check on the process at all stages.

Finding ways to make data analytics more transparent is an active research area. An important tool at present is the use of *Shapley values*. These approximate the importance of every subset of attributes to producing the correct outcome prediction (approximate because there are an exponential number of such subsets so a complete calculation would be too expensive to be practical for all but the smallest datasets). The Shapley value calculation allows the significance of each attribute to correct predictions to be measured, and so a ranked list of attributes by their impact on the outcome can be calculated. This often gives added insight into the system being studied. For each record, the role of each of its attributes in the prediction of its associated outcome can also be calculated, providing an even finer grained view of the reasons for the dependence of the outcome on the input attributes.

7.3.4 How good is this model?

Before the predictions of a model can be acted on, it is wise to have a sense of how good its predictions actually are. There are a number of metrics that aim to provide confidence in how well a predictor will perform in the field, that is when it is applied to previously unseen data.

Given a dataset, we could build a predictive model from it, apply it to the same set of records (hiding the attribute that is the outcome), and then compare the outcomes predicted by the model to the true outcomes that we already know.

If the task is classification, then the fraction of answers for which the prediction was correct can be converted to a percentage, and is called the *prediction accuracy*. However, this prediction accuracy, measured by making predictions for the same set of records that were used to build the model, will be very optimistic.

If the task was is regression, then the values produced by the prediction model can be compared to the actual outcome values from the data, and an aggregate score calculated. A common way to do this is to calculate the *root mean square error* (RMSE). This computes the difference between the predicted and actual value for each record, squares each one, sums them, and takes the square root of the sum.

However, a few records with large differences between predicted and actual value will tend to dominate this measure, so it is not a good estimate of overall performance. It is better to use the *mean absolute error* (MAE). This is calculated by summing the absolute values of the difference between the predicted and actual outcome value for each of the records, and then dividing by the number of records. This weights the errors equally across all of the records. The other practical advantage of the mean absolute error is that it is in the same units as the predicted quantity and so is directly interpretable.

To get a more reliable estimate of what the performance of a predictor is likely to be when it is used to predict previously unseen data (rather than the data on which it was trained) it is useful to divide the available dataset into two disjoint subsets, the *training set* and the *test set*. Typically, 75% of the records might be used for training and the remaining 25% for testing. When datasets were smaller, there was much agonizing about the relative sizes, but most datasets now are large and it does not much matter. This division should, of course, be done randomly so that any structure present in the dataset is destroyed. For example, it is common for a dataset to be captured in time order. Splitting the first 75% into the training set, and the remaining 25% into the test set means that the training data represents the system at an older time, and so it may not perform well on the test set records from a later time.

The training set is used to build the predictive model as before. Once the model has been built, it is applied to the records of the test set. The actual outcomes for the test set records are known, and so can be compared with the outcomes predicted by the model. Comparing the known and predicted outcomes can be used to calculate either a prediction accuracy or a mean absolute error. This test set accuracy is a much better estimate of the probable performance of the predictor when it is deployed on previously unseen data.

For any model, not all records will be equally easy to predict correctly. If we compute the performance based on one training set-test set split, then it is unclear whether the observed performance is the result of the choice of the prediction technique or a lucky distribution of records into the training and testing subsets. If easy records end up in the test set, a model might tend to look as if it is performing well; if difficult records end up there, it might look much worse. To tease apart whether it is the technique or the split, it is usual to repeat the training and testing process multiple times, each time dividing the available data into different training and test subsets, building models from the training subsets, and evaluating them on the test subsets.

Easy and difficult records will be randomly distributed across training and testing by this repetition. If the performances of these repeated experiments are comparable, then we can be confident that the prediction technique is performing well (regardless of how the records are distributed across training and testing) and so is likely to perform well on brand new data. If the performance of the repeated experiments varies widely then there are probably some hard-to-predict records in the dataset, and the performance depends on whether they fall into the training or the test set each time. This signals that there may be issues with brand new data that contains records like those that are hard to predict.

This repeated experiment framework is called *cross validation*. It is common to repeat the splitting process 5 or 10 times, depending on the complexity and cost of building each predictor.

We are often interested not just in how many prediction errors are made, but how they are distributed. For a classification problem with two possible outcomes (say, 'yes' and 'no') we typically want to see whether records where the answer should have been 'yes' were predicted to be 'no' more often than the converse.

To observe this behavior it is common to compute a *confusion matrix*. For a two-outcome classification, this is a 2×2 matrix whose rows correspond to the actual outcomes and whose columns correspond to the predicted outcomes for the test set. The entries in each square of the matrix count how often each of the possibilities occurred:

- A record was labeled 'yes' and the model predicted 'yes'. This is called a true positive, and counts how many times the model correctly predicted records from the 'yes' category.
- A record was labeled 'no' and the model predicted 'no'. This is called a true negative, and counts how many times the model correctly predicted records from the 'no' category. The sum of the true positives and true negatives divided by the total number of test records is, of course, the prediction accuracy.
- A record was labeled 'yes' but the model predicted 'no'. This is called a *false negative* – the model missed a record that should have been predicted to be in the 'yes' category.
- A record was labeled 'no' but the model predicted 'yes'. This is called a *false positive* – the model predicted a record to be in the 'yes' category, but it should not have.

Note that which is considered positive and which negative makes sense when the labels are 'yes' and 'no' but quickly becomes confusing when the labels have a less obvious orientation[5].

The number of records with each of the possible outcomes do not have to be the same. Especially in security and medical applications it is common to have unbalanced numbers of records: 95% of the records associated with one outcome, and only 5% with the other. In this case predicting every record to be in the largest class produces a prediction accuracy of 95%, but this is practically useless. The important measure is really the lift: the increase in prediction accuracy produced by the predictor compared to making the default prediction.

When the number of records with different outcomes is unbalanced it is useful to compute the *F-score*, It is given by:

$$F\text{-}score = \frac{tp}{tp + 1/2(fp + fn)}$$

where tp is the number of true positives, fp is the number of false positives, and fn is the number of false negatives. This score takes into account the imbalance between different numbers of outcomes, and so presents a simple but revealing estimate of a classifier's performance.

The false positive and false negative counts together make up all of the errors, but counting them separately reveals more about the fine structure of the predictor. Generally speaking, a good predictor will produce about the same number of each (and of course as few as possible of both).

However, sometimes the false positive rate matters much more than the false negative rate, or *vice versa*. This is especially true for security and medical settings. Consider a predictor for the risk that an air traveller is a terrorist. A false positive is an inconvenience – the wrongly predicted traveller receives additional searches and a slower passage through security. A false negative is much more consequential – the missed terrorist is allowed on board the plane.

However, in situations like this there had better not be too many false positives, even though they are not strongly consequential, for a second-order reason. If there are many false-positive predictions and this is detectable by the users of the predictor – for example, they keep screening passengers predicted to be terrorists, but never find anything – then they will lose confidence in *all* of the positive predictions. Predictors cannot be like the boy who cried wolf or they get ignored.

Most predictors have parameters that allow them to trade off the number of false positives against false negatives. This tradeoff is not usually smooth, so changing these parameters can reduce the overall error rate. For example, changing the parameters to produce 10 fewer false positives does not necessarily increase the number of false negatives by 10.

The best values for such parameters can be found by calculating the ROC (Receiver Operating Characteristic) curve. The model is built repeatedly with different parameter settings, and accuracies plotted on a graph whose x-axis is the false positive rate, and whose y-axis is the true positive rate. The resulting curve connecting the points describing each different set of parameters looks something like that shown in Figure 7.2. The overall best setting for the parameters for a general predictor is the point where the ROC curve is farthest from the diagonal line. In settings where low false positives are preferred to false negatives or *vice versa*, the ROC curve also suggests how much that will impact the overall accuracy. The area between the curved line and the diagonal line is also an indication of the power of the particular predictive model, and so can be used to compare one prediction algorithm to another using the same data.

For regression we typically want to see whether the model tends to predict larger values than the actual ones, or smaller. This is easily calculated by taking the mean error (that is, without the absolute value function). Again there might be a preference to predict at least (or at most) the true value, and parameters can be adjusted to try to make this happen. For example, a model predicting the risk of a particular crime across a set of locations might be better if it overpredicted the risk, rather than underpredicting it.

7.3.5 Selecting attributes

The datasets used for data analytics are seldom collected specifically for that purpose. They are often collected for some other organizational reason and repurposed, afterwards, for analytics. As a result the attributes associated with each record are not necessarily those that are most useful for predicting the outcome of interest. (Of

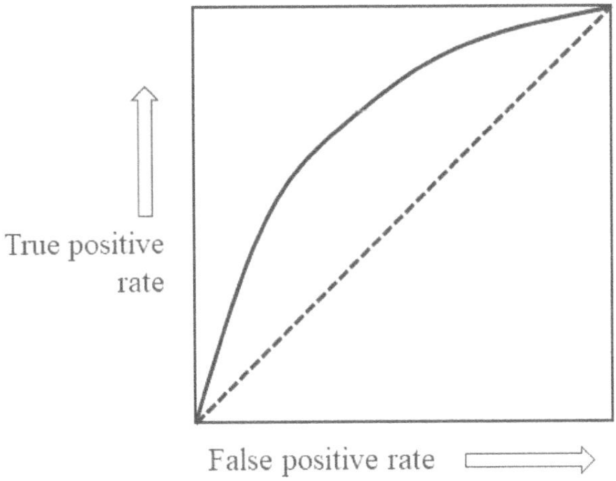

Figure 7.2: Shape of a Receiver Operating Characteristic curve

course, we cannot usually tell which attributes are most useful for prediction in advance anyway.)

If important attributes were not collected, there is not much that can be done about it, and it is rarely possible to know which attributes would have helped. It is more common to have attributes in the dataset that were collected on spec, in the hope that they might be important. Some data-analytic algorithms automatically ignore or discount attributes that are unhelpful, but most do not.

There are two common problems caused by the presence of extra attributes in the data. First, useless attributes increase the complexity and cost of the algorithms that build the models. The complexity of many algorithms increases as the square of the number of attributes, so having twice as many attributes as necessary increases the time to build a model by a factor of four.

Second, when two attributes are redundant, measuring more or less the same property, some algorithms (as it were) get distracted trying to explain the small differences between them. Of course, those doing the data collection do not knowingly introduce the same attribute twice, but it is easy to do so unwittingly because the attributes look very different, and it requires understanding of the system to see that they are measuring (almost) the same thing. For example, in an income tax setting there is a strong relationship between gross income and tax deducted because the majority of people earn income from a single source and have the tax deducted automatically by their employers[6].

Because of this, there are good reasons to reduce the number of attributes in a dataset when this is possible without losing information. This is called *attribute selection*. Attribute selection should always be done conservatively and cautiously – the process should be thought of as removing the least helpful attributes, not as trying to find the most helpful.

Reducing the set of attributes usually allows the model-building algorithms to run faster, and typically increases accuracy. A smaller set of attributes may also make it more obvious how the system operates and why it makes the predictions it makes.

When doing prediction, there is one particular outcome attribute. One simple way to reduce the number of attributes is to see whether there is any statistical relationship between the ordinary attributes and the outcome attribute. This can be done using something as simple as a χ-squared test. Typically, this will show that some attributes have a strong relationship with the outcome attribute, some have only a modest relationship, and some have none at all. Only this last category should be removed.

Other attribute-reduction techniques depend on using particular prediction algorithms. Some algorithms have a built-in way of counting how often each attribute plays a role in making internal decisions. Summing these counts over the entire model-building process provides an estimate of the overall usefulness of each attribute.

There is also a way to assess the usefulness of each attribute that works for any predictor. First, build the predictor using all of the attributes as usual. Then, for each attribute (a column of the dataset) permute the values and build the predictor again.

This permuting of the values breaks the association, in each row, between the other attribute values and this one. If an attribute is not important to making accurate predictions, then the permuting will have little effect on measured accuracy. If the attribute is important to making accurate predictions, then the predictor based on the permuted column will perform much worse than the original. Measuring the drop in accuracy as each attribute is permuted in turn allows attribute importance to be estimated: a big drop signals an important attribute, and *vice versa*.

Shapley values also allow the attributes to be ranked by their contribution to the correct outcomes.

All of these techniques allow attributes to be ranked by importance. The lower ranked attributes are candidates for removal. But the higher ranked attributes also show which properties of records contribute most strongly to the outcome being studied. Sometimes the set of important attributes is more useful than the predictions themselves because they reveal the important drivers of the system being modeled.

7.3.6 Making predictions in stages

Predictions can always be done by building a single monolithic predictor. For difficult problems, however, it may be more effective to build a *pipeline* of predictors.

Suppose that the goal is to predict whether or not each record has some property of interest, and we want the false negative rate to be as low as possible – we do not want to miss any records that have the property. We can build an initial predictor that is tuned so that its false negative rate is as small as possible, even though this almost inevitably means that its false positive rate will be high.

Records that this predictor says do not have the property are almost certain not to have it; but only some of those that are predicted to have the property actually have it because so many of them are false positives. It does not matter if half, or even more, of those predicted to have the property do not actually have it.

The records that this predictor claims have the property are sent to a second predictor which is tuned with the same bias against false negatives. The advantage for the second predictor is that it sees fewer records, and so can perhaps use a more expensive algorithm. The disadvantage for the second predictor is that distinguishing the two groups – those with the property and those without – is presumably more difficult (since if it was easy the first predictor would have done so). However, as before, this second predictor need only predict that records do not have the property if it is very sure.

The records that the second predictor says have the property, but which it may not be very sure about because of how it has been tuned, can be sent to a third predictor, and the process can continue for as many stages as necessary. It may even be possible to reduce the number of records down to a level where the final decision can be made by a human.

This idea can be extended to a pipeline of regression predictors. At the first stage, only records predicted to have very low scores are discarded. Some of the records passed to the next stage may still have moderately low scores, but the model for this stage will produce new regression scores that push some of these moderately low scoring records to even lower scores. As the process continues, the records that survive will tend to have high scores.

7.3.7 Bagging and boosting

Suppose that we trained a predictor by starting with a small batch of training records, then evaluating the model built so far using a test set, and then continued to train it with the next batch of training records, and so on. How would the accuracy measured using the test set grow as a function of the number of batches used so far? The surprising answer is that the accuracy grows initially very fast, perhaps reaching 80% of its final value after seeing only fifty or so training records; after that it flattens but continues to grow, just much more slowly.

Unfortunately, this does not mean that we only ever need to use the first fifty records to train a model. The final accuracy depends in a natural way on the size of the training set; it is the *rate* of improvement that slows as more and more training records have been seen.

Consider a classification problem with two outcomes. Before training begins, the boundary between records associated with the two outcomes could be anywhere.

However, once we have encountered one record with each outcome, this uncertainty has been reduced dramatically – we now know that the boundary must lie somewhere between them. If the next training record lies on the "outside" of the region where we know the boundary must lie, then it provides no new information and does not shrink the region where the boundary might lie. If, on the other hand, the next training record lies between the first two records, then it reduces the uncertainty about the region where the boundary lies, no matter which outcome it is associated with.

In the early stages of training, newly encountered training records are much more likely to be on the "inside" and therefore reduce the region of uncertainty for the boundary. As this region shrinks, training records are increasingly likely to fall outside this region and so they provide no new information. A record which would have shrunk the region, if it had been considered earlier, is uninteresting if the region has been reduced by some other record. But no matter how many training records have been seen so far, there will still be occasional records that lie inside the region of uncertainty and so reduce the uncertainty further. Improvement continues, but more and more slowly as it becomes less and less likely that the next record provides new information. Larger training data will always provide better accuracy than smaller training data, but the improvement in accuracy, in both cases, will still be concentrated in the earliest records encountered.

There is a way to leverage this rapid increase in accuracy based on the early training examples. It is called *bagging*.

The available training data is divided into small batches – in principle, randomly although this does not seem to matter much in practice. A predictive model is built from each of these batches independently (and possibly in parallel) in the usual way. Each of these models is fast to build because the training data it uses is small. They will not, individually, be very accurate but more accurate that you might intuitively expect because all the records look like early records in the scenario described above.

The complete predictive model that is deployed is the union of all of these simple models. When a new record is to be predicted, it is presented to all of the simple models, they all make their own predictions, and the overall prediction is either the plurality of the predictions made by each predictor (for classification) or the average of the predictions made by each predictor (for regression).

Each of the individual predictors is only moderately accurate, but combining their predictions produces an overall prediction that is much more accurate than any single one. This property is often called the *wisdom of crowds*. This property seems to have been first noticed by Francis Galton, who observed, at a fair in Devon, that the average of the guesses of individuals about the weight of an ox was much closer to its actual weight than the individual guesses were. Statisticians call this *variance cancelling*, and it describes the property that some estimates will be too high, some will be too low but, if the estimates are independent, then these errors will tend to cancel one another out.

For a test record, the individual predictors in this ensemble of predictors, each trained on a small batch of the training data, will make errors – predicting the wrong outcome class, or the wrong outcome value – but these errors will tend to cancel one another out. Many batches can trained in the same total time as one single predictor on the whole training data, and the ensemble prediction will typically be better than that of a single, monolithic one.

In bagging, every predictor is treated as the equal of every other and their contributions to the overall prediction are weighted the same. There is an extension of bagging that uses small batches of training data, but tries to choose them so that the resulting predictors increasingly focus on the hard-to-distinguish cases or, equivalently, the difficult parts of the boundary. This approach is called *boosting*. If bagging exploits the wisdom of crowds then boosting tries to exploit the wisdom of experts.

Each record in the training data is assigned a difficulty score, which is always normalized across the training data so that it behaves like a probability. (The sum of all of the difficulty scores for the training data is 1.)

For the entire process, the difficulty scores will be used as weights – a record that is considered more difficult is more likely to be selected. Selection is always with replacement: a record that has been selected once can also be selected again (and again) in the same batch. So every training set can contain repeated records.

The first small batch is selected from the training data with replacement. Because all of the difficulty scores are initialized to $1/n$, each record is equally likely to be selected. The first predictor is built from this batch.

Before the next batch is selected, the first predictor is used to make predictions for all of the training records. If the prediction is correct (for classification) or close (for regression) for a record its difficulty score is reduced. If the prediction is incorrect then its difficulty score is increased. These difficulty scores are normalized across the entire dataset so that they again sum to 1.

Now a second predictor is built by selecting another batch of records using the difficulty scores – a record with a greater difficulty score is more likely to be selected. The difficulty scores are not the same for all records, so records for which the first predictor performed poorly are more likely to be selected. This second predictor has specialized slightly in making predictions for records that are difficult.

The entire training set is then predicted by the ensemble of the first and second predictors, using the voting or averaging process described for bagging. The difficulty scores for each record are adjusted according to how well they were predicted by the ensemble. For classification, for example, a record might be predicted correctly by both the first and second predictor, by one of them, or by neither of them. For regression, an average error from the two predictors can be calculated, and the bigger this is, the more difficult the record is considered.

Now a third, fourth, fifth, and so on predictors can be built using exactly the same process. Successive predictors are learned from batches that contain a greater fraction of records with high difficulty scores, because these are more likely to be selected. Successive predictors become "experts" in predicting the correct outcomes for these more difficult cases.

Once training is complete, the ensemble of predictors is deployed just as in bagging. New records are predicted by all of the predictors and an aggregate prediction created by voting or averaging.

7.3.8 Anomaly detection

Usually, when we are making predictions, we want the predicted results to be accurate for typical records, which we expect to be representative of records we will see in the future. Sometimes there are records in the available data that seem quite different from the majority of records. In a clustering, they may not seem to belong to any of the clusters well; in prediction, they may often seem to be predicted incorrectly.

These records are usually considered to be *outliers* which is just a way of saying that they do not seem to fit the system we are studying. As we have seen, one reason for the presence of such records might be issues in the data collection and storage processes. But outliers might also be data that does not come from the system we are examining, but from some other system that exists alongside. In this case, we could call the outliers *anomalies*.

If we are only interested in the main system, then outliers are an annoyance that we may want to remove from the dataset so that the models built from it will be more sensible. However, in the adversarial systems typical of law enforcement, the separate system may be the one that is of greatest interest. In other words, we may want to examine the outliers carefully.

This will typically be the case when the dataset casts a wide net of actions and behaviors of ordinary people, but data about criminals is collected along with it. Examples include intrusion-detection systems in cybersecurity, CCTV, tax returns, and financial fraud. Most of the activities represented in such data are common and normal but, regardless of the particular differences of the criminal activity happening, there is a single, general difference – they are doing something that is not normal, and so not common. Anomaly detection refers to the process of looking for the existence of a separate, unusual process that is happening alongside the ordinary process that generated the dataset, without necessarily knowing how this other process works, just that it is different.

7.3.9 Ranking

In some settings, it is more useful to predict the ranks of a set of new records relative to one another with respect to some continuous property. Ranking is very natural for regression predictors – simply sort the records into descending order of their predicted regression scores.

The advantage of ranking comes when the decision to act on the results of prediction is independent of the prediction itself. This is often because of limitations to the capacity for action, or limitations that vary quickly. For example, suppose that a regression predictor predicts high risks for many city intersections as hot spots for crime on Friday nights. The number of units able to patrol intersections is limited, and so only the highest ranked (riskiest) may get patrolled. If the number of units is reduced because of illness or a large traffic accident that pulls away units, it is still obvious where the available units should be sent.

Contrast this with a classification model that predicts, say, high, medium, and low risk intersections. This is only useful if the number of units is exactly the right size to cover all of the high-risk intersections, or all of the high- and medium-risk intersections. If the number of available units suddenly gets smaller, there is not enough information to optimally allocate them.

Similar issues arise with, say, tax cheats. Having a ranked list of the most serious cheats allows audit capacity to be optimally allocated, even if this capacity changes dynamically. Many law enforcement issues are like this: in a perfect world, every incident would be handled completely, but resource limitations force triage.

7.3.10 Should I make a prediction at all?

There has always been a tendency to treat a predictor as an oracle. When it makes a prediction, the accuracy of that prediction can be judged based on the measures discussed previously, such as prediction accuracy or mean absolute error.

What is often ignored is that predictors are only trained on a finite amount of data, and they should only be allowed to predict outcomes for new records that resemble those on which they were trained. This idea of limiting predictions to records that resemble those trained on is almost never implemented, but ignoring it can be extremely dangerous.

A better approach to prediction is to require that two different models are built. The first is the predictor as before. The second is a clustering of *all* of the training data into a single cluster with a well-defined boundary. This boundary acts like a wrapper that specifies the space of data on which the predictor was trained.

When a prediction is to be made for a new record, it is first compared to the cluster. If it falls outside the cluster, the response should be "The predictor cannot predict the outcome for this record because it falls outside any data on which the predictor was trained" (in other words, "Don't know"). If it falls inside the cluster, then it can be predicted as usual.

Without the wrapper, most predictors will go ahead and make a prediction of outcome whether they have any real information to go on or not. This is dangerous for predictions that are at all consequential.

The wrapper should he constructed to be reasonably tight around the training data, but not too tight since there will be new records that are quite like the ones in the training set, but are not exactly like them.

Attribute	Outcome
1	A
2	A
2	A
3	A
3	B
1	B
1	A
2	A
3	B
1	A
3	B
2	A

	A	B
1	3	1
2	4	0
3	1	3

Table 7.1: Counting the matches between an attribute and an outcome to create a table of matches

7.4 Prediction techniques

We now turn to the algorithms that are used to build data-analytic models. Prediction models all learn the dependence of the outcome on the values of the attributes over all of the training records, and assume that this dependence continues to hold for new, previously unseen records.

Approaches can be divided into two broad categories: methods that learn the dependence by counting, and those that learn the dependence by optimization.

7.4.1 Counting techniques

Consider a classification problem with, say, two outcomes and a single attribute that has, say, three possible values. If we want to learn the way in which the outcome depends on the attribute we can count how often the six possible patterns of attribute value and outcome value occur in the training data, and use them to come up with simple rules on what to predict for a new record for each particular attribute value it may contain.

Table 7.1 shows a column of the dataset for the attribute, and the corresponding outcome labels. Counting the number of times each combination of attribute value and outcome value occurs produces the table of matches.

The table captures the way in which the value of the outcome class is related to the value of the attribute. The match is not perfect – sometimes an attribute value of 1 is associated with outcome A and sometimes with outcome B. That is not surprising: the prediction problem would be an easy one if the value of only one of the attributes was enough to determine the outcome. Each row of the table defines a simple rule based on the most common attribute value. Together they define this set of rules:

- if the attribute has value 1, predict outcome A
- if the attribute has value 2, predict outcome A
- if the attribute has value 3, predict outcome B.

Using these rules produces a prediction accuracy (on the training data) of 10/12, because of the 12 cases in the first table, 10 would be predicted correctly using these rules. This score (10/12) tells us, in a rough way, how much predictive power this attribute has. This process can be repeated for each attribute, one at a time.

We considered the attribute values in the example to be distinct codes, not numbers. If we do consider them as numbers, then we can derive a new set of rules based on the values of attributes. The new rules would be:

- if the attribute has value ≤ 2, predict outcome A
- if the attribute has value > 2, predict outcome B

and this has the same accuracy (10/12).

So for attributes whose values are categorical, chosen from a fixed finite set, we can use counting to generate small predictive rules and measure the predictive power of the attribute based on the accuracy these rules would produce based on the training data. For attributes whose values are numerical, we can derive similar rules based on inequalities, but there is more computation to do since we must consider many possible boundaries to consider. For example, we should also consider

- if the attribute has value ≤ 1, predict outcome A, otherwise predict outcome B

but this has accuracy 6/12 and so is worse.

These simple ideas lead to a predictor called a *decision tree*. Given a training set, all of the attributes are assessed to see which one, and with what set of rules or inequalities, would produce the greatest prediction accuracy for the outcome. This rule, treated as a test, is recorded as the root of a tree.

The training data is then divided into disjoint subsets, depending on how it satisfied the rule or inequality selected for the root, and the process repeated on each subset to create decision nodes at the second level. This process continues until the part of the training data remaining in a particular branch is all (or, in practice, almost all) labeled with one outcome. In that case, the process stops with a leaf, which is labeled with that outcome.

When a new record is to have its outcome predicted, it is first tested using the rule or inequality at the root. Depending on the result of that check, it passes down one of the branches; and subsequent checks determine the path it takes. Finally it reaches a leaf, and it is predicted to have the outcome associated with that leaf.

Decision trees are not powerful enough to be used as real-world predictors (although humans use them as a kind of checklist, for example, in medical diagnosis). However, they form the basis of a number of powerful predictors.

Random forests are rather like a bagged ensemble of decision trees, but with one extra feature. When each batch is selected to build a tree, not only are some records selected, but a subset of the attributes are selected as well. The resulting model uses the advantages of small training sets for quick training, but also gets the benefits of variance cancelling for attributes too. As with ordinary bagging, the result is an ensemble of decision trees, which are deployed for new records just as before.

Because the attribute that gets selected for each internal node of a decision tree wins a competition with all of the other attributes to do so, counting how often this happens estimates how important each attribute is. Because this competition is against a different set of attributes in each of the decision trees of the forest, this estimate is robust, and provides one way to rank attributes by their importance. (The permutation approach was developed for random forests, and also works well. Usually, the two attribute rankings broadly agree.)

An alternate approach to building ensembles of trees is called *gradient boosted trees*. These are also an ensemble approach, but instead of learning to predict the outcome, each tree after the first tries to predict the collective errors of previous predictors. They resemble boosted trees, except that the outcomes are errors not the class or values of the outcome.

The first predictor in the ensemble is built in the usual way as a single predictor. This predictor inevitably makes some errors. The second predictor then tries to predict corrections for the errors of the first predictor. The effect of these two predictor on the training data is calculated, and the third predictor tries to predict the residual error that those two have left. This process continues for as many steps as required.

When a new record is to be predicted, the initial predictor indicates the outcome, the second one applies the correction that it has learned that it expects to reduce the error, and so on.

Another important technique that is based on counting, but converts counts into probabilities, is *Bayesian prediction*. These are based on *Bayes Rule*, developed by an English clergyman, Thomas Bayes, in 1763. The notation $P[X|Y]$ means "the probability of X given that Y has already happened". Bayes Rule then says:

$$P[outcome|evidence] = \frac{P[evidence|outcome] \times P[outcome]}{P[evidence]}$$

If we want to compute the probability of a particular outcome ("the crime was committed by X") then we need to compute three probabilities:

1. The probability that if X had committed the crime, this is the evidence we would see, ($P[evidence|outcome]$);
2. The probability with which we would have assumed that X committed the crime if we had no evidence, that is, how inherently likely is it that X would commit such a crime, ($P[outcome]$);
3. The probability that we would find the evidence that we see at all ($P[evidence]$).

The usual use of this rule is to compute the probability of X committing the crime, as opposed to someone else (X not committing the crime). So the rule is used twice, once with $outcome_1$ (X committed the crime) and $outcome_2$ (X did not commit the crime). The left-hand side in both cases is interpreted as a probability, and the outcome with the greatest probability is taken as the model's prediction. So we have two uses of the rule:

$$P[outcome_1|evidence] = \frac{P[evidence|outcome_1] \times P[outcome_1]}{P[evidence]}$$

and

$$P[outcome_2|evidence] = \frac{P[evidence|outcome_2]P[outcome_2]}{P[evidence]}$$

The denominator is the same in both cases, and so only affects the magnitude of the answers, so we can ignore it because we only care about which left-hand side is the greater. This is just as well, since it is usually hard to estimate how likely a particular set of evidence is. Also $outcome_1$ and $outcome_2$ are mutually exclusive, so $P[outcome_1] + P[outcome_2] = 1$.

We can now see that the terms of the form $P[evidence|outcome]$ can be thought of as nudging the prior probability – the probability of the outcome before we consider evidence – higher or lower. The *prior* ($P[outcome]$) estimates how likely the outcome is inherently (and this is Bayes' main contribution to thinking about probability).

There are two mistakes that come from not thinking about the prior in a clear way. First, conspiracy theorists are those who ignore priors, and so give evidence more weight than it should have. There is a high probability that, if we are visited by a UFO, there will be strange sounds and lights in the sky so

$$P[\textit{sounds and lights}|\textit{ufo visit}]$$

might be of moderate size. But if we multiply this probability by a prior, $P[\textit{ufo visits}]$, that most people believe to be very small, then the resulting product, and so probability, becomes much smaller. In other words, hearing sound and seeing lights are not, by themselves, conclusive or even strong evidence for UFOs, so

$$P[\textit{ufo visit}|\textit{sounds and lights}]$$

will be small, using Bayes Rule.

The second mistake is the make the prior too large, and this is more common case in law enforcement. If we start with a prior with a large value for the outcome,

$$P[X\ committed\ the\ crime]$$

then it will take a very small value for

$$P[evidence|X\ committed\ the\ crime]$$

to reduce the overall probability from Bayes Rule. In other words, if the prior has a large value, it is difficult for the value to be altered much by the evidence. Large values for the prior tend to indicate bias, or jumping to conclusions.

This can happen in many different settings. A large prior for

$$P[crimes\ like\ this\ are\ committed\ by\ people\ from\ racial\ group\ Y]$$

feeds through to a large value for

$$P[crimes\ like\ this\ are\ committed\ by\ people\ from\ racial\ group\ Y|evidence]$$

unless the evidence compellingly suggests another possibility.

The role of a prior is also important in understanding settings that can be thought of as tests. Consider a polygraph test of a group of 100 individuals who are suspected of dealing drugs; and suppose that the accuracy of the polygraph is 80% (much better than it is in practice!). Suppose that 10 members of the group are actually dealing drugs and the other 90 are not.

Now suppose that an individual fails the polygraph test. What are the chances that he is actually dealing drugs? The most common answer is to say that there is a 80% chance, but this is completely wrong[7]. Of the 10 people who are actually dealing drugs, the polygraph results will find 8 of them (it is 80% accurate). But for the 90 people who are *not* dealing drugs, the polygraph will say that 18 of them actually are (again, it is 80% accurate, so it will report 20% false positives).

So the test will report that 26 (8 + 18) people are dealing drugs. Of these 26, only 8 are actually dealing drugs, so the probability that someone who fails the polygraph is dealing drugs is 8/26 = 31%. The reason for the difference is the prior: there is only a 20% chance that any particular individual is dealing drugs to begin with (before the polygraph) and ignoring this creates an entirely false intuition. (The original intuitive answer is to the question "how likely is it that someone dealing drugs will be detected by the test", a question that ignores the context, which is exactly what the prior forces us to pay attention to.)

We have discussed this in detail because ignoring or paying too much attention to priors is the source of much confusion about, say, the best course of action in an investigative setting.

Bayes Rule can also be used as a data-analytic predictor. However, one more step is required to make this practical.

The difficulty is the term $P[evidence|outcome]$ which is, in general, difficult to estimate. This is especially difficult in law-enforcement settings where the evidence might have been fabricated deliberately. However, even predicting from a dataset, this term can be difficult to estimate. It asks "for an given outcome, how likely is it that a record like this appears in the training data?" which is difficult to estimate.

The solution is the *Naïve Bayes Assumption.* This assumption assumes that each attribute (each part of the evidence) is independent of every other part; that is there is no correlation among the presence or value of one and the presence or value of another in the records. This assumption is hardly ever completely true (hence the "naïve") but it turns out to be quite workable in practice, unless there are many repeated or very similar attributes.

The term $P[evidence|outcome]$ can be rewritten as

$$P[attribute_1|outcome] \times P[attribute_2|outcome] \times \ldots \times P[attribute_m|outcome]$$

(dividing the evidence into its component parts, which are the attributes of the dataset) and these terms are easily derived from counts of the matches between each column of the dataset (each attribute) and the outcome, just as we saw previously for decision trees.

A Bayesian predictor computes these terms for every attribute, including the prior which, for each outcome, is just the number of records in the training set with that outcome, divided by the size of the training set. Prediction for each new record consists of applying the rule for each possible outcome, based on the appropriate probabilities derived from counts, and predicting whichever outcome gets the highest score. These outcome scores are (sort of) probabilities, so the model also provides an indication of confidence in the prediction. For example, if $outcome_1$ produces a value of 0.32 and $outcome_2$ a value of 0.29 then we would predict $outcome_1$, but with little confidence[8].

Bayesian prediction is useful in settings where there is class imbalance, that is one outcome is more common than the other(s). The prior, as it were, automatically takes into account the imbalance. It is often used in medical settings, where some diseases or conditions are rare.

When the domain of application is well understood, Bayesian predictors can be generalized to Bayesian networks. These are formed by a directed acyclic graph of Bayesian predictors, each one of which makes predictions about, say, one particular subsystem, and then passes its prediction to downstream Bayesian predictors. This kinds of connectivity is straightforward because all of the values are probabilities. The advantage is related to those we have seen for bagging: the prediction problem is decomposed into pieces that may be, individually, easier to train, and perhaps to understand.

7.4.2 Optimization techniques

The problem with counting techniques is that they consider each attribute independently of the others before combining them into a single model. When attributes have complex or subtle dependencies among one another, as well as with the outcome attribute, such techniques may struggle.

Another class of techniques treat the set of attributes all together, and try to construct the relationship between them and the outcome in a more holistic way. These all, in some way, try to learn or approximate the function that maps the input attribute values to the outcome.

One effective technique using this approach is called *support vector machines* (SVMs). These are naturally two-outcome classification models, although they can be generalized for regression and, with some effort, classification with more than two outcomes.

If we are given training data records with two possible outcomes, then a natural question to ask is whether there is a boundary between the records associated with the two different outcomes. This boundary becomes the model – the outcome for a new record is predicted based on which side of the boundary it falls.

Support vector machines assume that such a boundary is linear, that is in general it is a plane, usually in a high-dimensional space where it is called a hyperplane. The problem is that, given two sets of records, one for each outcome, there are many possible planes that separate them, each with a different position and orientation. Which one is the best? We want the boundary that will generalize the best so that previously unseen records will fall on the appropriate side of this boundary?

The key insight of SVMs is that a better question is: what is the thickest block that can be fitted between the two sets of records? Framing the problem in terms of a block ties the position and orientation of the boundary into a single problem. The center plane of the thickest block then becomes the actual separating boundary.

Finding the thickest block, given the sets of points, is an optimization problem, and not even a very expensive one, so this approach produces good boundaries at low cost.

The position and thickness of the block is determined only by the training records that touch it, and these are called the *support vectors* from which the technique gets its name. Note that all of the other records – those that are farther back from the block – play no role in determining its position.

The support vectors provide a way to understand why the accuracy of predictor building increases so sharply with the first few training records. Consider a sequence of training records. The first few are likely to be (temporary) support vectors since they delimit the space in which the eventual boundary will lie. Training records that do not "face" the other side have no effect on limiting where the boundary might be. As more and more training records are looked at, it becomes increasingly unlikely that they are support vectors and so the rate of improvement in accuracy slows.

Larger training data, though, will continue to contain an occasional support vector, and so there will always be slight improvements in the position of the block with larger data[9].

The second family of effective optimization techniques use *artificial neural networks*. Artificial neurons are based, loosely, on biological neurons. They are computational units with many inputs, each of which is weighted, the results summed, and then a non-linear threshold applied before an output is produced. Each artificial neuron produces an output that is a complex, non-linear function of its inputs.

These artificial neurons are combined into structures that take input attribute values, compute outputs for a first layer of neurons, pass these to a second layer, and so on, until an output is produced that is interpreted as a prediction. (Neural networks can be used for clustering, using a technique called self-organizing maps, but it does not work very well.)

The general training structure for a neural network is to present each record on the inputs of the network, see what value the network predicts, and then adjust the weights of each edge, working backwards through the network in such a way that, if the same record were to be presented again, the prediction would be slightly closer to the correct answer. Training records need to be presented to the network multiple times for the weights to converge to the point where the network produces accurate predictions. They are therefore relatively expensive to train.

In the last decade, new ways to structure neurons, and faster computational platforms have allowed some new forms of neural network data analytics. These are known collectively as *deep learning*. Conventional neural networks could not have many layers of neurons because the changes to the weights propagating back from the outputs and designed to improve further predictions become steadily weaker as they passed back through the layers, so that eventually the weights never change.

Deep learning is called "deep" because some of the initial progress arose from developing a way to increase the number of layers without running into this vanishing problem. Most deep learning today, however, does not use particularly deep networks. Instead they arrange the neurons in novel ways.

Deep learning approaches often produce a 3-5 percentage point accuracy improvement over predictors such as random forests or support vector machines. However, this is not guaranteed, and there are plenty of datasets where these older predictors perform as well or better than deep learning[10].

Neural-network techniques are especially effective when the outcome depends on the input attribute values in a non-linear way; and when the amount of information encoded in each attribute is small. That is why they have been successful for problems such as image recognition – each individual pixel contains very little information about whether an image contains a cat, for example – and for natural language.

7.4.3 Other ensembles

We have already seen that ensemble approaches such as boosting and bagging can produce better predictions without increased cost to build models.

There are other ways to use ensembles that are also effective. One way is to use *heterogeneous ensembles*. The idea is to either divide the data into subsets, or use the entire dataset, but train several models of different kinds (that is, using different algorithms). Each new record is then passed to every model, each makes its prediction, and the overall result is determined by voting or averaging exactly as for bagging.

The logic of heterogeneous ensembles is that some techniques perform better on certain kinds of records than others. Using multiple techniques allows the variance in errors that comes from the different capabilities of different predictors to cancel out. This is what we do as humans when we ask for advice from different kinds of people, rather than asking all of our peers, who are of similar age and experience.

Another way to use ensembles is called *stacking*. Here each member of a, usually heterogeneous, ensemble, produces its predictions, and a higher-level predictor is trained on *the predictions* of the first set. The higher-level predictor is learning patterns in the accuracies or inaccuracies of the first set of predictors, rather than properties of the data from the dataset itself. This is what we do when we learn which of a group of employees is good at judging a particular situation and then rely more on their judgment when such a situation comes up.

7.5 Social network analysis

Social networks represent the relationships among a set of people and/or organizations. This information is represented by a graph whose nodes are the people or organizations, with edges between them to indicate relationships. Often the edges have associated weights that represent the intensity of the relationship.

The main advantage of analyzing social networks is that, although they are created locally by the decision of one node to form (and maintain) a relationship with another node, there are deep social processes that lie behind these individual decisions. Once whole networks can be seen, regularities emerge as a consequence of these social processes; and often the global regularities have implications for the relationships at the local level. In other words, the process of social network analysis is: collect data on the local, pairwise relationships; integrate them into global knowledge; and then reconsider the local pairwise relationships in the light of this global knowledge.

Edges represent relationships, but the deeper meaning of relationships depends on how the social network is framed, and this can make a difference to how it is analyzed. Some of the meanings associated with edges are:

- The two people connected are likely to feel obligations to one another. This is the most common and general meaning of an edge, embodied in the idea of a "relationship", and includes the more specialized meanings.
- The two people can readily communicate with one another (but might not feel obligations).
- The two people collaborate on projects together.
- The two people influence one another.

These possibilities are often mixed together in the same relationship. For example, a Facebook friend relationship might include all four meanings, while a work relationship might include mostly the second and third meanings (communication and collaboration).

It is natural to think about the transitive nature of edges. If a is connected to b, and b is connected to c, then there is a natural way to think of a quasi-relationship between a and c, at least in terms of communication and influence. So we can reasonably consider how similar two arbitrary nodes are in terms of the number of steps along the shortest path that joins them (or even perhaps how many different paths join them, or the average number of steps along all of these different paths; and weights can be taken into account as well). So, in a social network, there is a kind of weak relationship or connection between *every* pair of nodes that have a path between them.

Until the advent of large online social-media businesses, collecting the data about social networks was challenging, and so only small-scale networks were studied. This is still true for social networks about criminals and their relationships since some of their more direct relationships (such as communication) are concealed, as much as possible, from law enforcement. However, some kinds of social networks can be inferred from the data collected routinely about criminals and crimes.

As social networks began to be studied at scale, many surprising properties were revealed. It is important to understand these, both to understand some aspects of criminal social networks, and to see how criminal networks are structured differently from ordinary social networks.

Here are some of these surprising properties discovered about social networks:

- The distance from any node to any other tends to be a logarithmic function of the total number of nodes. In other words, the *diameter* of a social network, the distance between the two most separated nodes, is quite small given the total number of nodes.

  When social networks were originally studied, and relationships in the network represented physical relationships in the real world, the intuition was that the distance between two people in the social network would mimic the distance between them on the surface of the earth. So people in large cities would be part of close, rich clusters while those in rural areas would be sparsely connected, and many steps away from those in cities.

Milgram showed that this was not the case, in an experiment in the 1930s that relied on ordinary real-world networks[11]. He gave packages to random people and asked them to send them to destinations distributed across the U.S. by sending their package to someone who they thought would be closer to the destination, and telling that person to follow the same strategy.

To his surprise, most packages took only a small number of steps to reach their destinations. The reason is that, although most relationships of most people were to those physically close to them, many people also had one or two relationships to people physically far away. These long-distance relationships were the key enablers of getting the packages delivered in few steps. Most packages took no more than six steps to reach their destinations, the origin of the phrase "six degrees of separation". This is also sometimes called the *small world property* of social networks.

It turns out that this mixture of "short" and "long" connections is typical of social networks and is what makes the distance between even the farthest nodes stay logarithmic as the number of nodes in the network grows.

If the edges are thought of as conduits of properties such as infection (literal or metaphorical) or communication, then such properties can spread and reach the entire network much more quickly than an intuitive view of the network would suggest. For example, if everyone has about Dunbar's number of connections then they can reach almost two million people in three steps, and a quarter of a billion in four steps.

- Nodes in the social network have properties determined by their *position* in the social network as a whole. Each node can be given a score based on its average distance (along paths of edges) to all of the other nodes. A node that has a short average distance is "in the middle" of the network, while a node with a high average distance is far from most other nodes, and so must be out towards the edge of the social network. This property of a node is called its *centrality* and high centrality, having short paths to most other nodes, is a useful measure of a node's importance in many kinds of social networks. For example, a node with high centrality can spread information to all of the other nodes more quickly than a node with low centrality.

  Another important property for nodes is called *betweenness*. This property is based on how many shortest paths between other pairs of nodes must pass through the node being considered. Nodes with high betweenness scores are bottlenecks between one part of the network and another.

  Nodes with high betweenness scores can be considered important for two reasons, depending on the meaning of edges in the network. A high-betweenness node may be a gatekeeper because it can prevent or enable flow from one part of the network to another. A high-betweenness node can also be important as a target: removing it has a disproportionate effect on the rest of the network, maximally disrupting activity that relies on edges.

- As we discussed previously, the number of nodes to which a given node is connected directly is constrained by Dunbar's number, with typical values of 125–150. This number reflects human capacity to keep track of other people at other than a cursory level.

  In a general social network, a node that has substantially more connections than this number may deserve attention. It is common to find individuals with many more than 150 "friends" but this almost inevitably means that many of these relationships are superficial. Individuals with many fewer than 150 "friends" may, depending on the context, be those who are socially isolated, but they may also be those keeping a low profile.

- In a social network, the number of triangles is a small, and quite predictable, function of the size of the network[12]. Normal social processes lead to triangle closure: when *a* knows *b* and *c*, it is likely that *a* will introduce *b* and *c* and they will form a relationship, producing a triangle.

  Social networks with many nodes representing criminals do not contain as many triangles as expected. This seems to be partly because of a concern for security; a sparser network structure makes it hard for an informer, say, to find out more about who else is in the network. It may also be a form of hoarding of expertise and social capital; the two people, if introduced, might cut the initial person out of future profitable crimes.

  Those who manage criminal networks cannot help but be connected in triangles, at least because they have to be able to communicate readily. This insight has been used to discover the command and control structure of criminal groups, by constructing the *Simmelian backbone* of the original social network.

  The Simmelian backbone of a social network consists of the original set of nodes, but the edge between *a* and *b* is weighted by the number of triangles in the original social network in which the edge from *a* to *b* is present[13]. Many nodes will have no edges connecting them to other nodes in the Simmelian backbone network and are discarded. The Simmelian backbone for criminal networks is typically much smaller than the network it was created from.

  The edges of the Simmelian backbone focus attention on nodes that participate in many triangles. If they do so only when they must, then these nodes are likely to be the important management nodes of the original social network.

  This has been applied to drug smuggling networks using relationships derived from intercepted phone calls and observed meetings, and does indeed find the important members of the group, even when they were being careful to conceal themselves[14].

- Social network edges plausibly represent the flow of information (friends pass on information to one another). What is less clear is that they also represent

> the flow of influence. It is not surprising that one person can influence another person with whom they have a relationship. What is startling is that this kind of influence travels long distances in a social network. Each node in a network is detectably influenced by friends of friends of friends, people three steps away in the network, and probably unknown. This applies to many properties, including happiness, weight, smoking, and generosity. Misery is also influential but to a lesser extent than happiness[15].
>
> From a law enforcement perspective, this means that attitudes, both positive and negative, can be "infectious". Negative influence needs to be defended against, and positive influence exploited.

Criminals are present in ordinary social networks, but they are not easily distinguished from everyone else. There are some situations where finding them might be of interest – for example, when they are violent extremists. The basic strategy for finding small criminal groups in the midst of large social networks is to look for structural anomalies, small groups of nodes whose connection structures are unlike the rest of the network. For example, they may have fewer relationships than others because they are concerned about security (or they do not have friends in the ordinary sense); they may be connected together in an unusual way (tightly coupled with one another, but weakly with anyone else); or they may be arranged in cells, the online version of typical insurgent group structures.

The difficulty with finding such unusual subnetworks is that real-world social networks are large, and they have many subnetworks – so many that exhaustive search is an impractical strategy. This kind of subnetwork is usually found only because one of their members is known and provides a starting point to look at a neighborhood.

One of the most common social networks in a law enforcement context are *cooffender networks*. The nodes of such networks are criminals, and the weighted edges count how many times each pair of criminals have cooperated in the same criminal act (that was detected). These networks are straightforward to construct since arrest records provide the necessary data.

Cooffender networks provide useful information about the criminal ecosystem. Reasons to cooffend include:

- The need for specific skills to commit the crimes. Cooffending rates vary by the type of crime, and are higher for crimes where multiple participants are clearly an advantage, and where the crimes are complex. This indicates that skill sets play a significant role in criminal cooperation.
- The need for psychological support. Rates of cooffending are high for young criminals, suggesting that having a partner is often desirable for support.
- Existing relationships, including family members, friends, and fellow gang members. The motivation for cooffending here is because it is convenient and habitual.

The countervailing motivation *not* to cooffend is the increase in risk that it brings. Collaborating with someone else in a crime, especially when the collaboration is new, risks the partner's incompetence, willingness to betray you, and a requirement to divide the proceeds among more participants. Cooffending is nevertheless common, with studies indicating that 80% of criminals will have cooffended at some stage in their lives.

Studies of cooffending networks in a location such as a city or a region show that they typically have one large connected component – a subgraph of nodes, each of which can reach any other node along cooffending edges – some smaller connected components, and then many pairs. About half of all of the active criminals will be cooffending, and so be included in this social network. The large connected component links together criminals by chains of cooffending with one another that are rich enough that there is a path between any two criminals in it. This component does not imply that there is a large organizational structure, but it does mean that everyone in the component could, with some effort, find everyone else via cooffender pathways. It also suggests that information may flow quickly and easily through this large group.

The next largest connected components are typically one-tenth the size of the largest connected component, and represent either criminals of minority ethnicity or who commit specialized crimes. The sizes of other connected components get rapidly smaller if the list of components is sorted by decreasing size.

The pairs presumably represent partnerships that have been effective, and so have no need to develop or involve others.

Cooffending is an important property to understand patterns of crime. Some crimes happen because one person decides to commit them and then recruits appropriate cooffenders to assist. But in many others, perhaps most, the dynamic is the other way round; a group of potential cooffenders get together first, and decide on the crime to commit second. The crime may well even be a crime of opportunity encountered by the group who were simply spending time together.

Cooffender networks are easy to construct for criminals who are arrested, but they always, of course, miss those who are active participants, but manage to avoid arrest. Although the criminal masterminds of detective fiction are mostly implausible, organized crime groups do have structures, including layers of management, that make it difficult to arrest some of the criminals involved. As a result, their existence will not necessarily be revealed in the cooffending network.

What about the social network of criminals more broadly than just based on cooffending? This would be a useful network to understand because criminals recruit from their social-network neighborhood, at least for unskilled criminal work such as selling drugs and violence. The social neighborhood of criminals also has some effect on how they choose their targets. So being in these social networks is a much riskier place than being in the rest of society. Those who are friends and relatives of criminals are victims of opportunity of crimes by the criminals themselves, but they also tend to become collateral damage in criminal-on-criminal violence. The social neighborhood of criminals is also where mentoring happens, and so provides indications of the criminals of the future. Collecting the data necessary to construct the social network of criminals and their connections is difficult because many of its members are not criminals. The development of online social-media may make this more plausible. Meanwhile we consider one approximation to such a network.

Another type of quasi-criminal social network is a *copresence network*. The nodes of these networks are the individuals present at police-involved incidents, and the weighted edges count the number of times that the nodes they connect were present at incidents in a given time period. The nodes are of three kinds: perpetrators (those arrested and charged), victims, and witnesses. (Unfortunately victims and witnesses are not usually distinguished in incident records.)

An intuitive view of such networks might suggest that they provide little more information than a cooffending network, because they contain criminals, some of whom are cooffending, and a random set of victims and witnesses. Nothing could be further from the truth. Victims and witnesses repeat frequently in such networks, and are often the connectors between different groups of criminals. This makes it clear that the risk of being a victim of crime, but also of being a witness, is heavily skewed. Presumably this reflects that some crimes are geographically skewed – if you live in a place with many criminals, you are more likely to be affected by crime – while others crimes are social-neighborhood skewed – if criminals know who you are you are more likely to be affected by crime. The converse is, of course, that people for whom neither of these properties is true are unlikely to be either targets or witnesses of a crime.

It is not obvious, but social networks also have hot spots. In a cooffending network, some regions (small sets of cooffending criminals) will account for a hugely disproportionate percentage of all crimes. In a copresence network, some regions (small sets of criminals, witnesses, and victims) will be present at a disproportionate percentage of police-involved incidents.

This provides the same kind of opportunities for better use of law-enforcement resources that we saw in discussing geographical and temporal hot spots. Paying attention to the most active cooffending collaborations or the most frequently encountered can reduce crime the most with the smallest expenditure of resources. Those who are frequently victims deserve some attention to understand what it is about them that attracts criminals to them, especially when it is not always the same criminals.

Social networks are difficult structures to analyze. Small networks can be visualized, but this gets rapidly more difficult as networks grow. The number of substructures in a social network grows exponentially with the size of the network, so clever algorithms are required to find and expose these substructures and their properties.

Here are some of the techniques that are used to analyze social networks:

- Investigate the neighborhood adjacent to one particular node (known as the ego network of that node). This usually involves looking at the number of immediate neighbors; the way in which these immediate neighbors are connected to one another (a star with no connections suggests a very different central node than one where all of the immediate neighbors are also connected to one another); and the number of nodes at distance two.

Nodes in social networks usually exhibit *homophily*, that is nodes which are connected by an edge tend to have similar properties. For example, our friends tend to be like us. So, if an ego network contains mostly nodes of a particular kind, but there are a few exceptions, then these exceptions may deserve special attention.

Social networks tend to have a structural homophily property called *assortativity*. Nodes with many attached edges tend to be connected to nodes that also have many attached edges (and, conversely, nodes with few edges tend to connected to nodes with few edges). So, for example, if a person has many friends, then it is likely that their friends will also be the kinds of people who have many friends.

The ego network of a node may show that it deviates from the expectation of assortativity, another reason why it might deserve special attention. For example, a criminal leader may be connected to many others, but these others are only sparsely connected to anyone else.

- Calculate measures of position for each node. We have already discussed measures such as centrality and betweenness. These can be calculated for all of the nodes in the social network, and the suggestions of importance that they provide matched with other knowledge of the social network.

- Calculate "distances" between pairs of nodes. Distances along paths are the basis of centrality, but centrality is an average calculation, and it sometimes interesting to look at specific path lengths. From the discussion of the small-world nature of ordinary social networks, we expect the every node can reach any other nodes in about six or seven steps. Cases where longer path lengths are required might suggest deeper investigation.

  Unexpectedly short paths are also a fertile ground for investigation. Short paths are naturally ways to connect to friends, and friends of friends. However, two random strangers are not likely to be connected by a short path. When this happens it can often be a sign of collusion. We mentioned the example of croupier and customer at a casino previously. Another setting where short paths have been useful is in insurance fraud. Suppose that an insurance company builds a social network based on physical addresses, phone numbers, and family relationships. When a car accident takes place, it is unlikely that the two drivers and the repair shop involved are all closely connected. When they turn out to be too closely connected in the social network, suspicion that the accident was contrived is justified.

- Apply clustering ideas to find subgroups or communities in the social network. Edge weights provide a natural measure of node-to-node similarity, so we can apply clustering algorithms to social networks to look at the groupings they might contain.

Clustering in social networks is more subtle than it seems. The difficulty is that, in an ordinary social network, most people are part of many communities. If the edges are undifferentiated ("relationship") then it is difficult to tease apart which edges are associated with which community.

We have already seen the issue, in embryo, in our discussion of Dunbar's number. Consider the group of approximately 12 ($= 3 + 9$) people closest to a particular individual. It is probable that the closest three form a community; they are probably immediate family and are the same inner group for all four members.

But consider the next layers of nine for each of these four people. These are probably the close friends and/or coworkers of each member of the family. There may be some small overlaps among the four groups of nine, but it is more likely that they contain different sets of people. So what are the communities in this group of forty people? Is it four groups of ten, or four groups of nine plus one group of four. Neither really captures what is happening from a social-network perspective. Each of these groups of nine does not make sense without seeing the one person who, as it were, nucleates the group. Now if we consider one person in any of the larger groups, they will have a set of four closest people, probably almost none of them among the other eight. Starting from a particular known person, the structure makes sense; but try and view the network without this starting point and the structure dissolves into a mess.

Specialized social networks, where the edges represent particular kinds of relationships, can have plausible communities, and these can be discovered using clustering methods. For example, in a typical drug distribution social network, there will be buyers (often far away), those who look after transportation, those who distribute the product to street-level dealers, those who handle the money, and those who manage the whole enterprise. The connections among them typically represent communication, which is kept as infrequent as possible, so the different parts of the organization are relatively easy to separate.

- Look for motifs, that is substructures which occur often usually because they serve some functional purpose. For example, in the drug-network example just mentioned, the part of the organization responsible for collecting the drugs, transporting them, and passing payments back to growers tends to have a similar structure no matter which drug (heroin or cocaine) and which source country (Colombia or Afghanistan). Law enforcement can look for sets of individuals who match the social-network pattern, and investigate them.

- Try to understand the network as a whole. The global structure of an ordinary social network emerges from the local pairwise connections that are made. Looking at the network as a whole can suggest places where anomalies are present since, as we have seen, there are expected regularities.

A special-purpose social network may also show, by its structure, something of its purpose; and certainly its scale.

Two different approaches have been used to understand social networks as a whole (as opposed to calculating properties of nodes or looking for local structures).

The first is *graph drawing*. This attempts to produce a rendering of the social network as a two-dimensional image that can be displayed (and increasingly as a three-dimensional image that can be walked through using virtual reality). The goal is to render the network so that as much of its structure as possible is made visible to human observers. As a result of making it as visibly clear as possible, the similarities among the nodes (equivalently, the lengths of the edges as displayed) will almost certainly be distorted.

The second is *spectral graph embedding* which uses the projection ideas we have already seen for clustering. A network with n nodes requires, in general, $n-1$ dimensions to render it exactly, that is with the edge lengths accurately representing the node-node similarities. Spectral embedding projects this $n-1$- dimensional space into a space of much lower dimension, even two- or three-dimensional, in such a way that it preserves as much of the similarity structure as possible. In other words, the rendered length of each edge represents the corresponding similarity as accurately as possible in the chosen number of dimensions.

Graph drawing represents the network in a visually pleasing way, at the expense (potentially) of accuracy. Spectral embedding represents the network accurately, at the expense (potentially) of not being visually pleasing. Both representations can be helpful to a user trying to understand the network as a whole.

The use of social-network analysis as a way to understand crime and criminal groups is still in its early days.

7.6 Natural language analytics

Natural language is another modality from which information useful to law enforcement can be gleaned. When we speak or write two different processes are in play. First, and obviously, we convey content. Second, and more subtly, we reveal a considerable amount of what is going on in our minds, most of it unconscious and so outside of our control.

The more direct role of natural language as conveying content can be useful for law enforcement in finding out about events, and understanding event dynamics in new ways. Many people post on Twitter, Instagram, and other instant-dissemination social media platforms. Even for emergencies, posts to these platforms may appear before an emergency call has been made. It has become relatively standard for law enforcement to track particular hash tags related to their jurisdiction, and also to track hash tags associated with events where there is the potential for criminal activity. It is not unheard of for crimes to be covered on cable news network before law enforcement even finds out about them.

The advantage of social-media platforms is that the information flows more quickly around a smaller circuit. If a crime occurs, and a bystander calls an emergency number, the information about the crime is known at that central location; but it then has to be disseminated to officers on the ground who can respond to it. In fast-moving situations, the time that this takes can destroy the ability of officers on the ground to build situational awareness in a timely way.

In contrast, if officers on the ground are monitoring real-time social media feeds, they get direct information about what is reported to be happening, as well as the data that they can see directly. Almost inevitably, emergency service calls are audio only, whereas social-media posts can include video, so that details at the site of an incident can be immediately understood. Many incidents can also be geotagged, so that it is clear exactly where the incident is. This makes it easier to build situational awareness, and to respond immediately.

Another advantage of social media is that many people will typically post, so there are multiple perspectives, and the number of posts is a rough and ready estimate of seriousness; whereas only a small number of people will call emergency numbers[16].

In well-structured environments, such as sports events or highway traffic, it is relatively straightforward to know what to watch for, and what the social-media posts mean. There are other settings where the data stream is large, and it is much harder to pick out what is significant. This is where automated analysis can help: using natural-language techniques to infer what posts are about, watch for key signals that indicate something that deserves law-enforcement attention, and calculate statistics that can detect sudden increases in discussion of particular topics[17]. This kind of analysis is useful for social unrest settings where there is a need to match law-enforcement resources preemptively to requirements.

Another place where natural-language analytics can be useful is to track marketplaces in the dark web, Recall that these sell both digital goods, that can be delivered over the Internet, and physical goods, which are delivered using physical mail. The kinds of information that law enforcement can get from analyzing the language of advertisements and other kinds of posts in dark-web marketplaces are:

- What is for sale? This provides intelligence on current trends in what is being offered for sale such as: stolen personal and financial data, stolen intellectual property, cyber attacks and attack kits, or new kinds of designer drugs.
- How are prices changing? Pricing is a useful surrogate for scarcity of many products. High prices suggest that interdiction efforts are working well. Low prices signal that new bursts of illicit products may be in the pipeline.

- What is being asked for? Knowing what potential purchasers are trying to buy provides information about the kinds of crimes that are being considered in time to do something about it.

Another target for natural-language analytics is forums where civil disorder is part of the discussion. For example, both religiously motivated and racially motivated violent extremists run forums where issues relevant to their communities are discussed.

These vary from public forums to forums concealed in the dark web. Public forums can provide intelligence about planned events, and also provide a measure of size and activity level of the group. The content of closed forums can often be extracted even from dark-web forums with some care. Analyzing the content of these forums can provide intelligence about more consequential events, and also suggest individuals who deserve attention.

Participants in such forums are usually identified by screen names. There are two ways to link these screen names to actual identities. The first is that people choose screen names that reflect something about themselves, and sometimes use the same ones, or small variants, in different places. Thus a screen name in dark-web forum may be linked to one in a more open forum where there is less effort to conceal identity. The second is that it may be possible to track the computer address from which the forum is accessed (even sometimes when concealed by the Tor routing mechanism). Computer addresses are not tightly bound to particular users, but knowing an address can provide at least a starting point for determining who is using a particular computer.

Forums are another example of a needle in a haystack problem since they are often large, and by far the greater proportion of the posts are irrelevant from a policing and intelligence perspective. Natural-language analysis must therefore start with a process to identify the small fraction of potentially interesting posts, and only then analyze the content of these posts.

Natural-language analysis can also be used to detect posts that use hate speech, abuse, and cyberbullying. There is considerable variation in the processes that are labeled in this way. Some forms express hatred towards another individual or group, driven mostly by the emotional pattern of the speaker or writer. Other forms are intended to get the target, or the target community, to behave in a different way, for example anti-immigrant hate speech aims, at least partly, to discourage further immigration and perhaps to force some immigrants to return to their countries of origin. Still other forms are intended to incite violence against the target or target community.

The legal landscape differs among countries. In the U.S. speech is protected and so hate speech by itself is not criminal. In other countries, various categories of targets are protected, and speech directed at them is considered hate speech. There is also considerable variation in the effect required of the speech to be considered hate speech – ranging from inciting violence to mocking or denigration.

There have been some efforts by social-media businesses to automatically identify and block hate or abusive speech. These have not been notably successful because it is a challenging analytic problem to distinguish hate speech from reasoned discourse that reaches a negative conclusion, because the legal framework is so variable, and because they do not really want to, because abusive language tends to make posts spread more vigorously and attract more eyeballs.

Online material may also disseminate information about how to commit certain kinds of crimes. While there is no hope of removing such content from the Internet, law enforcement may be interested in understanding what criminals are being told to do, so that they can better defend against it. Some law enforcement organizations have even experimented with their own dissemination, although perhaps largely tongue-in-cheek ("Worried about toxic chemicals in your meth? Bring it in to us and we'll check it for you, free").

There are two different mechanisms for natural-language data analytics:

- The *bag of words* approach. Each document is represented by counts of all of the words it contains. This representation destroys all of the effects of word order, since it is only the total number of times that a word occurs in a document that is recorded. Surprisingly, especially for a language like English where word order matters ("The man bit the dog" versus "The dog bit the man"), this representation is effective.
- The *deep learning* approach. Each word is represented in an encoding (typically a vector of size about 300) and the sequence of encoded words in a document is fed, in order, to a neural-network learner. This approach preserves the word order and so can use it to improve its prediction capabilities.

Most natural-language analytics looks at sets of documents rather than a single document.

Here are some of the questions that can be asked about a set of documents:

- What are the documents about? This reduces the content of a document to something much shorter, perhaps a set of topic words or précis. This makes it reasonable to quickly assimilate what a set of documents is about – its themes – and perhaps help to pick out the most interesting or significant documents among them.
- Are any of these documents interesting? Once the number of documents becomes large, approaches that rely on an analyst paying attention to every document, even a summary of every document, become impractical. An algorithm to select the (few) documents that are most significant is now required. This means knowing beforehand the words that make a document interesting, perhaps certain hashtags or important words ("traffic accident", "explosion", "gun shot").

- What topics are present in this set of documents? This is a more exploratory task that can start without any preconceptions about the content of the documents. It requires clustering the documents in a way that interacts sensibly with a clustering of the words. This is called a *biclustering*. Most people have encountered biclustering in the context of Google News – stories with similar content are grouped together, but the words that are the cause of each cluster are not prespecified, but emerge because of similarity of a group of stories. (This is essential because the set of topics that are associated with a cluster of similar stories being discussed changes from day to day.)

- How much of some property of interest does each document have? This computes a score for each document based on a set of signals that convey a property of interest. In the simplest case, the analysis begins with a lexicon, a set of relevant words, and just computes the total count of these words in each document. However, almost invariably some words are stronger signals than others so a score based on a simple sum will not produce accurate totals.

  Techniques that compute a score using a fixed point derived from the relevance of documents from the perspective of words, and the relevance of words from the perspective of documents provide good solutions. This approach has been used to label documents by their intent, level of deception, and fraudulence.

- Who wrote each document? There is often dispute over who wrote a particular document, particular if the document contains threats, hate speech, or a scam. Authorship can be decided from document style because each person has their own unique tells, not usually in the content-filled words, but in the smaller function words, and in the way punctuation and spacing is used.

- What are some internal properties of each document's author? Just as we introduce signals of authorship into the things we write, we also leak other aspects of our internal life. This signal is carried in a number of different ways, mostly by differences in word frequencies compared to our own baseline, or compared to other authors. For example, an author's poor health is signaled by using a smaller range of words over time than typical healthier people. In other words, healthiness is associated with greater variability in words used, but what those words actually are is not as significant.

  People who are depressed or have PTSD have characteristic changes to the frequencies of certain kinds of words they use. Personality (in terms of the so-called Big Five traits) can be determined robustly from the words used in writing[18].

Much of the research on natural language analytics has focused on English, with a much smaller focus on common European languages and Arabic. Little is known about how easily the techniques developed for these languages can be applied to other languages, particularly those that are quite different.

7.7 Making data analytics available

We have already discussed some of the reasons that the models produced by data analytics are not translated into changes in the way policing is done: unwillingness to believe models that contradict experience, models whose false positive rate is so high that they become distrusted, and so on.

There are also several structural reasons why data analytics does not have the impact that it could. First, the data analytics function is often separated from front-line policing, and put into a function called "analyst". The wall between the two functions raises the threshold for when a result is significant enough to be passed to the frontline officers – "that's interesting" is not enough. Analysts may not have the situational awareness to know that a particular result is very interesting at this moment.

This separation also enshrines the query mode of operation. The only way frontline officers can use the back-end data and models is by asking questions to the analysts. There is a case to be made that data-analytics tools should be made available directly to frontline officers who have much better awareness of the meaning or usefulness of models produced. There is still a role for analysts, but it is an offline role, exploring patterns of crimes and criminal behavior independent of particular incidents. There is a parallel here in the move to proactive policing. At present, many analysts are reactive (at one remove) to crimes as they happen; they can be useful in stepping back to use their analytic skills on the bigger picture of crime.

The second structural reason is that the line drawn from data-analytic modeling to actionable intelligence is not necessarily short or clear. This is partly because most officers do not have enough experience or training to understand what models can and are telling them; but there is also a need for developing better policy about how, for example, risk prediction should be turned into changes in policing.

The third structural reason is that models, if they are providing value-added, should constantly be generating surprise. After all, if what they show is already known, then there is not much point to building them. It is difficult enough to accustom an analyst to dealing with surprise from the modeling, but this becomes much more difficult if the surprise has to be mediated along a chain of potential users.

One potential way to improve the situation is the development of dashboards that can provide situational awareness, even in frontline settings. These require taking the results of models developed by data-analytic techniques, and synthesizing them, so that the key parts can be displayed in different settings, with varying levels of detail. So considerable detail might be displayed during daily briefings, but much less on a display in a patrol car. Such dashboards are a hopeful development, but they are still in development, and there are many potential pitfalls to their deployment before they can demonstrate their effectiveness in front-line policing.

7.8 Demonstrating compliance

One often-neglected role for data analytics is in investigating compliance and performance, and using this information to improve operations and personnel management.

For example, RMS data typically includes the time of call and the time(s) at which units reached the scene of the incident. The intervals between these can be analyzed and clustered to see whether there is any association between delays and, say, geographical areas. Data analytics can go beyond conventional statistical analysis because it naturally takes into account multivariate issues.

Data analytics for performance modeling can be used to provide better information to oversight bodies, for data-driven public relations, and to improve operations when issues are surfaced.

Data analytics can also be useful for personnel management. For example, when a call to police is made and units are dispatched, it is possible to predict properties of the incident even before units arrive. It is already typical for dispatchers to make assessments of the seriousness and urgency of a call based on what it said, and perhaps some background knowledge about the location. This second aspect can be refined using data analytics (based on the earlier discussion of hot spots) so that a more accurate prediction of threat level of the incident can be made. It is also possible to predict, for example, whether a call may be to a mental health incident, allowing a specialized response if that capability exists.

Data analytic systems can also track the kind of incidents in which personnel have been involved and build a predictive model of poor physical- or mental-health outcomes[19]. This makes it possible to plan personnel support before it is necessary.

Notes

[1]Indeed when a recent drawing produced the numbers 2, 3, 4, 5, and 6 an investigation was launched into the drawing process, showing that lottery operators themselves do not understand randomness.

[2]In one recent experiment, citizens in one region of a city complained that their response times had gone up when a well-known and well-loved pair of patrol officers retired. The data showed that, objectively, this was not the case, and so the perception could be safely ascribed to affection for the retired officers, and perhaps their detailed knowledge of the community.

[3]Building the models takes 90% of the project time but data cleaning takes the other 90%.

[4]"The data subject should have the right not to be subject to a decision, which may include a measure, evaluating personal aspects relating to him or her which is based solely on automated processing and which produces legal effects concerning him or her or similarly significantly affects him or her, such as automatic refusal of an

online credit application or e-recruiting practices without any human intervention." However, this "recital" is not included in the binding part of the regulations, and words such as 'solely' and 'legal effects' provide ample room for disputes.

[5]Of course, if there are more than two outcomes, say three, then the confusion matrix will be 3×3. The correct predictions will appear in the entries on the diagonal, and the errors in the off-diagonal entries. Non-zero entries in these off-diagonal entries show not only predictions for the wrong outcome, but also how these errors are distributed across these wrong outcomes.

[6]Of course, in income tax, it is the people for whom the relationship between income and deducted tax is not trivial who might warrant further investigation.

[7]If you guessed wrongly, almost all doctors make the same mistake about the results of medical tests, which have similar properties.

[8]Recall that these values do not usually sum to 1 because the denominator of Bayes' Rule is ignored.

[9]SVMs have a number of other attractive properties. They can easily be extended to allow some of the training points to lie within the block, but with a penalty cost. This enables a more subtle tradeoff to be made between the thickness of the block and a handful of support vectors that might be closer to the other side than the rest. SVMs can also handle the case where the two outcomes are not separable in the space spanned by the attributes by notionally expanding the space until they are. Careful choice of the expansion makes this only slightly more expensive, an approach known as the *kernel trick*.

[10]Deep learning techniques have produced much better results than older techniques on data where each attribute only contains a small amount of information about the correct outcome, for example images and language, both written and spoken. Here they have led to rapid progress in predicting from such data.

[11]J. Travers and S. Milgram, "An experimental study of the small world problem", *Sociometry*, pp. 425–443, 1969; S. Milgram, "The small world problem", *Psychology Today*, 1:61, 1967.

[12]If there are n nodes in the network, there are normally about $n^{1.6}$ triangles.

[13]B. Nick, C. Lee, P. Cunningham and U. Brandes, *Simmelian Backbones: Amplifying Hidden Homophily in Facebook Networks*, in: *Proceedings of Advances in Social Network Analysis and Modelling ASONAM, ACM & IEEE*, August 2013.

[14]D.B. Skillicorn and F. Calderoni, "Inductive discovery of criminal group structure using spectral embedding", *Information and Security*, 31:49–66, 2015.

[15]N.A. Christakis and J.H. Fowler, *Connected: The Surprising Power of Our Social Networks and How They Shape Our Lives – How Your Friends' Friends' Friends Affect Everything You Feel, Think, and Do*, Little Brown, 2009.

[16]These advantages are partially cancelled by people who see emergencies as filming opportunities, and ignore victims so that they can get better footage.

[17]K.M. Carley, M.M. Malik, P.M. Landwehr, J. Pfeffer and M. Kowalchuck, "Crowd sourcing disaster management: The complex nature of Twitter usage in Padang Indonesia", *Safety Science*, 90:48–61, December 2016.

[18]N. Alsadhan and D.B. Skillicorn, *Estimating Personality from Social Media Posts*, in: *SENTIRE Workshop, IEEE ICDM 2017*, 2017.

[19]S. Carton, J. Helsby, K. Joseph, A. Mahmud, Y. Park, J. Walsh, C. Cody, E. Patterson,
L. Haynes and R. Ghani, *Identifying Police Officers at Risk of Adverse Events*, in: *KDD '16*, 10pp, 2016.

Chapter 8
Case studies

In this chapter, we illustrate some of the data-analytic modeling possibilities that were discussed in the preceding chapters. These are small examples intended to show the kind of knowledge that can be extracted from fairly routine data collected by law enforcement.

8.1 Predicting crime rates

In the previous chapter, we discussed the idea that prediction can really only work to predict risk, not the possibility of a particular crime committed by a particular person. Risk is a useful property to predict, however, because it provides actionable information, although only with a general application.

The first example leverages a dataset that contains demographic attributes and law enforcement properties for a set of 1994 jurisdictions in the U.S. for which all of the data was available. This includes data from the 1990 U.S. census and the Law Enforcement Management and Administrative Statistics, a total of 123 attributes. Analyzing this dataset will show some of the properties of jurisdictions that are relevant to violent crime, and to explore what kinds of actions can be taken as a result of understanding these properties.

The immediate goal is to predict the risk of violent crime, which includes murder, rape, robbery, and assault. Jurisdictions where rape is not included in the counts of violent crimes were omitted.

A predictor using this data will be constructed. The outcome to be predicted is the risk of violent crime in each jurisdiction (really the normalized rate of violent crime, but we interpret this as a risk). Because the size of each jurisdiction is different, and especially they have different populations, we convert violent crime counts into violent crime rates, in units of violent crime per 100,000 population, and then

DOI: 10.1201/9781003126225-8

further normalize this into the range 0–1. These crime rates can now be naturally interpreted as the *risk* of violent crime in each jurisdiction.

Of course, the outcomes are known for all of these jurisdictions, because this is historical data, so we divide the available jurisdictions into a training and a test set. This setting makes it obvious why such a division always has to be done randomly – we want to make sure that a mix of jurisdictions of different sizes and characteristics is present in both training and test sets. We want to build a model that performs well on the test set, where we know the right answers (from the history) but the model does not.

Of course, these predictions are not directly useful unless a new jurisdiction is being opened, say because of suburban expansion, or because one existing jurisdiction is being split into two. In both cases, we might be interested in predicting the potential violent crime rate that might be expected in these new jurisdictions. However, as we shall see, there are other useful properties to be learned from building a predictive model for violent crime rates. In particular, by computing which attributes are most predictive, we can make inferences about the drivers of violent crime. This, in turn, suggests actions that could be taken to reduce violent crime.

Each record, describing a jurisdiction, consists of the values of a set of demographic attributes and a set of policing property attributes for that jurisdiction; and an associated violent crime risk score. Notice that this data, because it is collected on such a broad scale (the entire jurisdiction) does not allow us to exploit any of the properties of skew in the geographical distribution of crimes within each jurisdiction.

The histogram of violent crime rates – the outcome attribute values – is shown in Figure 8.1. As we expect, most jurisdictions are relatively safe and the higher the risk, the fewer the jurisdictions with such a risk. However, two interesting properties are visible in the figure.

First, there is a small peak at 0.5. This seems to show that jurisdictions whose rate of violent crime is exactly in the middle of the range are slightly more common than expected. This seem implausible, and suggests that something is wrong with the data from some jurisdictions. It is hard to see how this could be a consequence of poor data entry since any individual jurisdiction would not know what mid-range values for crime rates across all jurisdictions would be – recall that these values have been normalized to 0–1 from case counts. There is certainly something to be investigated here but it looks like a data-quality issue.

Second, there is a strong peak at the high-risk end of the distribution. In other words, there are more extreme high-risk jurisdictions than the global pattern of the risk data would indicate. One way to interpret this might be that there are two qualitatively different kinds of jurisdictions: ordinary ones that exhibit varying rates of violent crime but with a kind of Pareto or 80:20 distribution; and then a few (perhaps 40) that do not seem to fit this pattern, and where the risk of violent crime is extremely high.

It is tempting to explain the super-violent jurisdictions as being high-population centers, that is (roughly) larger cities. Although there is considerable disagreement

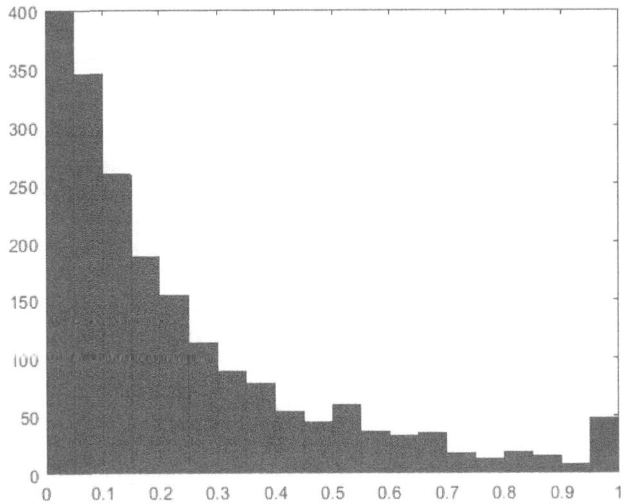

Figure 8.1: Histogram of violent crime risk

about the distribution of U.S. city sizes, the 40th largest is perhaps Omaha. The cities around this rank have populations around 300,000, so already much smaller than cities such as New York, Los Angeles, and Chicago[1]. So an explanation based on size or population density for these unusually violent jurisdictions seems at least too simplistic. So there is another property whose investigation might lead to greater understanding.

The prediction problem requires regression since we are predicting risk, a value between 0 and 1. A gradient boosting tree ensemble (xgboost) is a good fit for the problem. If we build a model using the training data with 200 trees, the mean absolute error on the test set is 0.09. In other words, this predictor is likely to predict violent crime risk for new jurisdictions or into the future with ± 10 percentage points of error. This demonstrates that the risk of crime is quite predictable from demographic and policing data, providing support for broadly sociological explanations of violent crime although, as we have seen, there is considerable subtlety underlying this idea.

The predictor itself is not directly useful, except in the special cases described previously, but the gradient boosting tree allows us to explore which attributes make the largest contribution to the model's prediction of crime risk[2]. Knowing which attributes matter to the risk of violent crime means that steps can be taken to reduce risk by altering these attributes when that is possible. Of course, demographic attributes can be altered, but only by macroscopic processes, and over relatively long time frames. Policing attributes, on the other hand, are under the control of law enforcement who can make changes to try and reduce the risk of violent crime. Discovering these attributes is useful to police forces because they can use the information to adapt their processes; but they can also use them to respond to pressures to "defund the police".

The most-predictive attributes in rank order (from most to least) are shown in Table 8.1. It is striking that they are *all* demographic attributes. Of course, the table does not tell us whether each attribute is predictive of higher or lower risk, but it seems straightforward that attributes broadly associated with poverty and social disruption might be positively associated with violent crime.

The lowest-ranked attributes are shown in Table 8.2 with those least associated with violent crime at the end of the list. This part of the list is a mixture of demographic and policing attributes. The policing attributes suggest ways that law enforcement can improve their performance. However, this list is the least predictive 30 attributes of 123, so presumably changing their values would have a limited impact on violent crime risk[3].

If we go down the ranked list looking for potentially significant policing-related attributes, then the most predictive one associated with violent crime risk is "total requests for police per 100K population" (rank 43), "percent of police that are African-American" (rank 52), and "total requests for police per police officer" (rank 68). The highest-ranked attribute, "total requests for police per 100k population", cannot be directly changed, since it is a property of the population, but it does suggest that tactics such as community policing might be effective. The attribute "percent of police that are African-American" is clearly a major opportunity for intervention. The attribute "total requests for police per police officer" is also actionable and provides evidence to present to city governments that staff levels do have an impact on reducing violent crime. However, these attributes all fall near the middle of the ranked list, so changing them necessarily can only have a limited effect on violent crime risks.

This first example shows how data-analytic modeling can increase understanding of the complex system of culture, demographics, and policing that drives violent crime. Rather than focusing on using a predictor directly, the understanding comes from seeing which attributes are important contributors to the predictions. (Of course, if the predictor is not accurate then the attributes it uses are not reliable or informative, so the predictor must work well to begin with.)

8.2 Clustering RMS data

RMS data contains a great deal of information about (a) the patterns of crimes and incidents that occur in each jurisdiction, and (b) the ways that officers deal with these crimes and incidents, especially their responsiveness and their interactions with the public. This data is often used for statistical purposes, but it is only just beginning to be used for data analytics. In this second example, we show how RMS data can provide a high-level snapshot of the activities and performance of a jurisdiction.

percentage of kids born to never married
percentage of kids in family housing with two parents
percentage of population that is Caucasian
percentage of households with investment/rent income
percent of persons in dense housing
percentage of population that is African-American
percent of family households that are large (6 or more)
percentage of families (with kids) that are headed by two parents
percentage of females who are divorced
number of kids born to never married
number of homeless people counted in the street
per capita income for people with Asian heritage
percentage of population that is of Hispanic heritage
percentage of people under the poverty level
percentage of households with public assistance income
percent of people using public transit for commuting
percent of housing units with less than 3 bedrooms
percent of vacant housing that is boarded up
total number of people known to be foreign born
percentage of population who are divorced
percent of people foreign born
percent of kids 4 and under in two parent households
median year housing units
percent of people who speak only English
number of people living in areas classified as urban
number of people under the poverty level
median owners cost as a percentage of household income – for owners with a mortgage
percentage of males who are divorced
percentage of moms of kids under 18 in labor force

Table 8.1: Ranked list of attributes predictive of violent crime rate

owner occupied housing – median value
percent of police that are Hispanic
median family income
percent of people living in the same state as 5 years before
police operating budget
percentage of people 16 and over who are employed in professional services
police average overtime worked
percent of officers assigned to drug units
police operating budget per population
percentage of people 25 and over with a bachelors degree or higher education
median gross rent
number of different kinds of drugs seized
owner occupied housing – lower quartile value
percent of vacant housing that have been vacant more than 6 months
number of officers assigned to special drug units
rental housing – median rent
number of sworn full time police officers
percent of police that are Asian
sworn full time police officers in field operations per 100K population
gang unit deployed
sworn full time police officers per 100K population
percent of police that are Caucasian
percent of people living in the same city as 5 years before
percent of housing without complete plumbing facilities
percent of population who have immigrated within the last 8 years
percentage of population that is of Asian heritage
per capita income for Native Americans
percentage of households with farm or self employment income
number of sworn full time police officers in field operations
percent of sworn full time police officers on patrol

Table 8.2: Lowest-ranked attributes associated with violent crime

Many jurisdictions have begun to put (sanitized) versions of their RMS data online, perhaps to see what data analysts can do with it. Of course, much more can be learned from such data when it includes the data that is removed before public posting, and so internal modeling can be much more powerful.

Here we use data from the city of Chicago as an example of what can be learned by clustering this kind of data, even when there is not much information about each incident.

We use a dataset of 35,479 records, slightly more than a month of incident data. For each incident, the following data is recorded:

- month,
- date,
- time of day,
- street address without the low digits of the house number,
- Illinois Uniform Crime Reporting codes,
- primary description of crime (for example, "narcotics"),
- secondary description of crime (for example, "possession, cocaine"),
- type of location (for example, residence, sidewalk, apartment, bar),
- arrest or not?
- domestic or not?
- beat number,
- ward number,
- FBI crime codes.

This data is extremely heterogeneous. Some attributes are numeric in the normal sense, for example times of day except that, as usual, there are issues because of the cyclic nature of times, so midnight, 24:00, is adjacent to 00:01, but does not look like it. Other attributes are numeric but structured in a way that does not match their numerical magnitudes. For example, the Illinois Uniform Crime Reporting codes have a hierarchical structure. The FBICD attributes are mostly numeric, and hierarchically structured, but some values can contain letters as well. The street address attributes are a mixture of numbers and words. The crime descriptions are short sets of words.

Data like this can be put into a database and queried, because each attribute has the same meaning across all of the RMS records. Some understanding of the domain is required to formulate reasonable queries. For example, it would be straightforward

M	D	Time	Block	IUCR	Primdesc	Secdesc	Loc	Arr	Dom	Beat	Ward	FBICD
6	10	7:45	021xx W Concord Pl	820	Theft	$500 and under	Street	N	N	1434	32	6
6	10	7:46	035xx W 24th St	2022	Narcotics	Poss: cocaine	Sidewalk	Y	N	1024	22	18

Table 8.3: Sample rows from the Chicago RMS data

to ask how many crimes of a particular kind occurred on each beat between 9 and 10 a.m.. But, as discussed earlier, to be most useful an analyst must think of queries that reveal interesting large-scale properties of the temporal and geographical distribution of incidents.

Heterogeneous data like this is easy to store in a database, because each attribute can have its own type, and attributes never interact directly with one another. Heterogeneity makes clustering difficult, because clustering depends on similarity. Some attributes have a natural similarity: times of day are similar when they are close (except on day boundaries) and dates are similar when they are close (except on month boundaries) Other attributes have a more complex kind of similarity; for example, the crime codes have a hierarchical structure so that FBI crime codes related to larceny all begin with 23. Textual descriptions have a complex similarity that depends on sharing the same words, a simple form of similarity, but also using words with roughly the same meaning ('car', 'automobile', 'vehicle'). Table 8.3 shows two rows from the RMS data, showing the heterogeneity.

Computing the similarity of two entire records based on the similarity of each of their attribute values requires a method for comparing differences in apples to differences in oranges. How should the similarity of each attribute be weighted compared to the similarity of all of the others? For example, if two records describe incidents that happened an hour apart, and with crimes that are one number apart in the crime codes, how similar are the two incidents?

One way around this issue is to map all attributes into a numerical form, using a hashing function that preserves some sense of similarity. Hashing does not guarantee that all of the semantic similarity between attribute values will be preserved but it can approximate it. The resulting dataset can be clustered based on the similarities between the hashed values and at least some sense of any clusters that might be present in the data exposed.

The clusters that results will represent incident records that are globally similar. This will tell us roughly how many different kinds of incidents there are, and how common each kind of incident is, which provides at least useful background information.

We can also get some further understanding of what clusters represent by overlaying values of each of the attributes, in turn, on a representation or visualization of the clusters. An attribute whose value plays almost no role in the clustering will seem to have its values distributed at random across the clusters. An attribute whose value contributes strongly to the clustering will have different values in different clusters.

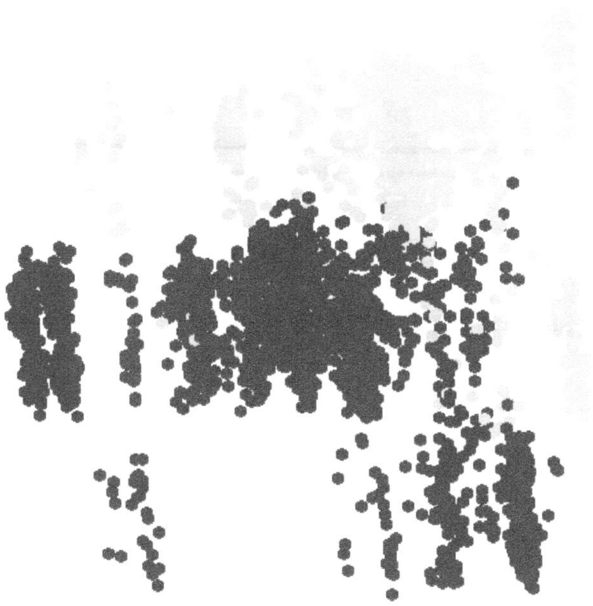

Figure 8.2: Clustering of incidents colored by arrest

We can use color coding for the values of an attribute to display this in a visualization. This helps to understand how each cluster depends on or represents particular attributes. For example, Figure 8.2 shows a three-dimensional plot of the clusters from the Chicago RMS data, colored by whether or not each incident resulted in an arrest.

We see that the arrest attribute is strongly associated with the structure of the clusters. The overall structure of clusters is repeated in two layers, the rear one (lighter points) corresponding to incidents that led to arrests, and the front one (darker points) incidents that did not lead to arrests. The macroscopic structure of the two layers is almost exactly the same – consisting of one or two larger clusters and a number of smaller clusters with quite strong structures[4]. So the variation between an incident that resulted in an arrest or not is being captured in the visualization by the dimension that is represented into the plane of the image. Other attributes that are associated or correlated with arrests (if there are any) will show the same pattern.

We can investigate what the other dimensions of the visualization represent by coloring the points according to the value of other attributes. Figure 8.3 shows exactly the same plot, but with the color based on whether or not the incident was domestic. The vertical variation in the plot clearly represents this difference between incidents that were domestic and those that were not.

Figure 8.3: Clustering of incidents colored by domestic or not

Figure 8.4 shows the same plot, with the color based on the IUCR codes. The left to right variation in the plot represents this difference between incidents – which kinds of crimes they represent. The FBICD, and primary and secondary description attributes produce a similar left-to-right gradient (not shown), which is what we would expect.

We can see that the clusters we observe in the plot are the result primarily of difference in outcomes, setting, and type of crime. In other words, the three axes of variation among these clusters are determined by three sets of attributes.

Although the plot is only three-dimensional, we can explore the possible effect of other, independently varying, attributes using the same color-coding approach. For example, Figure 8.5 colors the points in the plot by the time of day of each incident. The pattern *within* each of the clusters shows that time of day is more or less independent of the properties we have already considered, except that the distribution of dark points versus lighter points varies from left to right. So there is, as we might expect, some variation of crime type with time of day, but it is weaker than the other variations we have already seen.

This kind of clustering raises issues that could not be made visible using a query-driven approach. For example, how is it that incidents that result in arrests (Figure 8.2) are fairly similar, in all other respects, to incidents that do not result in arrests? Part of the answer is given by Figure 8.4 which shows that there are differences in arrest/no arrest rates for different kinds of crimes. Is this the full

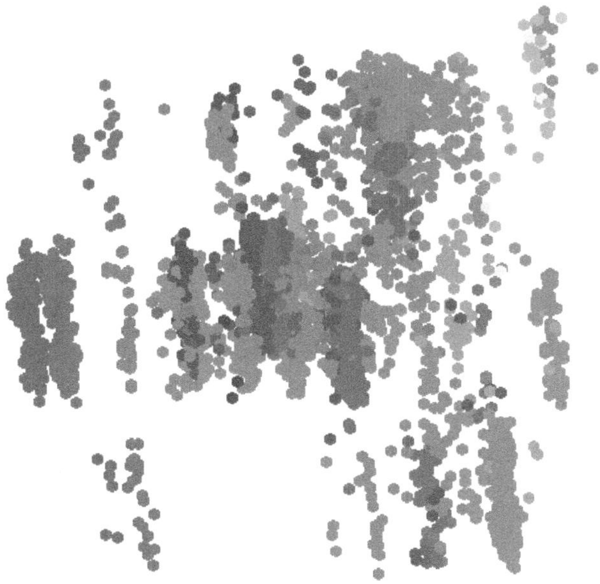

Figure 8.4: Clustering of incidents colored by IUCR code

explanation? We cannot tell from the limited data made public but it suggests a direction to investigate.

The effect of beat identity is shown in Figure 8.6. Again the pattern within the clusters (from left to right within them) shows that beat is also independent of the properties considered so far, including time of day.

Sometimes the coloring shows that a particular attribute is *not* associated with any substantial variation. Figure 8.7 shows the variation based on location of interest (residence, bar, street, and so on). The variation does not match anything about the structure of the clustering, indicating that this attribute is not significantly related to other attributes, and has little effect on the global clustering.

None of the properties inferred from this clustering is particular surprising, except perhaps that whether or not an incident results in an arrest seems to be independent of almost any other property of the incident.

Public RMS data such as this often does not include all of the possible attributes, and the omitted ones may allow more interesting conclusions to be drawn. For example, many RMS records include identifiers of the individuals concerned, including information about previous arrests or involvement in other incidents, and often contain more fine-grained location information.

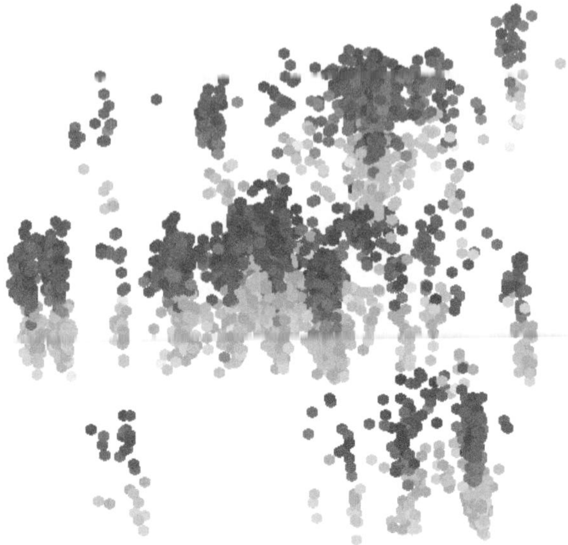

Figure 8.5: Clustering of incidents colored by time of day

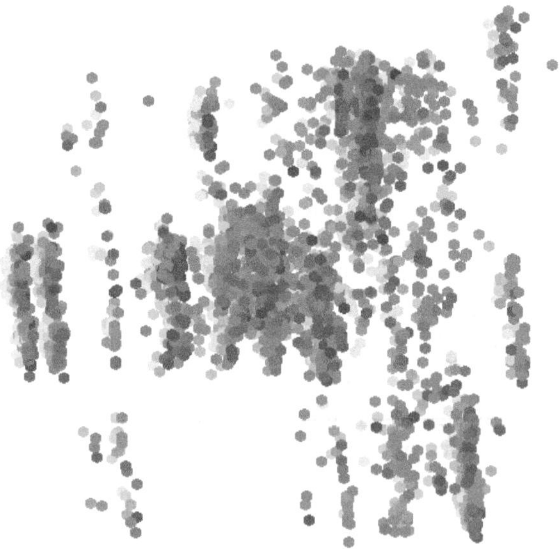

Figure 8.6: Clustering of incidents colored by beat

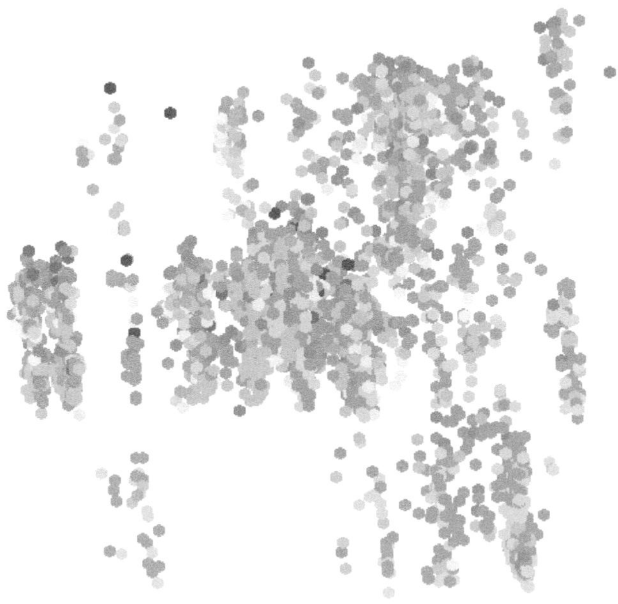

Figure 8.7: Clustering of incidents colored by location of incident

8.3 Geographical distribution patterns

It is also useful to be able to look at the distribution of crimes, especially from the perspective of hot spot policing. Our third example looks at the geographical distribution of crimes, which we expect, from the earlier discussion, to show considerable skew. The Chicago data also includes a geographical location for each incident, and this allows us to associate properties of each incident with the location where it happened.

There are 53 records in this data that do not have latitude and longitude information, even though these records do have address information. In at least some of the cases, this seems to be because the responding officers took the view that the location of the incident response had nothing to do with the location of the crime – cyberbullying and online stalking, and some frauds. While this is completely plausible and even appropriate, it does not seem have been considered in the design of the RMS system. This illustrates some of the problems of data quality, *post hoc* inference of what missing values mean, and failing to consider all of the reasonable values for attributes when an RMS system is designed.

Figure 8.8 shows a histogram of incidents by location on a map of the Chicago area, and Figure 8.9 shows the same information in plan view.

As expected, crime is concentrated in quite small areas. The high-density area

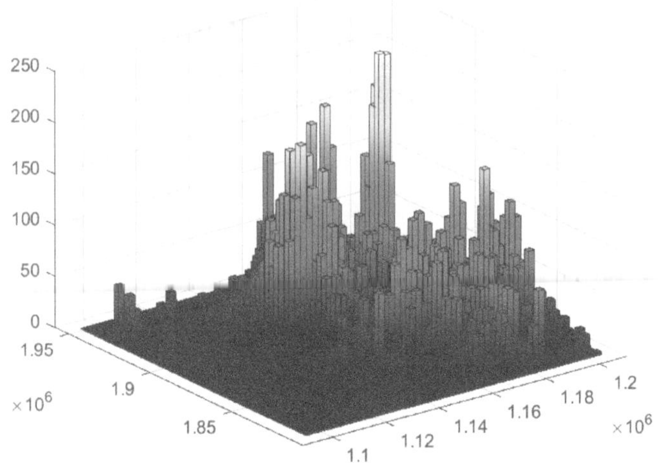

Figure 8.8: Histogram of incident frequency by geographical location, view from the North West

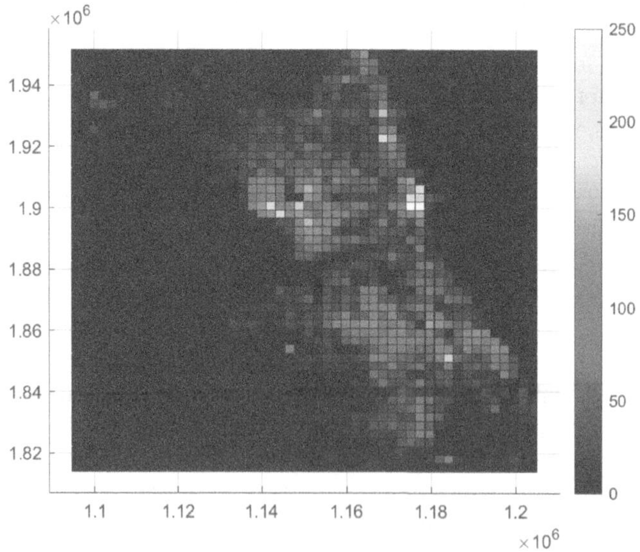

Figure 8.9: Same frequency data as Figure 8.8 in plan view, North at the top

Figure 8.10: FBICD crime codes by geographical location, North at the top

in white in Figure 8.9 is around North State St and Whacker Drive. The southern outlier is around S. Cottage Grove Ave and E. 79th Street, and the western outlier is on W. Flournoy Street. Even though Chicago is a high-crime city, there are plenty of locations in the city where crime is rare[5].

We can also plot the coordinates where crimes have occurred and color them using the attributes from the previous analysis. For example, Figure 8.10 shows the geographical distribution of crimes colored by their IUCR categories. It is clear, although not perhaps surprising, that the kinds of crimes committed are different in different locations. Notably the North-East of the city, which contains many of the wealthier neighborhoods, has many fewer serious crimes.

In contrast, Figure 8.11 shows the geographical distribution colored by the kind of location (residence, street, and so on) in which the crime took place. There is little association between the micro-location of the incident and the region of the city in which it took place. In other words, crimes that take place in residences (or on the street) are quite evenly distributed across the city.

Similarly, Figure 8.12 shows the geographical distribution labeled by time of day. Again there is little large-scale relationship between these two properties.

This kind of clustering is exploratory. It can suggest puzzles or anomalies that deserve further exploration, although, as we have seen, fine detail about location is needed to really make sense of crime occurrences. Such a clustering can also be reassuring to senior personnel, oversight boards, and the wider public since it can be used to show that the distribution of crime is not biased more than might be expected from other factors.

Figure 8.11: Kind of location (residence, street, bar) by geographical location

Figure 8.12: Incident time by geographical location

8.4 Risk of gun violence

In our fourth example, we look at the relationship between the risk of becoming the victim of gunshot violence and social-network position.

The conventional view of the risk of gunshot violence is that it is a consequence of individual risks (gender, age), situational risks (being in the presence of drugs), and community risks (poverty). However, as we have seen for hot spots, properties such as these might be necessary but they are not sufficient to explain who becomes a victim of gun violence. Individuals with similar apparent risks in these three categories nevertheless become victims of gunshot violence at highly skewed rates.

The social network in which criminals are embedded (their relatives and friends as well as cooffenders) plausibly explains the observed skew for three reasons. First, most violence occurs between people who know each other. Second, peer influence surely has an impact on stimulating violence especially in settings where issues around respect are a major driver of violence. Third, criminals primarily obtain guns from others (rather than buying them)[6]. As we have seen, the relationship edges in the social networks of criminals can play a number of different roles, and all are plausibly associated with transmitting the risk of gunshot violence.

Braga, Papachristos, and Hureau[7] collected data on the social network of criminals and associates in the Cape Verdean network in Boston. They collected the network starting from members of the Cape Verdean community known to the police and then their friends, and friends of friends, using data from Boston Police Field Intelligence data (those encountered together by police in a non-crime setting)[8].

The resulting social network contained 763 individuals, with 94% male, about half of Cape Verdean ethnicity and the remainder African-American, and about a third arrested at some time previously. The mean degree of the network was 3 but, as expected, this mean had considerable variance. The largest connected component of the social network contained 76% of the nodes (579 individuals). Situational and community factors were more or less the same for the entire population being considered. Individual's factors such as age, gender, and ethnicity, and simple social network measures such as ego network density[9] were only mildly predictive of the risk of gunshot violence. However, network proximity to another victim of gunshot violence was extremely predictive, with the odds of being a victim dropping by 25% for every step away from another victim. Looked at macroscopically, we therefore expect that the risk of gunshot violence will be high in some regions of the network and much lower everywhere else. In other words, being a victim of gunshot violence behaves like contagion by a disease – as soon as one person has it, their neighbors are likely to "catch" it, and their neighbors, in turn, and so on. Eventually, the contagion dies away, only to flare up somewhere else. The "ordinary" risk factors such as demographics and poverty play the role of susceptibility, but the conversion from potential victim of gun violence to actual victim of gun violence depends on the structure of the social network, and very strongly so.

A similar analysis in Newark[10] showed similar results. The social network in this case consisted of those arrested, those given city ordinance violations, and those encountered in field intelligence operations. Edges were created whenever two individuals were involved in the same activity. The resulting social network contained 10,731 individuals, about 4% of Newark's population; and about 7% of the network members were known to police as gang members. The largest connected component contained 17% of the nodes, so a much smaller fraction of the total than the Cape Verdean network.

First, approximately 33% of all shootings in Newark, fatal or not, occurred within this network, representing such a small fraction (4%) of the Newark population. Second, even within this social network, the risk of gunshot violence was highly concentrated, with many densely connected clusters of individuals experiencing no gunshot violence at all.

In an analysis of gang murders in Chicago, a similar conclusion was reached: "gang murder is best understood not by searching for its individual determinants but by examining the social networks of action and reaction that create it. Gang members do not kill because they are poor, black, or young or live in a socially disadvantaged neighborhood. They kill because they live in a structured set of social relations in which violence works its way through a series of connected individuals."[11].

These results show that the social-network environment of criminals and those connected to them is more important for understanding the risk of gun shot violence than larger scale properties that are often considered explanatory: situation, demographics, and community. As we have come to see from the intersection of criminal activity and hot spots, risk concentrates far more than environmental factors can explain. Models based on environmental factors cannot explain why *this* person commits or is a victim of a crime, as opposed to *that* person. Social-network position provides the beginnings of such an explanation: *this* person commits or is a victim of a crime because s/he is in a particular position within a social network. Social-network analysis provides a way to predict risk at the level of individuals, not just interchangeable people living in the same environment.

The difficulty with leveraging this kind of analysis is collecting the data to form the social networks required. Inevitably there is uncertainty in the risk predictions because the network contains only the nodes and connections that are visible to police (and researchers). In all of the examples above, the social network went far beyond a cooffending network to include other members of the community who were observed spending time with the "obvious" members, those already known to police.

The cooffending part of the social network is straightforward because the data needed to build it is collected routinely. However, extending the cooffending network to include those connected to criminals (who may or may not be criminals themselves) is difficult. The use of intelligence gathering encounters captures connections based on public social activity. Recording data from such encounters is increasingly deprecated because of its potential for bias (or the appearance of bias) against particular communities. Intelligence gathering encounters can usually happen only in very public places, such as sidewalks. Seeing two people eating at a restaurant together is a public encounter in one sense, but in most jurisdictions probably cannot be entered into an intelligence repository.

It is also impossible by definition to capture private social activity, and so add links to the social network that represent family relationships, unless criminals volunteer them. Relationships with those who are geographically remote, sustained by online activity or phone calls, may be important but are also invisible to these kinds of network-construction techniques.

An interesting open question is the extent to which police forces can enhance cooffending networks by observing connections on online social-media platforms. On the one hand, this would reveal connections that could not be captured in the real world, for example to gang members who are physically remote but collaborating in the same criminal enterprise. On the other hand, most people use the same social-media platforms for all of their social interactions of any intensity so it will be more difficult to extract the connections that are strong enough to convey risk in the sense we have been discussing. There might also easily be pushback on privacy grounds even though, ironically, many thousands of businesses are gathering the same information and leveraging it vigorously.

8.5 Copresence networks

The previous section shows that social-network position is just as important as geographical position for understanding the dynamics of crime – what crimes happen where, and with whom. The practical difficulty is that, while cooffending networks can be constructed from arrest data, capturing the social networks that surround criminals – their relatives, friends, and neighbors – is more difficult and expensive. In the previous examples, the cooffending network was enriched by adding data from intelligence interviews, but these are becoming increasingly unpopular, and are no longer permitted in some jurisdictions. Copresence networks provide a way to approximate the richer networks that surround cooffending networks.

Most police forces capture identities of victims and witnesses, as well as perpetrators, in RMS incident data. Often each individual is assigned a unique code. This means that if an individual interacts with police more than once, these interactions can be connected to each other.

RMS data, therefore, allows a richer social network to be inferred, the *copresence network* whose nodes are all of the individuals who interact with police at incidents, and whose edges capture the number of times individuals are present together at the same incidents. Unfortunately, few RMS systems distinguish between victims and witnesses, although these are usually very different roles. In other words, copresence networks generalize the idea of cooffending by including perpetrator-victim, perpetrator-witness, victim-victim, victim-witness, and witness-witness connections.

Does it make sense to collect these other connections? A naive view would be that victims and witnesses are a random sample of the ordinary, non-criminal population, so that the copresence network would have a core that looks just like the cooffending network, and a fringe of non-criminals with very weak connections to the cooffending network. This is far from the case.

Criminals commit crimes in their environment; indeed, crime pattern theory suggest that most criminals hardly ever step outside the physical environment defined by their residence, work, and the route between them. Criminals choose their victims, at least partly, from those who are physically available to them. It is not a surprise, then, that victims of one crime tend also to be victims of others because they are in a geographical hot spot of some kind. The same argument suggests that witnesses to one crime are also witnesses to others, because they are present in the same geographical hot spots. Victims and witnesses therefore are far from random because of the skew we have seen in the distribution of crimes.

Cooffending networks reveal the hot spots of collaborative crime which, as we have seen are quite strong. If a particular criminal always committed crime that victimized the same victims, and were observed by the same witnesses, then adding the copresence network to the cooffending network would provide no genuinely new information. They would still form a periphery to the cooffending network, just with more heavily weighted edges.

However, if the same person is the victim in crimes committed by *different* criminals then this is new information which might, for example, suggest a pattern that is being used for targeting. Similarly, if the same person is a witness to crimes committed by different criminals, then this is new information about overlapping criminal activity. The presence of victims and witnesses in the network adds paths between criminals, revealing that they are similar because of similar targeting choices or because they choose similar geographical or social locations for their crimes. Sometimes the victims or witnesses are themselves criminals, but this was not obvious to the officers who attended the incident.

It turns out that the structure of a copresence network is much more subtle than it might appear, with criminals connected to one another by paths passing through victims and witnesses. The result is a social network that includes a mixture of the cooffending network, the crime pattern network, and the geography in which criminals act. The resulting networks are qualitatively different from the networks based on cooffending plus intelligence interviews, which capture who criminals hang out with, rather than those they victimize.

To make these ideas concrete, the copresence network for a small city over a single year of RMS incident data was calculated, and its properties explored. The RMS data contained 46,668 incidents, in which 12,375 individuals were charged, the vast majority – 11,863 – exactly once. As expected, the distribution of charges per person was highly skewed, with one individual charged 50 times in the year.

The copresence network constructed from this RMS data has nodes that are individuals: perpetrators, victims and witnesses. The weighted edges represent simultaneous presence at incidents. When three or more individuals were present at the same incident, this was represented by a clique, that is the weights on each pair of connections were increased by one. Only the 26,146 individuals who were present with at least one other person were retained, since the others have no effect on the structure of the network (they are isolated nodes). Of these, only 3,359 had total incident edge weight of at least 2, so most people (87%) are only present at one incident with one other person.

The copresence network has a large connected component containing 9,973 of the nodes and, of course, many of these must be connected to the component via a single edge. The remaining connected components are of much smaller size: the second connected component has size 76, then 67, 48, 46, and so on, with a long tail of pairs, for a total of 4,939 connected components. Note the *extreme* skew in connected component sizes.

Cooffending networks typically also have a large connected component, showing that any criminals in each particular environment are connected to one another, at least indirectly. However, the large connected component of the copresence network is not just the large connected component of the cooffending network with a few non-criminal additions, as we shall see. Many of the paths that connect criminals into the connected component pass through non-criminals.

In the following examples, the social networks are based on embedding the networks using spectral graph embedding[12]. Nodes that are similar to one another will be placed close together, whether they are connected or not. Nodes that are dissimilar will be placed far from one another, so that "arms" in the figures represent different clusters of nodes. This is in contrast to the approach used by Papachristos and colleagues described earlier, which are based on properties of each node derived from the social network, but not on the social network itself.

There are a number of ways of thinking about the core of a social network: is it those members who interact with police most often, or those who are most strongly connected to one another? Figure 8.13 shows the copresence network of the largest component of individuals who were present at at least 40 incidents in the year, those who interact with police frequently. Nodes are colored in red if the individual was ever arrested in the course of the year, and green otherwise. The size of the symbol is proportional to the number of arrests. Given that nodes appear in this network interact with police a lot, the surprise in this figure is that it includes some victims and witnesses.

This group who interact with police extensively split half and half between criminals and others. Note especially that non-criminals are *connectors* between different subsets of criminals. In other words, there are criminals who are not present at the same incidents but who are connected in the copresence network because they are present at an incident with some witness or victim, who is then present at some other incident with another criminal. This shows that cooffending networks are not enough to explain all of the criminal dynamics.

It is startling that, in a medium-size city there are non-criminals who are present at incident at least 40 times a year. There are a number of possible explanations for these frequently encountered non-criminals. They could be Neighborhood Watch citizens who call the police regularly and so become witnesses for many incidents, but this suggests something close to vigilante patrolling. They could victims

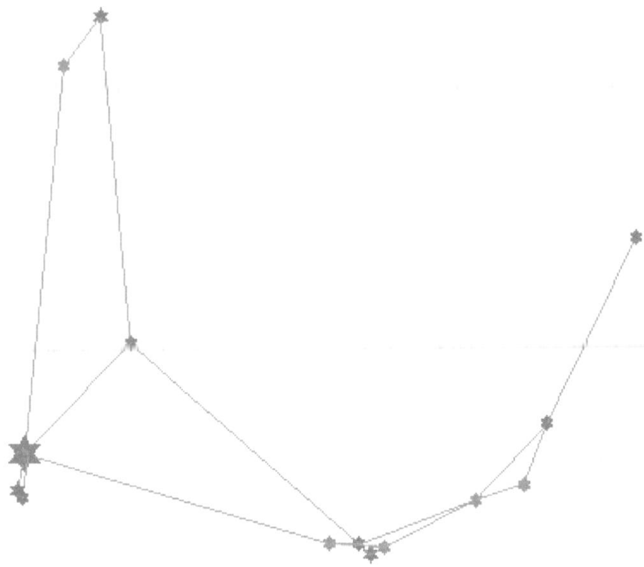

Figure 8.13: Copresence network of criminals (red), victims and witnesses (green), present at at least 40 incidents in a year

whose lifestyle or personal characteristics invite crimes, those who behave in foolhardy ways, flashing cash around while drunk (although being robbed 40 times in a year might cause some lifestyle changes). It is possible that they play a role such as a club bouncer or a store detective which naturally involves calling police to incidents routinely. But it is more likely that they simply happen to be around when crimes happen because they live, work, or hang out with criminals. In other words, they are either opportunistic victims or witnesses because of social and geographical proximity to criminals.

But notice the critical fact: all of these individuals encountered police at least 40 times in a year. They are the low-hanging fruit of reducing policing workload: using well-known suppression strategies for the criminals but, less obviously, developing strategies to manage the workload created by the non-criminals. There is some evidence in the dataset that some of the non-criminals are police groupies, and appear whenever they see flashing lights, that is they are not really witnesses but claim to have been to attract police attention.

Another way to focus on a core group in the copresence network is to focus on the nodes with stronger ties, that is those edges with large weights because of frequent copresence. Figure 8.14 shows the largest component of the network in which every edge has weight at least 5. Again it is clear that the non-criminal members of the copresence social network play an important role as connectors between otherwise separate groups of criminals.

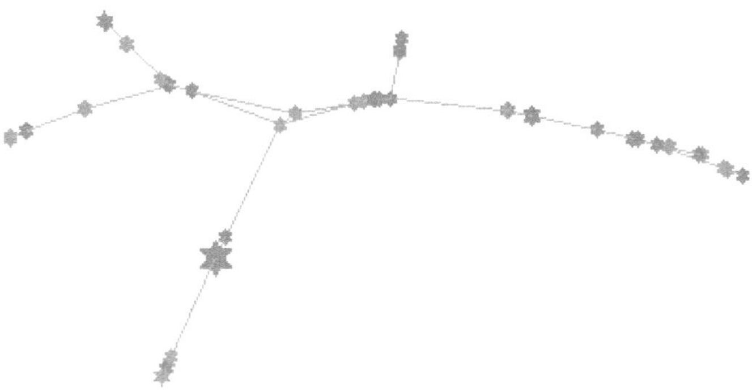

Figure 8.14: Copresence network of criminals (red), victims and witnesses (green), with edge weights at least 5

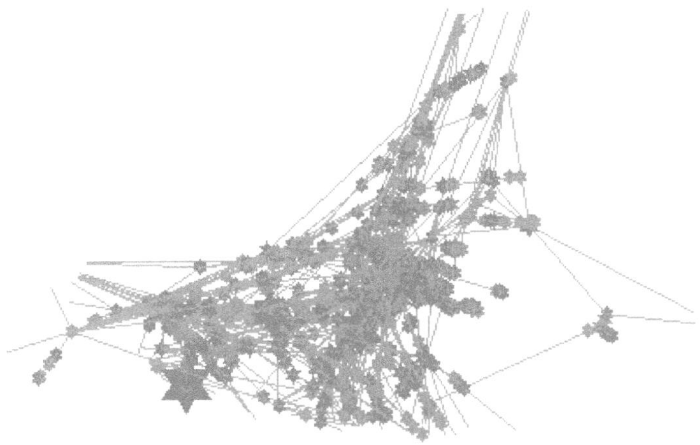

Figure 8.15: Copresence network of criminals (red), victims and witnesses (green), where individuals were present at at least 2 incidents, and every edge has weight at least 2

We can also consider the subnetwork of nodes who interact often with police and each other in this copresence sense. Figure 8.15 shows the copresence network in which each node has been present at at least two incidents, and each edge has weight at least two. This arguably represents all of the interesting interactions among criminals. The network is complex, and the figure zooms into the central region.

The figure shows that the structure of the most active criminals is not an organized one, with some central criminals who commit most of the crimes, and then layers of less active criminals. The often-arrested criminals (the larger stars) are not central nodes, and indeed there are no central nodes. The structure is more like an ecosystem of criminals and non-criminals with many interactions that bind both criminals and non-criminals into a tight social network. One definite conclusion is that the victims and witnesses are not peripheral players in a criminal ecosystem but rather central figures in the interactions among criminals.

The data required to create and analyze copresence networks is (almost) available in RMS incident data. Differentiating victims from witnesses would enable more subtle analysis, since these two kinds of individuals play very different roles in crime incidents.

8.6 Criminal networks with a purpose

Groups of criminals engaged in complex crimes, often spanning countries and even continents have a structure that reflects their functional needs. Social-network analysis of such networks can reveal this functional structure, and perhaps the importance of each component. As we shall see, it is also possible to reveal the dynamic behaviors of such a network.

We use data collected about a drug smuggling network in a North American city. Police acquired warrants to intercept telephone calls between group members over 11 time periods of two months each. The initial warrant applied only to two individuals who were suspected of running the network, and was gradually expanded as phone calls involved more and more individuals. Police listened to and transcribed each phone call and were therefore able to determine whether the individuals involved in each call were members of the group, and also what role each individual played. Over the 11 time periods, police interdicted the drug shipments, but did not arrest any group members[13].

Intercepting, transcribing, and analyzing phone calls is expensive. Here we examine what can be learned simply by analyzing the metadata of these intercepted phone calls, that is how many times each individual phoned each other individual. These call produce a social network in which each node is an individual and each edge is weighted by the number of calls between them. (The edges are actually directed because each call is initiated by one of the participants.)

The social network actually consists of 11 subnetworks, one for each time period. Spectral embedding can create a representation of this network projected into 3 dimensions[14]. The result is shown in Figure 8.16.

In this figure there are four arms, three easily visible and the other into the plane of the image, and these correspond exactly to four subgroups of the entire network. The lower arm corresponds to the cocaine distribution subgroup, the arm going into the plane of the network corresponds to the hashish distribution subgroup,

Figure 8.16: Social network of a drug smuggling network, showing each participant's position at each of the 11 time periods (key participants in red)

the upper left arm corresponds to financial management, and the upper right arm corresponds to foreign suppliers and a transportation connection. The more central each point is in this embedding, the more important and well-connected is the corresponding individual.

The important fact is that this determination of the structure of the network is derived from relatively superficial information about the network activities: who phoned whom. Getting this data is much easier – in some jurisdictions it might not require a warrant, and in others the burden of justification is much lower than for a warrant to listen to the content of calls. It is also cheaper since there is no need to listen to and transcribe conversations. And yet much of the information derived from the more complex and expensive interception is available.

Recall that although drug shipments were interdicted, members of the network were not arrested. Unsurprisingly, this caused increasing suspicion within the group since it must have seemed clear that something was wrong, but not clear exactly what. The most obvious conclusion was that some members of the group were purloining the drug shipments for themselves.

Figure 8.17 shows the trajectories of five key players: 1, the group chief, 3, the head of the hashish subgroup, 87, the head of the finance group, 76, the head of

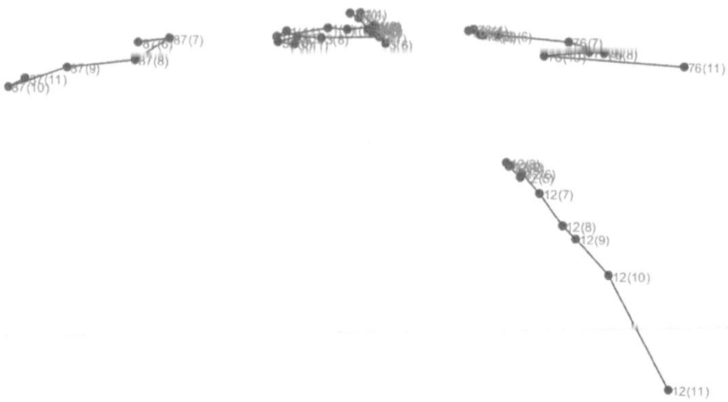

Figure 8.17: Position of five key players over 11 time periods (with the rest of the network not rendered)

the transport subgroup, and 12, the head of the cocaine subgroup. Through the 11 time periods, there is a general outward movement as each senior member becomes suspicious of the others. This is especially true of 12 whose distance to the rest increases rapidly over time. (From the analysis of the directed version of the network it is possible to tell that this distancing is caused by 1 and 3, rather than by 12. This agrees with information gleaned from the content of the calls. In other words, suspicion falls on 12 and the cocaine subgroup.)

Because the social network over the 11 time periods is integrated into a single embedded graph, it is meaningful to measure the diameter of the graph over time, that is the average distance between all pairs of nodes. The result is shown in Figure 8.18. In the early time periods, the diameter increases as new members are discovered and added to the network. Then there is a period of stability. But by time period 7, interdictions have passed beyond bad luck and into something more suspicious for group members, and the diameter increases rapidly until the last time period.

Spectral embedding techniques have great potential to provide insights from data that is cheaper and easier to collect than conventional warrant-based interception of communication.

8.7 Analyzing online posts

Law enforcement are interested in analyzing the natural-language content of online posts because they may be crimes in themselves in some jurisdictions (hate speech), but may also provide early warning of certain kinds of other crimes. For example, some posts in a white-supremacist forum may be aimed at decreasing immigration

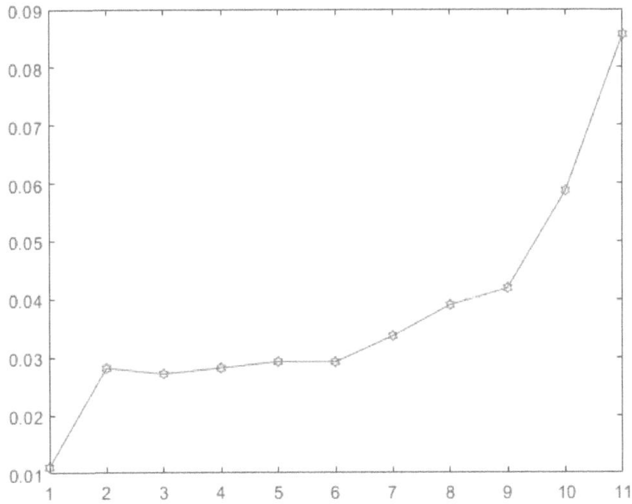

Figure 8.18: Diameter of each time slice of the social network on the same scale

from certain countries by spreading abuse aimed at that community, but other posts may be about planning real-world attacks against that community.

Predictive models based on natural language are attractive. For example, it would be useful to be able to predict school shootings, or suicides, or violent extremist attacks based on the language used in social-media posts. Some progress is being made in this direction, but as usual predictive techniques are better at predicting risk than predicting particular actions.

Unfortunately the public does not understand why particular events of this kind cannot be predicted. "After all", they say, "the evidence on their Facebook page or tweets was unambiguous". What is not so easy to see is all the similar social-media posts that did *not* lead to a bad event. In other words, the false positive rate from such predictions is too high to make the predictions actionable.

However, there are two problems where natural-language predictive approaches can be helpful. The first is to discover, for example, hate speech in large social-media settings or forums. The second is to discover intent to commit a crime (or to commit suicide) as long as this is treated only as a prediction of risk. Detecting intent may be the basis for action, but not forensic action.

There are two main approaches to detecting the signals of a particular mental state. The first is based on a lexicon, a set of words that is considered to be the signals for the appropriate state. Each document can then be scored by how many of these signal words it contains, and the greater the signal the more that it is considered to be expressing the property. Building an effective lexicon is a difficult problem because of the inherent ambiguity of language, and because we do not necessarily understand which words express a particular property. Practically, online posts tend to use informal language and contain prolific spelling mistakes so that it is difficult to match the words that actually appear in the post with the lexicon words. In some communities, an in-group shorthand language is developed, perhaps even deliberately, to make posts harder to understand by outsiders.

Lexicon-based approaches are usually used with bag-of-words approaches, since all that is needed is to count the frequencies of words.

If we wanted to build a lexicon that would capture documents expressing anger, then starting would be easy: "anger", "angry", "mad" (but this is already ambiguous), and then a long list of epithets that might also convey anger but which vary a lot by cultural subdomain. To further complicate matters, some words that often convey anger can be used in a jocular sense, where their angry meaning is defused.

One of the ways in which deep learning has been applied to natural-language data analytics is to build representations of words and pieces of words (n-grams) encoded in (typically) 300-bit strings. These representations are built from large sets of documents by taking a sliding window across the texts, and training a neural network to predict the middle word of each window from its neighbors. The non-linearity of the neural network step tends to map words with similar meanings close together in the 300-dimensional vector-space representation.

Given an initial lexicon, even a small one, new words can be added to it by including all the words that are close enough in this 300-dimensional representation. This process adds words that are semantically similar to the initial set. Better still, it also adds pieces of words that have similar meanings because they will also be close in the representation. For example, if we start with "anger" and "angry" then "angered" will probably also be included because it is likely to be a neighbor of the initial words. The representation is also likely to capture obfuscated versions like "@ngry" and misspellings like "angre" because of the substrings that overlap with the base word. The use of embeddings has expanded to applicability of natural-language data analytics to the informal language that is used online (and so made it much more useful in practice). Starting points for lexicon-based analysis have been much improved by the development of systems such as Empath[15] (and before it, LIWC[16]). These consist of predefined sets of words associated with meaningful categories. For example, Empath has lexicons associated with syntactic categories, topical groupings (for example, "social media"), and affective states, such as emotions or moods. These lexicons are generated by analysis of a large corpus of amateur writing, using a skip-gram neural network approach that produces a 150-dimensional vector space representation of sufficiently frequent words. Word-word similarity is based on cosine similarity in this vector space. It also has a mechanism for creating new lexicons by seeding them with a few representative words, and the Empath tool will then fill in other similar words.

A second approach is to use deep learning directly. This means processing the words in each document in order, unlike the bag-of-words approach, and so this approach has access to more information about each document. The current state-of-the-art is to use biLSTM (*bidirectional long-short term memory*) deep-learning networks. These explicitly leverage the fact that the significance of a particular word in a document does not depend only on its immediate neighbors, but also on words that appeared earlier – hence the long-short – or, in some languages, words that have not been seen yet (verbs in German) – hence the bidirection.

We now consider applying these analysis ideas to natural language data of the kind that may be of interest to particular parts of law enforcement. This includes language collected from social media, from online forums, from intercepted emails, and even from offline documents such as ransom notes.

8.7.1 Detecting abusive language

Lexical approaches can work in a flat way, by selecting as complete a set of words as possible that represent or encode the property being detected. However, making sure that the lexicon includes *all* of the relevant words is difficult. One strategy that helps is to consider intermediate states of the property being detected, and predicting the presence of such intermediate states in a document. This tends to improve the coverage by finding more subtle signals, and also increases confidence that the lexicon is detecting the desired property.

As we have seen, the question of when language is abusive is a difficult one, with different jurisdictions using slightly different criteria. In some cases, the issue is a law-enforcement one, because certain kinds of language use is illegal. In others, it is a business issue because sites want to ban certain kinds of language because the use of such language on a site negatively impacts their brand.

Detection of abusive language can be improved by considering intermediate level constructs that are significant for abusive language. Being abusive requires certain attitudes, and perhaps emotions, on the part of the author; if these are not present, it is unlikely that a particular document is abusive, even though it might contain some abusive words.

Othering is the mental framing of some group of people as qualitatively different from oneself, and this has been suggested as a prerequisite for abusive language. In other words, we are not usually abusive about a group with which we identify; abuse is directed against "them" not "us". Othering is partly expressed lexically (in the use of pronouns such as us and them) but can also be expressed in more subtle ways that are not easily captured by a lexical approach. For example, boasting about the qualities of one particular group can, in some settings, be a subtle way of putting down the obvious contrast group. "We are great" can imply that "they are not". If othering is not present in a document, then the presumption that it is abusive becomes much weaker.

Another intermediate level construct is subjectivity, since most abuse is based on internal mental models that are not objective – abuse is not argument. Abuse uses negative language, but negative language is not abuse if it is based on evidence, or even on reasoned argument. Separating negative content that is attitudinal from negative language that is abusive is helped if the context can be determined to be objective or subjective. Subjective language can be separated from objective by considering the pronouns ("I think", "we think", "I feel" are much more subjective than "people think"); and by emotional tone, since objective language tends to be informative. Models that predict if the content of a document is subjective or objective help to disambiguate the negative valence words that are present.

Emotions expressed in documents may correlate with abuse: for example, anger and disgust may correlate with abusive language, and the presence of joy may suggest that a document is not abusive. However, emotions are short lived, lasting typically only minutes. An occasional document, written in anger, may contain abuse, but we are used to people expressing themselves intemperately when emotional, and such documents may not be useful for larger purposes. A social-media site might block such a post, but it is unlikely to be of interest as hate speech. Because emotions are so short-lived their practical role as signals of abusive language must be weak.

Much online language is informal, so using a lexicon based on formal language tends to miss important signals. For example, it is common to see variants such as 'cr@p' either to be cool or because of concern about language-filtering tools. Words like this are almost certainly intended as abusive, but will be missed by a standard lexical approach. This can be partly avoided by constructing n-grams from the lexicon, that is contiguous substrings that appear in abusive lexicon words, and looking for these substrings as well.

Lexical approaches almost invariably use a bag-of-words model of each document, counting the frequencies of all of the words that appear in the document, but ignoring their order. In languages like English, where word order is important, this obviously loses information about document content.

One way to leverage these specific models based on different modalities is to build a predictor for each one (an othering predictor, a subjectivity predictor, an anger predictor, and so on) and then combine their predictions by voting or averaging to form a *heterogeneous predictor*. In other words, this is just an ensemble predictor, as in bagging, except that each individual predictor uses a different predictive technique. The overall predictor acts like a committee where each expert gives an opinion about whether a particular document is abusive, and then the committee as a whole votes on their overall decision.

An alternative is called *stacking*. Here individual predictors are built using different predictive techniques (the same othering, subjectivity, and so on predictors), and each make their predictions on the training data. However, this set of predictions then becomes the training data for another predictor, and this second-stage predictor learns to the predict the outcome from the *outcomes* of the earlier stage. In other words, rather than combining the earlier predictions using, say, voting the second-stage predictor learns when to pay more attention to one of the earlier predictors,

Model	F1-score	Accuracy
Subjectivity	0.625	0.853
Othering	0.870	0.940
Character n-grams	0.895	0.950
Word n-grams	0.879	0.944
Disgust	0.552	0.838
Joy	0.008	0.748
Anger	0.527	0.833
Negative mood	0.623	0.855
Empath word categories	0.660	0.852
BiLSTM	0.889	0.946
Stacked predictor	0.906	0.954

Table 8.4: F1 score and accuracy for predictors using various properties of abusive language

and when to pay more attention to another. When a new record is presented to the ensemble, it is predicted by each of the earlier stage predictors, and then the final prediction looks at their predictions, and makes the final determination. Stacking is like learning that each of your friends gives good advice about certain topics, but less good about others. When you have to make a decision, you can ask all of your friends, but rely more on the advice of some than others.

An experiment was aimed at detecting abusive language in a mixed corpus of documents: a corpus collected by Google as part of their Perspectives project, a corpus collected for a project on hate speech, and an insult corpus. The results are given in Table 8.4. Only 25% of the documents in the corpus were abusive, so the F-score is reported as well as the accuracy.

Subjectivity is moderately helpful in predicting abusive language, but othering is much more successful. The character and word n-grams do not use an intermediate model but instead address the weaknesses of conventional bag-of-words approaches by considering small sets of adjacent words (word n-grams), and by looking inside single words (character n-grams). As expected, these are both strong predictors.

Negative emotions are only slightly predictive, while joy, a positive emotion, is entirely useless. This is consistent with the view that abusive language primarily comes from attitudes, rather than emotions.

Negative mood is moderately predictive. The role of moods is not well understood, but they are longer lasting than emotions, so it is possible that they more consistently signal negative content; that is, when in a bad mood, generating abusive language is more likely.

The deep learning predictor performs strongly, as expected, but only at the same level as the lexical predictors based on n-grams. Combining all of the outputs of the individual models and using a stacking predictor produces the best overall performance, but is only very slightly better than the character n-grams and biLSTM models.

Overall, either a stacked predictor or just a biLSTM will perform well on this problem. Such a predictor could be deployed to label, or block, abusive posts on a social-media site. But, by building a separate predictors for each modality, we learn something about how different mental states contribute to abusive language.

Using a predictor (xgboost) that ranks attributes by how much they contribute to each prediction makes it possible to understand what kind of language conveys abuse. The stacking predictor shows which individual predictors make the greatest contribution to the overall prediction. These are, in order: the biLSTM, character n-grams, the Empath word categories, subjectivity, word n-grams, and othering. This is slightly surprising since othering, by itself, performs much better than subjectivity. However, in the context of all of the subpredictors subjectivity helps the overall prediction. This implies that it correctly labels some documents that other subpredictors find difficult.

We can also look inside each of the predictors to see which individual signals are predictive of abuse. For example, the Empath word categories that make the greatest contribution to predicting abusive language are: swearing terms, negative emotion, Internet terms, dispute, writing, and ridicule.

For the subjectivity model, the top ranked signals are: ‘it’, ‘bitch’, ‘you’, ‘please’, ‘there’, ‘which’, and ‘me’. These words can be signals of objectivity (presumably “it”) as well as subjectivity (presumably “bitch”).

For the anger model, the top ranked signals are: ‘bitch’, ‘shit’, ‘hate’, and ‘remove’. In fact, ‘bitch’ ranks near the top of the many of the lists, suggesting that misogyny is deeply involved in online abusive language.

Lexical approaches can be useful to detect particular properties in language, provided that some plausible starting point can be imagined. As a result, progress has been made with automatically detecting properties that psychologists already understand, and so can suggest such starting points.

8.7.2 Detecting intent

Properties for which there is no deep psychological modeling are more difficult to detect, because there is usually no clear starting point. One such property is intent. There would be great practical usefulness in being able to distinguish when a violent extremist is planning an actual attack, rather than simply talking about one; or when a high school student is planning a gun attack at school or a suicide, rather than simply expressing dark thoughts. The difficulty is to differentiate armchair talk of action from the intent to act.

Intent is an example of a property that we understand as humans, but find it difficult to codify. Other examples are properties such as remorse or sarcasm.

The starting point for intent is the observation that "I will <action verb>" and "I am going to <action verb>" are basic intent phrases. They rely both on the use of a first-person pronoun ("you will" is an order, and does not signal intent), a desire verb, and its relationship to an appropriate action verb. In most practical cases, the right action verbs will need to be selected to make the predictions useful ("I'm going to have another cup of coffee" is intent but not of much interest to law enforcement.) There are also a range of relevant desire verbs: "I plan to", I want to", and perhaps "I need to".

We illustrate how to develop an intent model for white supremacy, using posts from the Stormfront and Iron March forums which are hidden in the Dark Web, and the manifesto of the Christchurch shooter[17]. As with many forums, the language needed considerable cleaning up, in particular removing quotations. Quoting from other sources, often news media but sometimes other posts in the forum, seems to be a common form of participation. It allows members to post even if they have nothing in particular to say, and so feel like they are a part of the forum's community. However, they must be removed before attempting to detect intent, since second-hand intent is not useful for law enforcement. A set of Wikipedia articles was also added to the corpus. Their style guidelines disallow intent so this provided a contrast set of documents that models should all predict to be free of intent.

Documents vary in length considerably, and intent might be quite a localized property, so documents were divided into segments at sentence boundaries and semi-colons. An initial labeling is generated by labeling segments that contain one of the two templates with an appropriate desire verb. The desire verbs were initialized as an obvious set: 'want', 'need' 'going', 'have', 'about', 'planning' (to) and 'will'.

A FastText embedding was computed for the entire Stormfront corpus, producing a 200-dimensional word-embedding vector space. These desire verbs were generalized by computing a hypercone prism based on the average of the initial set, producing a set of 596 desire verbs.

Initial labels were generated for the documents: +1 if it contains an instance of the template, 0 if it contains a negation, question, or second- or third-person pronoun, and 0.5 (unknown) otherwise.

The difficulty with properties like intent is that there are no corpora with labeled data. Getting such a corpus would require large-scale human labeling about which there might even be significant disagreement. To learn an intent model requires bootstrapping, and bootstrapping quite conservatively. This is done using two concurrent learners, one based on n-grams and the other using a deep learning biLSTM. Each learns a model of intent, the two predictions are merged, and then each revises its model based on the updated labels, until the process has converged.

The n-gram learner learns whether each n-gram is predictive of intent by considering how often it appears in a document tentatively labeled as containing intent as opposed to one that does not. n-grams at the extremes, based on the ratio of their occurrence in intentful versus non-intentful segments, are taken to be signals of intent or non-intent. Segments are relabeled as intentful if they contain only intentful n-gram, and non-intentful if they contain only non-intentful n-grams. They are labeled as neutral if they contain none of these n-grams or more than one with contradictory senses.

In parallel, the deep learners takes a random sample of the tentatively labeled data and trains on it, treating any label greater than 0.5 as 1 and any label less than 0.5 as 0. The resulting model is then used to relabel all of the records based on the deep learner's predictions.

These two sets of new labels are then reconciled. Each model can propose segments whose labels were unknown before but have now acquired a label, but it can only propose as many as had that label on the previous round. This is to prevent the models from converging too quickly. Any record proposed by either model is relabeled, unless the labels contradict, in which case it is relabeled as unknown. Once the merge mechanism has labeled a record it is never altered subsequently.

After a few rounds, the labels have converged and the model can be used to predict previously unseen segments.

A model of intent could be used in several different applications. For example, a social robot could use an intent model to detect the needs and potential actions of the humans around it to interact with them safely and effectively. However, we are interested in detecting intent for bad or criminal activities. In other words, we are interested in a model that combines intent with particular kinds of potential actions.

This could be done in a number of ways. For example, one straightforward approach would be to look for segments that contain both intent and some signal of targeting. One combination that has been explored is intent + abusive language, since these together might signal intent to do harm to the abused group.

This requires measuring the abusive intent of a segment, as well as its intent. This can be done using the approach described previously, and so an abusive score can be generated for each segment. Taking the product of abusive language score (in the range 0–1) and intent score (also in the range 0–1) is a good way to find appropriate segments. Here are some examples of high-scoring segments from different places:

- Stormfront: "we need segregation from these stupid filthy diseased savages", abuse: 0.96, intent: 0.97 (we need), product 0.93.
- Stormfront: "don t refer to us as a bunch of hillbillies or we ll kick your ass", abuse 0.90, intent 0.99 (we ll kick), product 0.90.
- Iron March: "he is a fucking retard and i want to organize a massive troll on him", abuse: 0.95, intent: 1.0 (I want to organize), product: 0.95.

- Manifesto: "we will kill you and drive you roaches from our lands", abuse: 0.97, intent 1.0 (we will kill), product: 0.97.

Using the product means that a segment only gets a high score if it contains high values for both intent and abuse.

One further step is required to produce an overall abusive intent score for an entire document (that is, multiple segments). Some care is required because a document can express abuse in one segment, and intent in another, but the document is still relevant. A useful way to compute a composite score is to compute the maximum abuse score and the maximum intent score in each sliding window of three segments within a document. The abusive intent score for the document is the maximum of the product of abuse and intent in each of these windows. This effectively smooths the presence of abuse and intent distributed through the document.

Since we do not have labels for intent, the performance of the system can only be validated by looking at examples like those shown above, but also be comparing its labeling to those produced by humans. Agreement with human raters was around 80% (which is about as well as humans tend to agree). In fact, humans tend to see intent where there is none (for example, "well i decided to join the group to educate the morons and counter their ridiculous posts with facts", not intent because past tense). Some examples such as "old barry might want to think about keeping his ass at home" are perceived by humans as a threat, and so as implicit intent, but there are no explicit linguistic signals for a model to detect. The human scorers also seemed to view "need" as a very weak form of intent (as in "we need to fight").

Predictors of interesting properties of natural-language posts on forums and social-media platforms are most useful for focusing analyst attention on the important few documents out of the extremely large set of documents that are created and posted online. It is impossible to look at hundreds of thousands of documents exhaustively hoping to find the critical few. Predictors like this (which, again, are predicting risk, the risk that each document contains the property being looked for) can reduce the set to be searched to a manageable size. Note that it is important that such predictors miss as few of the documents with the property as possible (false negatives) even if this means that they flag documents that do not contain the property.

8.7.3 Deception

Another language property that can be detected computationally, and which is of considerable interest in law-enforcement contexts is deception[18]. Deception here means someone saying or writing something that they know not to be true (not misinformation, which the speaker or writer might believe to be true).

Early work on deception discovered that, in free-format documents, there are four strong signals of deception:

1. A decreased rate of first-person pronouns;

2. A decreased rate of exclusive words, words such as "but" and "or" which introduce increased complexity;

3. An increased rate of negative-emotion words; and

4. An increased rate of action verbs.

The intuition about these signals is perhaps that reducing first-person pronouns creates psychological distance from the deceptive statements. Reducing exclusive words reduces the cognitive load associated with creating deceptive content. Increasing negative-emotion words may be a consequence of a subconscious awareness of doing something socially disapproved of. Increasing action verbs may be an effort to keep the narrative moving and provide fewer opportunities for doubt.

Of course, these are all relative changes in word rates, so they cannot be used to declare that *these* documents are deceptive and *these others* are not. But these word rate changes can be used to rank a set of documents of a similar kind from most to least deceptive; and perhaps to detect when someone is being deceptive when they usually are not (comparing against a baseline).

Experiments have shown that humans are poor both at being deceptive and at detecting deception. This is not surprising since the ability either to be deceptive or to detect deception would have value in human groups, and so there must always have been a kind of arms race between the two abilities. A stalemate between the two must therefore have been the normal state of affairs through human history.

Law-enforcement personnel, even when trained, are not particularly better at detecting deception than ordinary people, although they think they are. Ordinary people score badly at detecting deception because they miss it; law-enforcement personnel score badly because they over count it ("everybody lies"). (This is starting to change as the signals described above are being included in training.)

The nature of the signal of deception shows why we, as humans, are very poor at detecting it. We are not equipped with the "hardware" to notice when certain classes of words are being used at higher or lower rates than usual. However, software is able to track word rates quite readily, and so rank any given set of documents.

This model of deception assumes that the documents being assessed are free form, that the author or speaker is able to write or say whatever they wish. It is useful for looking for deception in documents like forum or social-media posts.

However, for law enforcement one of the key places where the ability to detect deception would be useful is in interrogations. In an interrogation there are two parties, the questioner and the person being questioned. The person being questioned is no longer speaking freely, but is instead responding to questions, and this changes the dynamics of language use.

In particular, conversations are full of (unconscious) mimicry – we tend to recycle the word patterns of the people we are speaking with. This breaks the direct use of the deception model. After all, a natural form of question is "Did you ..."

which forces an answer of the form "Yes, I did ..." or "No, I didn't ..." with a first-person pronoun in it. So a model that depends on rates of first-person pronouns is bound to be affected in a dialogue setting.

The deception model can still be applied but its use is more complex. The effect of mimicry dies away after about 50 words, for then the writer/speaker is once again using their own words. So in an interrogation, (the initial part of) each response must be processed to have the effects coming from the words in the question removed. This can be done, and the effective level of deception estimated[19] but it is more complex, and would be difficult to do in real time.

There is a further complication, and that is the interaction of mirroring and rapport with detecting deception. Interrogators are often trained to build rapport with subjects, and one straightforward way to do this is to mirror their movements and language patterns – to reflect back at them aspects of their behavior. This is remarkably effective, and works powerfully at an unconscious level. In one experiment, a waitress received much larger tips when she repeated orders back verbatim (even though this sounds and seems a bit awkward) than when she summarized them; and retail staff trained in the same way generated greater sales and more satisfied customers[20].

However, in interrogation settings, increased rapport between questioner and subject increases the blindness of the questioner to deception, and so comes with a substantial cost.

The best solution would seem to be to use an automated tool to detect deception, and let the questioner establish rapport, but such a system has not yet been built.

8.7.4 Detecting fraud in text

The Securities and Exchange Commission (SEC) requires publicly traded companies to file quarterly reports of their performance. Sometimes it decides that a particular quarterly filing was fraudulent, that is intended to mislead the market about the performance and prospects of the company. However, these determinations that a particular quarterly filing is fraudulent are (a) conservative, since the SEC will not declare a filing to be fraudulent unless it is very sure; and (b) much delayed, up to 10 years after the filing was made. There has been obvious interest is using data analytics to predict whether or not a quarterly report is fraudulent immediately after it is filed.

One obvious way to do this is to look at the financial statements, the summary balance sheets of the business for each quarter, that are included in each filing. However, this turns out to be extremely difficult to do. Prediction accuracies are low and it is not clear why this is so.

Looking at the textual part of quarterly reports turns out to be much more useful. Each report contains a section called the Management Discussion and Analysis (MD&A) which is a free-form discussion of each company's performance and prospects over the quarter, and looking ahead.

The deception model discussed previously might be expected to perform well is detecting fraudulent MD&As but in fact does not. This seems to be because business communication does not use first-person pronouns much (favoring the passive voice) and these pronouns are a major part of the deception model's signal. Negative-emotion words are also rare in business writing and so in these MD&A sections.

However, a support vector machine predictor was able, with some care, to distinguish fraudulent reports from non-fraudulent ones with a per-quarter accuracy of 88% based on SEC labeling of fraud[21]. Since the SEC is conservative in its determination of fraud, the real performance is probably slightly better than this.

Looking at the temporal behavior of the regression score from this predictor shows that there is a characteristic dynamic to producing fraudulent MD&As: in the few quarters leading up to a series of unequivocally fraudulent reports the truthfulness of reports starts to decrease. Sometimes this is simply a wavering, and would not be classified as fraudulent by the model. At other times, one report is clearly fraudulent, but then the next few will be less so, before a clear sequence of fraudulent quarters begins. These single-quarter fraudulent reports are almost never labeled as such by the SEC, even when they detect the longer sequence, but detecting such a warning quarter would be extremely valuable.

Interestingly, the end of a sequence of fraudulent quarterly reports is typically clear cut, with the truthfulness returning to high levels at one particular quarter and staying there. Presumably this is either because the fraud is detected and the people responsible fired, or there is simply a turnover of personnel which replaces the fraudsters. In some companies there is a sequence of frauds, then a return to truthfulness and then, a year or two later, a return to fraud. This suggests a culture of fraud in the company.

Some of the most predictive words of this fraud model are 'acquisition', 'acquisitions', 'months', 'sales', and 'legal' although it is not the use or non-use of these words that is predictive, but changes in the rates at which they are used, compared to some hypothetical normal MD&A.

It might seem surprising that language patterns indicative of fraud could be detected in a document that, in most companies, is prepared by a committee most of whom, presumably, are unaware of the fraud. However, it turns out that the language patterns used by, say, a CFO who is committing fraud are picked up by those writing the MD&A (another example of verbal mimicry) and make their way into the eventual document[22].

In another example, the Scamseek project labeled online solicitations for financial products as fraudulent or not, but required a large team and several years[23]. Fraud seems difficult to detect compared to other properties signaled by natural-language patterns. Since most language use has a large unconscious component this cannot be because fraudsters are more motivated or better at concealment.

8.7.5 Detecting sellers in dark-web marketplaces

In the marketplaces in the dark web, there are a mixture of sellers and buyers. Law enforcement has an interest in both. In principle, those who act in the dark web do so anonymously, but this is not completely true.

First, there are hints that the anonymizing of mechanisms such as the Tor router are at least partly transparent with sufficient skill. This is partly because of timing – the Tor routing network is intended to obfuscate the mapping from inputs to outputs by moving requests around randomly, but users do not want to wait long for responses, so there is pressure not to delay requests too long. As a result a request exiting the Tor network may be potentially mapped to the same request entering the network, breaking the supposed disconnect. Second, people tend to use the same or cognate handles in multiple places, and so it may be possible to tentatively connect a dark-web user identifier to one in the open web, and so perhaps to an identity. Third, it is easy for even moderately knowledgeable users to make a mistake that reveals their real IP address. This might be because of misconfigured settings, the use of another piece of software or a plugin that is not careful about keeping secrets, or because of downloading and opening some object that contains the functionality to "phone home" when it is opened.

Law enforcement might be interested in any buyer who can be identified because they are likely to use whatever product they bought to do something illegal. But sellers are higher-value targets. First, arresting sellers prevents them from continuing to sell their illicit products and so has a larger effect. Second, knowing who sellers are may enable their sources of supply to be traced in turn, and still greater disruption caused by closing them.

The number of posts on a dark-web marketplace is large, and buyers outnumber sellers by a factor of at least four. A human reader can readily distinguish a buyer from a seller, but the scale of the problem makes this impractical. So there is considerable usefulness in being able to automatically detect sellers.

The basic content of the posts of a seller and a buyer are not very different. They both mention a kind of object and its properties, and do not use conventional phrases from classified advertisements such as "for sale" and "wanted to buy". Furthermore, the same individual may sometimes be a seller and sometimes a buyer.

In an experiment to understand the natural-language differences between sellers and buyers, the content of a malware dark-web forum was collected[24]. We have already seen that a corpus can be used to create an embedding in which words with similar meanings (as used in the corpus) are placed close together; and words with opposite meanings are placed far apart. A word embedding using singular value decomposition was created from all of the posts in the forum (this is a technique with a long heritage, and is the basis for generalization in, for example, Google's web search).

This embedding can be explored using queries. For example, the query "X" returns the words closely associated with this word, and the query "not(X)" returns its antonyms, both within the context of the particular corpus.

It is quite obvious that a strong signal of being a buyer is the use of thanking words. Unfortunately, many, many variants of "thanks" are used, although they are all similar within the singular value decomposition embedding.

So the language used by sellers can be identified by using queries that contain "not(thanks)". For example, the query "config and not(thanks)" returns "cracking, also, forums, premium, files, sites, may, link, account, pc, must, text, username, change, serial, download, cracked, list, private, keygen", all of which are plausibly associated with sellers and/or experts.

The query "proxy" is interesting because the words ("do, not, have, sufficient, rights") appear in the result. A search of the forum shows that these words occur whenever a link that leads to a potentially high quality product (a paywall, effectively) is present in a post.

The words associated with the query "not(thanks)" lead to a lexicon that is associated with sellers: "account, accounts, addresses, also, bad, change, combo, configs, cracked, cracking, did, doing, dont, download, fake, files, forums, has, keygen, link, list, little, may, method, must, normal, own, pc, premium, private, serial, show, sites, some, staff, text, username, using". This lexicon can be used to automatically extract the posts associated with sellers for analyst attention. (There are also hints, for example the appearance of the word "staff" in this list, that many of the sellers are also the moderators and managers of the forum itself. This is not surprising, but it does show that malware sellers are entrepreneurial in the sense of setting up their own distribution channels; and are able to collaborate with one another.)

Another experiment of the same kind used Latent Dirichlet Allocation, a topic-clustering technique, to cluster the posts in a completely unsupervised way, that is without any input about what the topics should be about[25]. The goal of this work was to identify the most proficient cybercriminals because they would be associated with a cluster containing references to high-end or sophisticated cyber products. But they also found clusters that were related to buyers. One was based on the words "nice, good, work, man, share, brother, test, love, thank, hope, job, check, mate, wow". The tone here seems different from the buyers in the earlier experiment. The forums were collected 5 years apart so it is hard to know whether this reflects a change in language, or simply a different forum environment.

All of these examples show how data-analytic approaches can be used to understand human behavior, especially as it is expressed in natural language.

8.8 Behavior – detecting fraud from mouse movements

One reason why interesting properties can be detected in natural language is because we "leak" our mental state into the ways we use language. The same thing happens with behavior: the awareness of doing something illicit is often visible in body language, and we cannot easily hide these leaked signals. Implicit awareness of this channel of information is revealed by the use of words such as "skulking" and "furtive" – behaviors that ordinary people understand and detect intuitively.

One set of movements that have been used to detect fraud is the way that people use their mouse when visiting a web site: both how the mouse is moved, and how long it takes. For example, an online mortgage application site typically asks questions about income, other financial commitments, and willingness and ability to make payments. Those who are being deceptive have characteristic patterns of both movements and timing. For example, they may repeatedly visit and alter the field in which they specify the amount they are asking for; or they may take longer to answer commitment questions. Automatic form filling by some other piece of software can also be detected straightforwardly[26]. This approach is being commercialized and businesses are running this kind of predictive model as a first-stage filter on their potential customers in businesses such as insurance and money lending where a web-based interface is used.

Data-analytic models applied to behavioral data are still in their infancy but there is a great deal of potential to detect potentially criminal behavior in this space.

8.9 Understanding drug trafficking pathways

Illegal drugs in a particular jurisdiction may be produced locally (a meth lab), grown locally (marijuana), or grown far away, processed somewhere en route, and then sold locally (typically plant alkaloids such as heroin and cocaine). The chemical composition of a plant-alkaloid drug when it is interdicted by law enforcement typically contains both traces of the process used to refine it from the plant precursor, and various chemicals (adulterants) that have been used to cut it, to increase the volume for sale. The trace chemistry of a drug sample therefore acts as a fingerprint that hints at its provenance.

The cost of chemical analysis is not trivial, so it is usually only done for large seizures. For each seizure, multiple samples can be taken and their chemical compositions analyzed.

We consider a dataset of seizures of a common illegal drug, cocaine, and the chemical profile of the samples taken from each seizure. What can we learn from this? First, we can get a sense of the typical adulterants and how common they are. In this dataset, they include, in decreasing order of occurrence: levamisole (a medication with major side-effects[27]), phenacetin, dexamisole (another medication with major side-effects), caffeine, creatine, diltiazem (a medication for high blood pressure), sucrose, mannitol, lactose, glucose, inositol, lignocaine (aka lidocaine), benzocaine, paracetamol, procaine, (another local anesthetic), aspirin, sorbitol, fructose, chloroform, phenobarbitol, maltose, nicotinamide (vitamin B3), dextromethorphan, theophylline (used to treat COPD), creatinine, ketamine (an antidepressant and pain reliever), and several more. This list by itself should discourage illegal drug taking.

Figure 8.19: Clustering of drug samples by chemical profile, color-coded by seizure

These adulterants are consistent with those found all over the world[28]. They appear to be chosen because (a) they are available and cheap, and (b) they mimic the action of cocaine in simple tests. For example, a common way to test for cocaine is to put some on the tip of the tongue and observe local anesthesia. Lignocaine, benzocaine, and procaine will simulate or enhance this effect. Cocaine also tastes bitter and caffeine, paracetamol, and aspirin have similar bitter tastes. Cocaine's melting point is also easily tested, so it is important that adulterants have a similar melting point.

Second, the refining process leaves traces of the chemicals used, especially solvents, and so reveal the favored refinement process that produced each sample.

Looking at the patterns of chemicals in the samples from a single seizure can show whether the seizure is the output of a single trafficking pathway or not, and looking for the same adulterant pattern in different seizures can show when a different delivery pathway passes through a single supplier. Both provide information about processing and delivery mechanisms that can then be leveraged for interdiction. For example, if a drug dealer in a Western country has created an integrated supply pipeline, then the samples from an interdiction of one of their shipments should all have the same chemical profile. On the other hand, if the drug dealer buys from an intermediate market, then samples from an interdiction might be expected to show much more variability in chemical profile.

Figure 8.19 shows a clustering of several thousand drug samples based on their chemical profiles. The clustering uses singular value decomposition. Each point is color-coded by the seizure from which it came.

An integrated supply chain would be detectable as points of the same color (and so from the same seizure) clustered close together. This is manifestly not the case; there is some clustering of points of the same color, but it is not strong. We can conclude that the processing labs for cocaine are not tightly integrated with the delivery organizations. Rather, in both directions there must be some shopping around: delivery organizations buy from multiple processing labs, and processing labs also sell to multiple delivery organizations; or there are wholesalers who buy from labs and sell to delivery organizations. This is supported by Kenney[29] who argues that, in Colombia, the idea of drug cartels with organized and tightly controlled, vertically integrated supply systems is largely an illusion.

The clustering also provides a sense of how many different patterns of adulterants there are. The figure does not contain tight clusters of points, so there are obviously not a small set of "recipes" that different processing labs use. However, we can get a sense of the large-scale differences in chemical use by looking at the clustering overlaid with the concentrations of particular adulterants.

The basic shape is a large V or butterfly. The left-hand grouping (shown in Figure 8.20) is related to the use of solvents such as benzene, hexane, isobutylacetate, toluene, methyl ethyl ketone, and several others. The right-hand grouping is related to concentrations of acetone (shown in Figure 8.21), mesitylene, and several others. The points at the bottom of the V are related to concentrations of fructose (shown in Figure 8.22) and sucrose, while the points at the top of the V are associated with cocaine variants such as ecgonine. So the vertical variation seems to be associated with the quality of the refinement process and the use of volume-increasing additives, while the horizontal variation is associated with major variants in the refinement process.

These figures also suggest further directions for investigation. For example, the fairly tight cluster at the top left (colored yellow) is strongly associated with the use of methyl acetate, so at least this seizure seems to have a consistent fingerprint.

The examples in this chapter have provided a sense of the variety of ways in which data-analytic ideas and techniques can be applied in law-enforcement contexts.

Notes

[1]This is further complicated because law enforcement jurisdictions do not necessarily match census-based definitions of cities.

[2]The question of whether these attributes *cause* changes in the risk of violence is a subtle one. In a controlled experiment environment, it is usually claimed that a variation between the control and the experiment group associated with a variation of outcome qualifies as causative. In the natural experiments that data analytics embodies, the variation is the chance variation between one jurisdiction and another, but when a consistent agreement can be seen between the variation of an attribute

Figure 8.20: Clustering of drug samples overlaid by concentration of benzene

and the variation of the outcome, we can, perhaps with less certainty, argue that it is causative.

[3]Interestingly, the percent of female police officers was not collected.

[4]Although it is hard to be sure of the density of points in such a clustering, so there may be more incidents in one layer than in the other.

[5]One pitfall of this kind of analysis is that many incidents in which citizens come to police headquarters are geolocated at that headquarters in the RMS record. So the hottest hot spot is often police headquarters! This illustrates another weakness in the design of RMS systems.

[6]Even in the U.S. where guns are readily available, there are rudimentary checks designed to prevent criminals buying guns through ordinary retail channels.

[7]A.V. Papachristos, A.A. Braga and D.M. Hureau, "Social networks and the risk of gunshot injury", *Journal of Urban Health*, 89:992–1003, 2012.

[8]This kind of investigation would not have been possible without field intelligence, which is one argument for using it. In general, collecting information about the social network of criminals is difficult, except for the cooffending subnetwork.

[9]Ego network density is the fraction of one's neighbors who are connected to one another.

[10]A.V. Papachristos, A.A. Braga, E. Piza and L.S. Grossman, "The company you keep? the spillover effects of gang membership on individual gunshot victimization in a co-offending network", *Criminology*, 53:624–649, 2015.

Figure 8.21: Clustering of drug samples overlaid by concentration of acetone

[11]A.V. Papachristos, "Murder by structure: Dominance relations and the social structure of gang homicide", *American Journal of Sociology*, 115:74–128, 2009.

[12]F.R.K. Chung, *Spectral Graph Theory*, Number 92 in CBMS Regional Conference Series in Mathematics. American Mathematical Society, 1997; U. Luxburg, "A tutorial on spectral clustering", *Statistics and Computing*, 17(4):395–416, December 2007.

[13]C. Morselli and K. Petit, "Law-enforcement disruption of a drug importation network", *Global Crime*, 8:109–130, 2007.

[14]D.B. Skillicorn, Q. Zhen and C. Morselli, "Modeling dynamic social networks using spectral embedding", *Social Network Analysis and Mining*, 4, March 2014.

[15]empath.stanford.edu/

[16]liwc.wpengine.com/

[17]D.B. Skillicorn and B. Simons, *A Bootstrapped Model to Detect Abuse and Intent in White Supremacist Corpora*, in: *IEEE International Conference on Intelligence and Security Informatics*, 2020.

[18]B.M. DePaulo, J.J. Lindsay, B.E. Malone, L. Muhlenbruck, K. Charlton and H. Cooper, "Cues to deception", *Psychology Bulletin*, 9:74–118, 2003; M.L. Newman, J.W. Pennebaker, D.S. Berry and J.M. Richards, "Lying words: Predicting deception from linguistic style", *Personality and Social Psychology Bulletin*, 29:665–675, 2003; L. Zhou, D.P. Twitchell, T. Qin, J.K. Burgoon and J.F. Nunamaker Jr., *An*

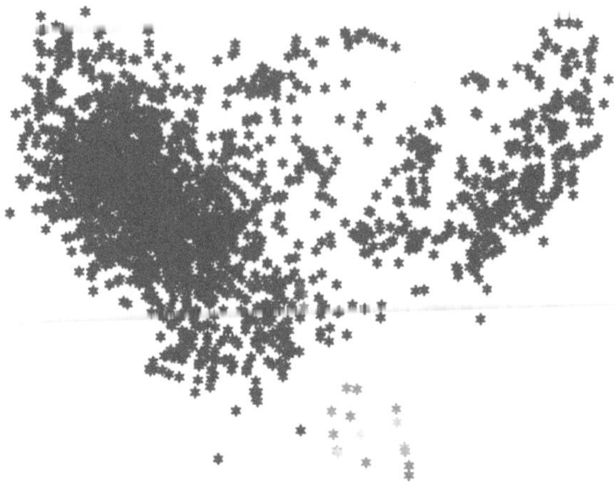

Figure 8.22: Clustering of drug samples overlaid by concentration of fructose

exploratory study into deception detection in text-based computer mediated communication, in: *Proceedings of the 36th Hawaii International Conference on Systems Science*, 2003; L. Zhou, J.K. Burgoon, D.P. Twitchell, T. Qin and J.F. Nunamaker Jr, "A comparison of classification methods for predicting deception in computer-mediated communication", *Journal of Management Information Systems*, 20(4):139–165, 2004; J.K. Burgoon, L. Hamel and T. Qin, *Predicting Veracity from Linguistic Indicators*, in: *2012 European Intelligence and Security Informatics Conference*, pp. 323–328, 2012.

[19]C.E. Lamb and D.B. Skillicorn, "Extending textual models of deception to interrogation settings", *Linguistic Evidence in Security, Law and Intelligence (LESLI)*, 1(1):13–40, December 2013.

[20]R.B. van Baaren, R.W. Holland, B. Steenaert and A. van Knippenberg, "Mimicry for money: Behavioral consequences of imitation", *Journal of Experimental Social Psychology*, 39:393–398, 2003; C. Jacob, N. Guéguen, A. Martin and G. Boulbry, "Retail salespeople's mimicry of customers: Effects on consumer behavior", *Journal of Retailing and Consumer Services*, 18:381–388, 2011.

[21]D.B. Skillicorn and L. Purda, *Detecting Fraud in Financial Reports*, in: *European Conference on Intelligence and Security Informatics*, 2012; L. Purda and D.B. Skillicorn, "Accounting variables, deception, and a bag of words: Assessing the tools of fraud detection", *Contemporary Accounting Research*, 2014.

[22]P.R. Murphy, L. Purda and D. Skillicorn, "Can fraudulent cues be transmitted by innocent participants?", *Journal of Behavioral Finance*, 19, 2018.

[23]J. Patrick, *The Scamseek Project – Text Mining for Financial Scams on the Internet*, in: *Data Mining: Proceedings of the 4th Australasian Workshop on Data Mining*, Springer LNCS 3755, pp. 295–302, 2006.

[24]N. Alsadhan, D.B. Skillicorn and R. Frank, *Comparing SVD and word2vec for analysis of malware forum posts*, in: *FOSINT 2017 Workshop at Advances in Social Network Analysis and Mining (ASONAM 2017)*, 2017.

[25]J.W. Johnsen and K. Franke, *Identifying proficient cybercriminals through text and network analysis*, in: *18th International Conference on Intelligence and Security Informatics*, 2020.

[26]J.L. Jenkins, J.G. Proudfoot, J.S. Valacich, G.M. Grimes and J.F. Nunamaker Jr, "Sleight of hand: Identifying concealed information by monitoring mouse-cursor movements", *Journal of the Association for Information Systems*, 20(1):1–32, 2019.

[27]K.C. Lee, B. Ladizinski and D.G. Federman, "Complications associated with use of levamisole-contaminated cocaine: An emerging public health challenge", *Mayo Clinic Proceedings*, 87(6):581–586, 2012.

[28]O. Kudlacek, T. Hofmaier, A. Luf, F.P. Mayer, T. Stockner, C. Nagy, M. Holy, M. Freissmuth, R. Schmid and H.H. Sitte, "Cocaine adulteration", *Journal of Chemical Neuroanatomy*, 83–84:75–81, 2017.

[29]M. Kenney, "The architecture of drug trafficking: Network forms of organisation in the Colombian cocaine trade", *Global Crime*, 8(3)233–259, 2007.

Chapter 9

Law enforcement can use interaction too

We have already seen that criminals communicate at global scale, and this has effects on the way crimes are carried out. Law enforcement can benefit from global communication as well, but it is more difficult.

There are two main impediments: inertia, and differences across jurisdictions. Crime has, until recently, been a mostly local phenomenon, with both criminals and targets contained within a single geographical area. It is taking some time to adjust, mentally and practically, to the fact that many crimes have a component that is non-local, and might be global.

Of course, law enforcement in different jurisdictions have always communicated and cooperated, but the mechanisms are typically:

- Slow, at least compared to the speed of cyberspace, often relying on phone calls or emails. Always-on communication platforms such as wikis or Slack are not in common use. This is in contrast to, say, the signals intelligence organizations within the Five Eyes, who routinely communicate new information within minutes to their peers in other countries.
- Often reliant on personal contacts to disseminate information or to ask questions. As we discussed earlier useful information is stored in databases, but access to these stores of data is often limited to personnel from the force to which they belong. Someone from another jurisdiction must interact with, and interrupt, someone else in order to formulate a query and get a response.
- Point to point, so that disseminating information widely takes a long time, and may easily miss some places where it would be relevant.

In other words, communication across jurisdictions has high friction, and therefore requires effort from everyone involved. The costs of wide communication are

DOI: 10.1201/9781003126225-9

obvious, while the benefits are more nebulous, and often asymmetric, generating work for one jurisdiction and rewards for the other.

9.1 Structured interaction through transnational organizations

Umbrella organizations, such as Europol and Interpol, were partly set up to assist with communication and information dissemination, but their mechanisms have failed to keep pace with modern communication. For example, for Interpol to issue a *Red Notice* (an international wanted person notice) a country has to have followed its usual warrant for arrest process, then notify Interpol, where a specialized task force evaluates the request, before disseminating it[1]. This is a high bar, and a process that is almost impossible to happen even at the speed of air travel, let alone the speed of the Internet. There is little information available about the time it takes to issue a Red Notice, partly because it depends on the speed of the processes of the country requesting it. An arrest or detention pursuant to a Red Notice usually requires an extradition hearing, for which the country that made the original request must provide much more information than required for the Red Notice. There can be long delays before extradition, even in clear-cut cases.

Interpol also manages other kinds of notices:

- Blue notices – locate and identify an individual;
- Green notices – warn about the activities or threats of a person;
- Yellow notices – locate and identify a missing person;
- Orange notices – warn of an imminent threat;
- Purple notices – provide information about the modi operandi of criminals;
- Black notices – seek information about unidentified bodies (John/Jane Does).

There is also a special notice that can be issued by the United Nations about someone who is subject to U.N. sanctions.

There has been considerable controversy about Interpol notices, mostly because some countries that issue them have used them in ways that do not meet the highest standards of international practice. Like many mechanisms, it is also much easier to issue a Notice than to remove one. The process of appeal by an individual who is the subject of a Red Notice is long and difficult.

Interpol also maintains databases of criminals with an international footprint, and these can be accessed by police forces in member countries. Members can issue *diffusions*, which are more informal requests for information and action. These can be circulated to all Interpol members, or only a subset, but their existence is recorded in Interpol databases, and so can be queried by any member. At present, there are about 10,000 Notices and about 50,000 diffusions issued each year.

While some kinds of crimes naturally involve international cooperation, for example drug smuggling and people trafficking, there is less awareness that many lower-level crimes, especially those in cyberspace, are international in important ways.

Part of the reason why communication across jurisdictions is limited for law enforcement is that different jurisdictions can be very different. Differences exist at a number of levels:

- The legal systems consider the same activities as serious crime in one jurisdiction, minor crime in another, and perhaps not even a crime at all in a third[2].
- Law enforcement is often given an exception to normal data-privacy rules, but because it is an exception, it has a tight local focus. Typical exceptions allow police to see data that would normally be considered private from their own environment, but not to share it with those from outside that environment. This includes law enforcement from other jurisdictions.
- Resource limits means that certain crimes considered important in one jurisdiction are necessarily considered of much lesser concern in another, even though they are illegal in both. It is hard to convince law enforcement in the jurisdiction where a crime is minor that it is worth their effort to help law enforcement in a jurisdiction that considers it much more significant.
- Even when two jurisdictions agree that a particular action is criminal, the way crimes are labeled makes it hard to work out the mappings to the criminal codes of the two jurisdictions. Notably, many cyber crimes have been, as it were, retrofitted into existing categories of crime but this has been done in different ways in different places.

  For example, deploying ransomware could be considered an offence under Section 430 of the Canadian Criminal Code (mischief), but also under Section 340 (extortion). In the U.K., ransomware is an offence under Section 3 of the Computer Misuse Act (1990!). And many countries have yet to explicitly criminalize computer misuse.

Again the contrast with signals intelligence is instructive: a new cyber threat is significant, and in the same way and with the same intensity, for every signals intelligence organization, no matter where in the world. As a result, the channels for disseminating the details of such a threat flow smoothly and quickly, at least among allies.

The same cannot be said for a new idea for a crime. The new variants of ransomware, for example, are increasing the extortion pressures associated with it, but there is no structured way to disseminate the existence of this new kind of attack rapidly and widely to all law-enforcement organizations in all countries, but they all would benefit from knowing.

9.2 Divisions within countries

In countries with federal systems of government, police force jurisdictions are often divided in complex, potentially overlapping ways. For example, in Canada the Royal Canadian Mounted Police (RCMP/GRC) act as federal police, but also as contract police forces for some provinces. Other provinces have their own police forces (for example, the Ontario Provincial Police and the Sûreté du Québec); but within those provinces both major and minor cities have their own local police forces (for example, the Toronto Police Service).

As well as these regional divisions, there are also divisions of responsibility for certain crimes. For example, the RCMP is responsible for national security, border integrity, and critical infrastructure protection; but only coordinates cybercrime across the other police forces.

In Australia, each state has its own police force that has jurisdiction in all communities in the state, while the Australian Federal Police are responsible for investigating crimes that tend to cross state boundaries such as human trafficking. Cyber crime is a federal issue if the target is government, but a state issue otherwise which guarantees huge duplication of skills and effort.

Crimes that require complex actions by criminals and have been a problem for a long time (drug and human trafficking, money laundering) have caused most jurisdictions to create first task forces, and then eventually specialist organizations with well-defined powers and responsibilities. Cybercrime is too new to have gone far down this pathway so collective action among police forces remains problematic.

From these small examples it is not clear what the lines of communication might or should be within a single country. No federal country has a system that is noticeably better than all of the others. The problem becomes even more difficult when international cooperation is required. Many countries form blocs within which cooperation is close, but many of these blocs are historical accidents, and cross cut the ways in which criminals choose to operate. Some governments are willing to provide safe haven to criminals, as long as they do not commit their crimes within those countries. One reason for doing so is that these criminals act against those countries' enemies but can be disavowed. They may even receive covert state-sponsored support. Sometimes it is just too difficult for the countries concerned to root out the criminals and they are tolerated as a nuisance.

For any particular might-be criminal issue, the people responsible in two different countries might sit in very different places in the hierarchy, and they might struggle to find one another, let alone begin a dialogue.

Communication between police forces can be considered in three categories: sharing of information about crimes and criminals; sharing of data collected by investigations and by large-scale surveillance; and sharing of data-analytic models.

9.3 Sharing of information about crimes

Police forces know a lot about the crimes committed in their jurisdictions, and data like this has been collected for more than a century.

Most are willing to share snippets of this information with other police forces. For example, query-driven approaches to data mean that another force can ask a question ("Has this person been arrested in your jurisdiction", "Have you seen a crime with these characteristics") and receive the response to an appropriate query from that jurisdiction. In other words, seeing through a window into another jurisdiction's data about crime or criminals is well-established and straightforward (once the right person to issue the query is found) – but it will usually be slow.

Sharing an entire dataset is much more problematic. Mostly, the rules that enable the collection of such data prevent it being widely shared[3].

Police forces can freely share knowledge about criminal methods with others. Intelligence gathering, for example by crawling the dark web can reveal information about new forms of crime, or old forms that look as if they may be making a comeback, and passing this information on to jurisdictions where these might be exploited helps everybody. However, there is no widespread, timely mechanism, organized mechanism for doing this, even between jurisdictions within a single country or region. Even when the underlying data cannot be shared, inferences from it are readily sharable with police in other jurisdictions but again there are few standard mechanisms.

9.4 Sharing of data

When it comes to sharing what might be called "raw data" the situation is more complex and nuanced.

First, data protection and privacy legislation may rule out come kinds of sharing and make others hard to decide. Data collected by law enforcement for the purposes of detecting and prosecuting crime is normally regarded as exceptions to privacy rules, but the exact details are often complex, and vary significantly from country to country[4]. For example, the European Union's General Data Protection Regulation contains an exemption for law enforcement. However, it is not obvious whether this exemption applies to data analytics that uses personally identifiable information unless it is directed at a particular crime. It is even more unclear if, say, data about police-involved incidents becomes part of a disciplinary process involving an officer. And the use of data such as RMS records for human-resource purposes appears not to be covered by the exemption, so that the full provisions of GDPR apply. But all of these examples have yet to be fully tested legally.

Success stories have worked around these issues by finding ways to encode the data so that it is still valuable, but is no longer personally identifiable, and so does not raise privacy issues[5].

For example, images collected during child pornography investigations are hashed, so that the image itself is converted into a string. A database of these strings can be freely shared, as can the function used for the hashing. If a new image is encountered in another jurisdiction, it can be hashed and compared to the images in the database to determine if is a new image or not. If it is not, then its previous history can help to detect child-pornography distribution networks.

Data such as local drug prices can also be freely shared, and is useful to other jurisdictions because it is an indicator of success at interdiction – prices rise when more drugs are stopped and more dealers and chemists are arrested.

Open-source data can also be freely shared. This is useful because it means that every force does not have to watch every possible online source if they know that another force will pass on anything that seems relevant to them.

Data that is collected as the result of surveillance, or other kinds of operational data, are harder to share for political, social, and practical reasons. Sometimes one force will pass a tip to another force that they have discovered some activity that they think will be of interest to the other force – either because the criminals involved are in the other force's jurisdiction or because the target is.

Scaling up this informal mechanism would enable data analytics with a greater scope. For example, different cities, states, or provinces would be able to notice common patterns, perhaps the result of the spreading of techniques among criminals. Also, of course, using larger datasets for data analytics makes it easier to see the outliers.

Some data is collected because of long-standing practices, for example taking the fingerprints or DNA of those potentially involved in a crime for elimination, or collecting information about locations and travel plans to check alibis. Other data is collected under specific judicial authorization based on a warrant, for which a probable cause bar is set higher.

The collection and retention of fingerprints and DNA is tightly controlled using rules which have been worked out relatively slowly and often with adversarial relationships with the legal system. Newer forms of data, especially data from cyberspace, do not have the same historical track record, and the framework for collecting and retaining them is correspondingly messy. For example. licence-plate capture data can be retained for periods ranging from a month to forever, depending on the jurisdiction.

The collection and retention of quasi-personal data such as IP addresses, licence plates, CCTV images and other data that comes from newish technology is still a matter for dispute, at least in part. The collection of data such as emails and texts is shoehorned into existing law about the interception of physical mail, with which it does not fit very well. This can be seen clearly in the furor about the use of "fake" cells towers which are used to collect data about criminal communication under warrant.

This uncertainty about exactly how data can be collected, used, and preserved makes it difficult for police forces in different jurisdictions to share data with one another. This simply has not been enough of an issue for there to be settled law or regulation about much of it. As a consequence, police forces are reluctant to share data because of a fear of violating some constraint that might involved them in high-profile legal wrangling.

There are also considerable practical limitations on how data can be shared. Police forces may use incompatible RMS systems; there are at least tens of different systems, and even police forces in the same country may have made different choices about which one to use. Sharing data can require a non-trivial amount of work to map the data from one format into another and, again, the work falls to one party and the benefit to the other.

Other kinds of data are also difficult to share. Should data be exported from a database to a spreadsheet (with the possibilities of corruption discussed earlier), or should a subset of the database be shared instead? Is a flat file better? Although the answers to these questions are conceptually straightforward, they cause practical difficulties and can consume inordinate staff resources on low-level work.

Another reason why data is not shared is a fear that doing so will reveal mistakes made by the sharing force. In other words, sharing data always carries potential reputation risk. Performance statistics are implicit in RMS data, and so one force can be compared to another. Data analytics may reveal issues that the force whose data they were found in may not even be aware of.

All of these issues are magnified when the sharing happens across international borders. Now, the rules about data sharing are more complex, the definitions of what constitute offences are different, the formats are even more likely to be incompatible in complex ways, and national pride is at stake.

9.5 Sharing models

Sharing the models produced by data analytics is less of a problem from a regulatory viewpoint, because they represent systems at a level above personally identifiable information. Issues of incompatibility remain and are perhaps worse.

Some kinds of models transfer from one jurisdiction to another. For example, we have seen how RMS data can be used to find geographical hot spots, and to cluster incidents. These models are built in the same way wherever they are applied (with the constraint that RMS systems differ in how they capture location data). For example, the models we built as case studies to cluster incident data, based on the inherent properties of each incident and on the locations at which they took place, are straightforward to apply to a different jurisdiction – with the exception of the Illinois criminal codes, and the fact that the geographical locations were based on an Illinois state reference point. There is pressure from the builders of RMS systems to use standardized descriptors, but many jurisdictions do not want to deal with the discontinuity between old and new systems that this creates.

Analysis of social-network data or natural-language documents can be done in the same way in different jurisdictions. For example, abusive language or intent model like the ones we looked at as case studies can be deployed across different forums, although the question of how to adapt them to other languages, especially synthetic or agglutinative languages is still very much a research question. Also even for the same base language, the patterns of informal language between, say, a U.S. forum and a U.K. forum might be moderately different.

A less obvious limitation is that each force must be capable of interpreting the results of using a model. This turns out to be a subtle issue. The early development of data analytics, in the 1990s, tried to package up model-building techniques into black boxes, so that models could be built by pressing a single button.

This did not work for two reasons. First, knowing what kind of model to build requires understanding of the domain of application, and also of the properties of the model-building algorithm itself. No algorithm will work well in every setting (but may well still produce "results") and so the person doing the analytics needs to know when the fit is wrong and the results untrustworthy. This is partly an issue of training and partly of experience.

Second, understanding the model's output requires deeper understanding than a black-box approach can provide. Each model produces slightly different results, and knowing how to interpret these as actionable takes some skill.

In these early systems, analysts used to build a model, look at its test-based performance, but be unable to take the next step and decide what to do (differently) as the result of having the model.

This issue means that the usefulness of building a model in one jurisdiction and then giving it to other jurisdictions is limited, unless that jurisdiction already has the expertise to interpret it.

9.6 International issues

The international scope of crime raises particular issues that increase the pressure to share, despite the difficulties.

For crimes that take place in, or leverage, cyberspace, it is increasingly unlikely that the criminal is in the same country, let along the same jurisdiction, as the victim. Attempting to investigate, let alone prosecute, such a crime within a single jurisdiction is doomed to failure. Increasingly, investigation and prosecution are not workable from a single-jurisdiction perspective.

Different nations have always had an ambivalent attitude to sharing information related to crime. On the one hand, Westphalian principles, the touchstone of international relations, say that each nation is solely in control of what happens inside its own borders. On the other hand, there have always been transnational crimes and criminals who moved across borders to try and evade capture.

We have already discussed the mechanisms for international warrants and extradition via Interpol. Some countries have provisions for hot pursuit by officers of one country into the territory of an adjoining country, for example Brazil and Paraguay, or the countries of the Schengen region in Europe. Under these rules, officers are typically limited to detaining a suspect until local officers arrive, but the exact details of how much violence they may use to restrain the suspect are rarely clear.

These hot-pursuit rules have historically been based on geography – officers can pursue into an adjacent country, but flying to a distant country does not count as "hot" pursuit. In one sense this is reasonable; getting to a distant country takes enough time that there is potentially a window to involve the law enforcement of that country. However, travel times continue to decrease, so that this window might be less than an hour in many parts of the world.

A wider use a hot pursuit has been invoked in the past few decades because of the rise of non-state actors (violent extremist groups)[6]. Many countries have launched operations into the territory of another (the U.S. in Afghanistan, Turkey in Iraq, India in Myanmar); these are often impossible to characterize as purely military or purely policing because they have elements of both.

Complexity is added because privacy regulations such as GDPR apply to the data of E.U. citizens wherever in the world they are. So a police force that monitors the activities of E.U.-based criminals taking place outside the E.U. has to take into account the protections afforded by GDPR. Few local police forces have the capacity even to consider such issues.

The balance between national sovereignty and mutual cooperation has always been variable across the world. Not all pairs of countries have extradition treaties; and many might give lip service to sharing information on crime and criminals but do not do so, perhaps as an expression of national pride, because they cannot afford the resources, or because it might show their incompetence.

The problem of prosecuting crimes that are committed in one jurisdiction by criminals in another is still open. Extradition of the criminal to the jurisdiction where the crime was committed is the standard mechanism, but when some countries do not allow extradition they become magnets for criminals committing long-range crimes.

The U.S. has tried a name and shame approach, where they indict those they believe to have committed long-range crimes, knowing that there is no realistic possibility of prosecuting them. This, of course, shames the country providing them protection as well but, so far, this has produced little result.

There have been some success stories in areas such as human trafficking and money laundering, but others areas such as drug trafficking have remained stubbornly difficult. Part of the problem is that criminals are able to move their operations from jurisdiction to jurisdiction whenever one becomes more difficult to operate in. The problem is global and the solution will have to be global.

The whole area of the clash between nationally based law enforcement and international, mobile criminals is still developing, as nationals realize that the modes of operation of the past century must adapt to not only a global village, but one that exists substantially in borderless cyberspace.

Notes

[1]There are signs that some countries do the minimal amount to follow their own processes, wait for some other country to make an arrest pursuant to a Red Notice, and only then actually construct the case necessary for an extradition. This brings the entire process into disrepute, makes Interpol's decision to actually issue a Red Notice more difficult, and puts the arresting country in a difficult position.

[2]An interesting case is the U.K.'s National Police Computer system which shares information about people and objects of interest between the U.K. and the Schengen area of Europe. As the U.K. exits the E.U. the way in which this sharing happens will presumably have to change, and in the direction of making sharing more difficult.

[3]This also prevents academic research on law-enforcement data.

[4]And this is normally further complicated because privacy legislation is a moving target in many countries as they try to catch up to the impact of cyberspace on personally identifiable information.

[5]A note of caution: it is almost impossible to deidentify data that has several attributes. Although any particular attribute might have a wide range of values, the number of records with a particular combination of values is almost inevitably small. Knowing just a few attribute values may be enough to identify the record. This problem has bedevilled census statistics for a century – knowing that a family has six children is enough to uniquely identify them in almost any census tract. An individual computer can be almost completely identified by web sites based on the its version of the operating system, browser, and browser addons even though it seems like there cannot be all that many permutations of these properties.

[6]L.M. Beehner, "A means of first resort: Explaining "hot pursuit" in international relations", *Security Studies*, 27(3):379–409, 2018.

Chapter 10
Summary

Two technological changes have altered the face of policing and related areas such as national security, financial regulation, and border control. The first change is the growth of cyberspace. Up to, say, 1990 cyberspace was a platform used by governments and academics for communication. The development of the World Wide Web changed it into a way to access all of the world's information, and encouraged businesses and, more slowly, governments to make their organizational knowledge available on web sites. The development of ways to change browsers from passive receivers of knowledge into active ways to post content and interact with businesses, governments, and with others has made cyberspace the place where knowledge, action, and socializing all happen. As such, it is a core service almost everywhere; and some would argue critical infrastructure, and so access to it a right. This has been realized even more strongly as the 2020–21 pandemic forced online interaction in ways that might otherwise have taken a decade.

The second technological change is the development of data analytics as a way to understand complex systems. From the Enlightenment, rigorous ways to understand natural systems were based on controlled experiments, but these are limited to systems that we can carefully control (who gets the drug and who gets the placebo) and experiments to test hypotheses that clever people must imagine in the first place. In contrast, data analytics enables natural experiments, in which systems are not manipulated, but just observed. Models are built that try to explain underlying properties of the system that are consistent with the observations. The role of the person trying to understand the system is to select from among the most plausible models those that seem most explanatory, and these are taken as explanations of its inner workings[1]. In a law-enforcement context, this means that forensic, consequential results from data analytics are less common than intelligence results, providing insights or hints about the operation of the system being considered, usually a crime of some kind.

DOI: 10.1201/9781003126225-10

Developments in both technologies are rapid. While most law-enforcement personnel have some knowledge of these areas, it is hard to see the big picture, and to know which areas are, or may soon be, the most useful. This book has tried to provide the right kind of background for frontline policing, for data analysts within law enforcement, and for management.

All of us use cyberspace, probably every day, but the view as an individual user does not reveal much about its inner workings. Some understanding of these workings is important to understand the impact of cyberspace on crime. After all it is the nature of crime to use the non-obvious features of any environment.

Cyberspace consists of a set of nodes (computers, phones, web servers, clouds but less obviously switches, printers, and Internet of Things devices such as doorbells and earbuds). These nodes can be divided into those that are human-facing (computers, phones, printers), those that are in the core of the Internet (web servers, clouds), and the nodes that control the movement of data at all scales (network switches, cell towers). All of these nodes use one of only a few different substrates (processors – Intel, AMD, ARM – and operating systems – Windows, iOS, Linux) because it is easier to implement different functionalities in software than to build many different forms of specialized hardware. This monoculture means that a way to manipulate or attack one node is also automatically a way to manipulate or attack many millions of other nodes. The use of monocultures means that cyberspace is fragile, but the economics drives monocultures anyway.

These nodes are connected by pipes that move the data between them. The pipes ranges from the high-capacity undersea cables that move data between land masses, to the wifi within offices and homes, down to the Bluetooth connection between a phone and a set of earbuds or the momentary connection between a phone and a purchase terminal. All pipes are just data movers, so that all of the control of exactly how data of different kinds is moved (how it is encoded, how fast it can be passed, and so on) must be done by the nodes at the ends. Since the same pipes are used in many different contexts, and the rules about how to use them must be understood by many different nodes, they are another monoculture, with the same risks.

The need for backwards compatibility means that it is impossible to upgrade the basic infrastructure. When changes have been wanted or needed they have been built on top of this basic infrastructure, creating a baroque structure of *ad hoc* and often rickety superstructure.

These nodes and pipes together form what we have called cyberspace which connects every country in the world, and about half of its population. However, it is useful to think of it as consisting of two distinct parts, based on which set of communication rules are used. The first consists of the hard-wired connections, wifi, and the various short-range connections that developed from the original Arpanet, and inherits its modes of operation. The second is the collection of wireless cellphone networks which have the same functionality but achieve it in a different way. Because this part of cyberspace is privately owned, it can in principle be upgraded by design, but there are still many constraints, and cell-networks are mostly pipes rather than nodes.

Not every computer is connected to cyberspace directly. Some organizations, primarily military, run so-called air-gapped networks in which the computers are connected to one another within the network, but not to the larger Internet. Such network use the same node and pipe technologies and rules as the rest of cyberspace, so if a way can be found to reach them, they are vulnerable in the same way as the rest of cyberspace (and despite the best efforts of their owners, they are often breached, perhaps because their separation encourages complacency).

Cyberspace is used for many things in which people are not directly involved (large computations, for example), but the main interface to cyberspace for most people is the World Wide Web, accessed via a browser. The WWW is a bipartite system, with users and their web browsers on one side, and web servers on the other, connected by pipes. When the Web was invented, browsers were passive displayers of content, but they are now extremely interactive. This interactivity has become a conduit for many useful activities but also makes the WWW a major target for criminals.

Most web sites are available to everyone, but there are two parts of the Web (and partly of cyberspace as well) that have limited access. The first is the deep web which consists of those pages that exist only transiently, for example when someone logs into their Amazon account and looks at their purchases.

The second is the dark web, a set of web servers that are accessible to all but via a mechanism that obscures the connection between each browser (and its user) and the web site. The most common part of the dark web consists of special web sites that can only be accessed via the Tor routing system, which bounces traffic randomly between a set of intermediate nodes, before sending it on to its final destination. Dark-web web sites will only accept incoming traffic from Tor routing nodes.

The dark web is a place for dissidents, but also for criminals to talk, plan, buy and sell. Their actions may be observable, but (in theory at least) these actions cannot be tied to the browser that is doing them.

Cyberspace was designed for a simpler environment, and just grew into what we have today. It was originally designed to be highly distributed, and so there is no overall control of any of its aspects. Global decisions are made, fractiously, by a loose consortium of governments, owners of infrastructure, large platform owners, businesses that have a stake in its operation, and ordinary citizens.

Many sensible changes that would improve usability or security would have to be agreed by everyone, and implemented simultaneously, and this complexity has so far defeated any but incremental changes. Even these incremental changes do not necessarily move in a consistent direction. For example, in 2021 many browser designers, as well as large Internet businesses, are trying to find a way to protect individual user's data even though access to such data is one of the main ways that businesses monetize their web presence. There are a variety of proposals, most of which are at least partially incompatible.

There are a number of impacts from the existence and structure of cyberspace. Most obvious is its scale and reach. Many of its users do not have anything more than a rudimentary grasp of geography, and yet can reach anywhere and a serious fraction of everyone (which is part of the reason why spam is a problem).

Cyberspace contains a large fraction of the world's knowledge. Not all of this knowledge is accessible to everyone. Important parts such as academic research and some kinds of news are sequestered behind paywalls. Finding knowledge relies on the use of search engines, and these are increasingly being distorted by the search-engine businesses who are trying to drive users towards pages that benefit them (and so not necessarily where those users wanted to go). So some of the world's knowledge is becoming increasingly difficult to find.

Cyberspace also contains much of the world's data because connecting data repositories to cyberspace makes them accessible remotely. This means that businesses can interact with their customers directly, and that their staff can continue to work even when they are remote. This is a problem for law enforcement because this data is valuable. Unlike the world's knowledge, the data held by a business includes intellectual property, trade secrets, development plans, current sales, and personnel information. Making such data available to their collaborating businesses, staff, and customers by making it available in cyberspace also makes it at least potentially available to criminals.

Another property of cyberspace that is important for law enforcement is the speed of action and interaction. Email and texts means that criminals can communicate with one another quickly, including in rich ways that include photos, videos, and recordings. Criminal activities that use cyberspace can happen quickly and at scale: sending a scam or phishing email, transferring funds in the financial system, or altering a plan because of noticing some action by law enforcement.

Cyberspace does not respect national borders, so criminals can live in one place, launch a criminal activity in another, and have it have its effect in yet another. This makes investigation and prosecution difficult because the rules are typically different in all three places, and they may be far apart, with different cultures and languages.

As well, the connection structure of cyberspace does not respect the surface of the earth. Many law-enforcement organizations have developed close working relationships with their neighboring countries, and not so close ones with countries further away. They have trouble adjusting when they suddenly have to interact with law-enforcement organizations that are geographically far away. Many supra-national organizations are based on geography as well (for example, the European Union) but these often crosscut the relationships required for investigation and prosecution.

Law-enforcement organizations face a special problem because of the differences between countries, and sometimes within the same country. First, legal systems differ both macroscopically and microscopically, so that what constitutes a crime can vary from one jurisdiction to another. Second, what constitutes an acceptable investigation process can also differ (for example, from common law to

Napoleonic legal systems). Third, administrative boundaries inevitably create friction for any kind of collaboration, from sharing information to working together. Fourth, data formats differ between jurisdictions so that, even with the best will, there are practical low-level impediments to sharing information.

Cyberspace originated in a system in which all of those involved were trusted, or at least subject to organizational sanctions if they misbehaved. As a result, security was never prioritized in designing what became the Internet, and its subsequent explosive growth and diversification has similarly prioritized the next great thing over increasing security. Security is not the kind of property that can be retrofitted easily, so the improvements that have been made are piecemeal and weak.

Because the original users were trusted, identification and authentication were not prioritized either. As a result, matching an identity in cyberspace to an actual person is extremely difficult. Even matching an action in cyberspace to the device that instigated it is difficult. The problem for law enforcement is that attribution of a crime to the criminal who did it is problematic, and even then devices can always be reported as stolen or hacked.

It is typical of law-enforcement settings that there is an asymmetry between attack and defence. Criminals need only succeed in one way, but the defenders (both targets and law enforcement) are expected to succeed against every attempt at a crime. The scale and speed of crimes committed leveraging cyberspace makes this asymmetry much more impactful.

The design of cyberspace means that all of the traffic that passes through switches is visible to them and, as a result, visible in principle to other nodes as well. The only way to hide content from a completely public gaze is to encrypt it. However, this does not protect the patterns of communication themselves (who is talking to whom, when, how often, and how much). These patterns cannot be concealed because the switches need to know where to send each new piece of information.

Encryption hides the content of communication from anyone who does not have a decryption key. Encryption is a two-edged sword because it hides legitimate communications, but also the communications of criminals and violent extremists. There is nothing that can be done about this; the regularly repeated discussions about ways to make only criminal communications accessible to law enforcement are completely unworkable.

Although encryption protects data "in flight" (as it moves) and "at rest" (when it is stored), it must be decrypted in order to interact with it. If the data is valuable, then this should only be done in a safe space, on computers protected from unauthorized access[2].

Maintaining such safe spaces is difficult because of the numerous possible ways to intrude illegally. The easiest way to get access to a safe space is with the unwitting collusion of one of those with legitimate access to it, using phishing or spearphishing to place malware within it. This malware can then open the metaphorical door to illegal access. Safe spaces can also be accessed by direct cyber attacks, using the pipes themselves to introduce malware without any user involvement. This is substantially more difficult and has, so far, primarily been the domain of state-based groups.

One of the successes of cyberspace is that so much of it is invisible to its users. The average person using their web browser to do their banking or to purchase something online is aware of only a small fraction of the infrastructure and activities that make this possible. One of the side effects, however, is that crimes are more invisible. Steal my wallet and I will find out quickly; steal from my bank account and I may not notice for weeks. Send me a phishing email, and I may not notice that it installed malware for a similarly long time (if ever). This means that when law enforcement finds out about a crime in cyberspace, the trail is often already cold.

The legal environment within which crimes involving cyberspace are named and prosecuted also has difficulty keeping up with the rapidly changing technical possibilities. Legislators are not often technically aware, and so cannot assess how to frame criminal behavior in cyberspace, nor to estimate its seriousness. Judges face similar issues, both in the issuing of warrants and the trying of defendants. Rather than creating new offences for crimes involving cyberspace, many countries have put cybercrimes into categories that were designed for crimes in the physical world.

The existence of cyberspace has changed the face of crime. First, there are new crimes that exist only because cyberspace exists. These include: destruction of online structures such as web pages, extortion based on ransomware or denial of service attacks, theft of data such as intellectual property or personally identifiable information, identity theft, and online worldwide sales of illegal tools, physical and software-based. These all have analogues in traditional crimes, but they are crimes in cyberspace, not because of cyberspace.

Second, there are crimes that are qualitatively different because they happen in cyberspace. These include: spam, scams, financial crime, pornography (especially involving children), and theft leveraging online shopping. These differ from their traditional versions because they have greater range and speed.

Third, there are crimes that are, in a way, conventional but are more convenient to carry out in cyberspace. These include disseminating hatred, stalking, and digital vigilantism.

The existence of cyberspace has also changed the way in which the value produced from a crime is concealed so that it can be used safely. The cash economy is dying out as the use of cards increases. There are still crimes where cash is used for anonymity, but they are shrinking as cryptocurrency begins to replace them, or where online illegal businesses can masquerade as legitimate ones and accept cards themselves. This simplifies the money laundering problem for criminals since they no longer have to worry about converting cash into value in the financial system. However, financial-system transactions are (in principle) trackable so the role of layering has increased. Money laundering as a service is becoming increasingly popular because it breaks the link between the proceeds and the crime that produced them, a necessary part of the offence. At present, law enforcement is losing the upper hand in detecting money laundering. Unexplained wealth orders look like a workable solution, but they require a change in perspective because they reverse the burden of proof.

Because cyberspace reaches everywhere it is available for interaction among criminals. This includes finding other criminals with special skills and knowledge, learning techniques and skills, and finding and purchasing tools.

The second technological change that is changing policing is the development of data analytics. While the ability to act in cyberspace gives an advantage to criminals, the existence of data analytics provides law enforcement with a huge advantage – if they can leverage it well.

Data analytics involves building models of systems based on the outwardly observable data about them. In a law-enforcement context, the systems of interest are either particular crimes, or the activities and relationships of criminals. For a particular crime, the observable data includes the scene, interviews with witnesses and victims, forensic evidence, and alibis. The actual underlying system is who committed the crime and how they did it. A model of the system must explain all of the observable data, but that does not necessarily mean that the model has actually discovered the crime (although it may have)[3].

For the activities and relationships among criminals, the goal is a model that helps to understand the system. Again the model must be consistent with the observable data, but its internal structure is one plausible explanation of the observed system.

There are two different kinds of models. Clustering models place the observations in groups, clusters, that make it possible to see the similarities between groups of observations rather than just the similarities between observations. These clusters often suggest higher-level structure that can be understood in the context of a crime or crimes – there are a set of burglaries that all happen in this particular area between midnight and 2 a.m., for example. Humans are good at detecting these kinds of patterns, but they perform poorly when the data is large or the similarity between observations are subtle, and data-analytic algorithms can help here.

Clustering can also be a useful tool to demonstrate compliance by showing that police actions are consistent with the clusters detected. For example, response times to an incident tend to be proportional to how far they occur from typical patrol locations. Clustering by time and distance can show that there are few anomalies, and so response times are what they should be.

The second kind of model is used for prediction. Such models learn, from historical data, how outcomes depend on observables of the system. They can therefore be used to predict what outcome is likely given a new set of observables. Predictive data-analytic models are part of a move towards policing that is more proactive, that is not just solving crimes as they happen but working to reduce the rate at which crimes happen. Predictive models that can predict actual crimes ("Col. Mustard in the library with a candlestick") are totally implausible, but the *risk* of crimes in particular places at particular times can plausibly be predicted. Predictions can be based on properties such as place (geographical location), time, weather, people who might commit a particular crime, and the social and social-network position of those involved.

In predicting risk, a critical property is that almost all risks are skewed, often extremely so. Statistical models of crime are perhaps not helpful for deciding on responses to risks because properties such as averages conceal the effect of skew. Paying attention to skew allows the prediction of low-hanging fruit, activities where a small intervention can have a large effect on crime rates.

Another advantage of predictive models is that many of them provide a ranked list of the attributes, ranked by their contribution to the overall prediction. This provides a great deal of understanding of which observables are having an effect on the outcome; and this understanding can often be directly leveraged. For example, it may be possible to tell how to alter an environment to make it more resistant to crime, or how to hire to make a police force more effective.

However, the risk of crime in a particular setting depends on microscale properties of the setting. Existing attempts to predict risk have tended to use much more macroscale properties and so, as we have seen, they tend not to be reliable at predicting risk. There is an opportunity to collect better microscale data, perhaps from RMS incidents, and try to build better performing models.

Social networks capture information about relationships and so are important ways of understanding how criminals function within their environment, and also how they act together to commit crimes. Most clustering and predictive models are applied to data consisting of records, each with values for a set of attributes, but social networks require different analysis techniques.

Social networks have the same properties of skew that we have seen in other contexts: the significant parts of a social network, no matter how we think of "significant", are only a small part of the whole network. Within a social network of criminals, those who are responsible for the most crime will tend to be small islands of connected nodes; and the risk of being a victim of gunshot violence also tends to concentrate in small islands within the network. As usual, this provides low-hanging fruit for law-enforcement attention.

The edges of social networks usually model relationships, but many properties act as if they flow along these edges: risk of being the target of violence, influence, drug use, and attitudes. In other words, a relationship is not just a connection but a conduit.

The structure of the social network as a whole reveals properties of individual nodes and regions that are not visible at the level of individual nodes and edges. For example, properties such as centrality and betweenness capture how important each node is in the entire social network, and correlate with ideas of importance (and so reasonable investigation targets) within the group that the social network represents.

Criminals tend not to form the same structures that are observed in ordinary social networks. For example, criminal social networks contain fewer triangles than ordinary networks; but the command and control of a criminal group tend to participate in triangles for functional reasons. Looking for the triangles can help find which members of a group are running it.

We can also look for subnetworks in a social network, but this is a subtly difficult problem because a social network is the union of many overlapping subnetworks. One exception is the social networks of criminal organizations that have functionally differentiated subgroups, for example drug and human trafficking networks.

All of this data analytics requires collecting data, both about criminals themselves, and about ordinary citizens. There are two main reasons why data has to be captured about non-criminals. First, it allow data-analytic modeling of what normality looks like, which makes it easier to detect and understand abnormality. Second, it may not be possible to separate data about criminals from data about everyone else until after the data has been collected and analyzed[4].

Ordinary citizens are wary about data collection by law-enforcement and intelligence organizations. Which particular forms of data collection will trigger suspicion and pushback are difficult to predict, and vary from country to country; as will the arguments that are advanced for why a particular form of data collection is improper. Part of this is the result of citizens drawing a mental line from data collection, to suspicion, to tainting.

Law-enforcement organizations that are planning to collect new forms of data, or older forms at larger scale, should think carefully about the rationale for doing so, and be prepared to defend it carefully and non-defensively. Data collection that seems like an obvious benefit to law enforcement may seem anything but to ordinary citizens.

Some data is collected in small quantities and under warrant. Such data collection is usually not problematic, since it is widely understood that this is only allowed by demonstrating a basis for suspicion. However, there can be public resentment if the warrant-granting process is seen to be unfair or to be used improperly, or if the collection of data from a particular target also captures data about neighboring (physically or in cyberspace) people.

High-volume data is almost always more problematic. This is partly because of the "collection equals suspicion" feeling that many have. Data captured from CCTV or body cams do not seem to cause problems for citizens, perhaps because they have become used to video surveillance, and perhaps because they sense that not much analysis can be done with it. The resistance to facial recognition systems suggests that this latter is the most important issue.

Data from cyberspace is more difficult. Many people do not realize what can and is being collected, and there is often outcry when they do realize. In cyberspace it is difficult, perhaps impossible, to collect data only from targets so the data collection is inherently wider than it, in theory, could be.

One of the difficult problems with data collection at present is how to fuse data of qualitatively different kinds into forms that are meaningful to those using the data-analytic systems. Current systems can do this for queries – a query about, say, a person using their name as an identifier will often produce all of the information known about that person, their actions, relationships, vehicles, and belongings in one single framework. But we do not know how to integrate fusion into data-analytic systems well. This is partly because the data about two people will have different content, and so it is hard to do even simple things like decide how similar they are.

Bias can be an issue at every stage of data analytics: data collection, modeling itself, and use of the outputs. The problem of bias is that the difference between the real world and what is being represented is systematically wrong, usually too simple. There is no straightforward way to detect bias, so those who design and implement data-analytics pipelines must be conscious, at every stage, of the possibility of bias and actively work to minimize it.

Data analytics produces four main kinds of models. A clustering provides understanding of a system based on the similarities among the observables of the system, and so draws attention when there are groups of occurrences or people that resemble one another, without having to think of the reasons they might be similar in advance. A predictor provides a mapping between observables and outcomes. As we have said, the outcomes of interest in law enforcement are almost always assessments of risk or, symmetrically, advantage. An anomaly detector points out the observations of a system that are not consistent with the rest of the system. Since crimes are not the usual behavior of society, and criminals do not behave as others, anomaly detectors can highlight criminal activity, even in large datasets. A ranking is a form of regression-based predictor that orders observations by the intensity of some property that they exhibit. This enables resources to be concentrated on the parts of a system where the rewards are the greatest.

Data analytics is a new way of viewing complex systems. Making the results of data analytics actionable is limited by the cognitive change required to take inductive modeling seriously, and by the normal resistance to change in any organization. Data-analytic modeling extends activities carried out by law-enforcement personnel that are common but not well-codified – the intuition that many officers have gained from long experience, and the training which is based on experience but not necessarily based on solid data. The role of data analytics in workflows is therefore subtle, since the workflow component that it enhances is not explicitly recognized in many law-enforcement contexts.

One of the biggest advantages that criminals have over law enforcement is that smarter criminals can be part of a world-wide fraternity that can easily share all kinds of information, quickly and easily. In contrast, law enforcement works in silos defined by the administrative choices of each country and region, and each country's legal system. Interaction is possible across silos, but there is considerable friction in doing so. Any request for information costs the jurisdiction being asked (time, effort) but advantages the jurisdiction doing the asking. This asymmetry always make sharing difficult, and will only improve when information can be made available in shared repositories. Then any jurisdiction can access it directly without requiring the effort of an intermediary. Jurisdictions that shelter their data from their own frontline personnel behind a groups of analysts will not be able to make the data sharable with those from other jurisdictions.

The ease with which information can be shared differs depending on what kind of information it is. Sharing individual facts is typically straightforward. Once the volume increases, sharing becomes more problematic, and sharing of entire repositories is typically impossible, both for legal/political reasons, and for practical ones such as differences in formats. Sharing models should be easier, because they contain less personally identifiable information, but it is still rare; a part of this is that it requires skill to interpret models, and a model developed in one context may be hard to understand in another.

Those who work in law-enforcement will be aware of some of the changes that the existence and widespread use of cyberspace have made to policing and intelligence. Perhaps fewer are aware of the changes that data analytics is making to policing. This book has tried to fill in the gaps and at least provide a starting point for deeper exploration.

Notes

[1]Although this might seem like a lower standard than "conventional" science, science also makes no claim that its models are true, simply the best approximation to truth known at the moment. So Newton's Laws (really theories or models) of motion were approximations that were serviceable for three hundred years. By 1900, a growing list of exceptions had been detected and had to await Einstein's theories of relativity for a more accurate model of motion.

[2]Interaction without decryption is possible, for example using homomorphic encryption, but it is expensive, slow, and limited.

[3]Agatha Christie used to come up with scenarios in which all of the observable data was consistent with more than one actual system, and so with more than one perpetrator. Her skill was to make the systems incrementally more complex so that skillful readers were more likely to choose the more complex solutions – but few readers actually found the system that was revealed by Poirot or Marple.

[4]Bible, Matthew 13:24–43.

Bibliography

N. Alsadhan and D.B. Skillicorn, *Estimating Personality from Social Media Posts*, in: *SENTIRE Workshop, IEEE ICDM 2017*, 2017.

N. Alsadhan, D.B. Skillicorn and R. Frank, *Comparing SVD and word2vec for analysis of malware forum posts*, in: *FOSINT 2017 Workshop at Advances in Social Network Analysis and Mining (ASONAM 2017)*, 2017.

L.M. Beehner, "A means of first resort: Explaining "hot pursuit" in international relations", *Security Studies*, 27(3):379–409, 2018.

A.A. Braga, A.V. Papachristos and D.M. Hureau, "The concentration and stability of gun violence at micro places in Boston, 1980–2008", *Journal of Quantitative Criminology*, 26:33–53, 2010..

P.L. Brantingham and P.J. Brantingham, *Environment, Routine, and Situation: Toward a Pattern Theory of Crime*, in: *From Routine Activity and Rational Choice: Advances in Criminological Theory*, volume 5, pp. 259–294. Routledge, 1993..

J.K. Burgoon, L. Hamel and T. Qin, *Predicting Veracity from Linguistic Indicators*, in: *2012 European Intelligence and Security Informatics Conference*, pp. 323–328, 2012.

M. Campobasso and L. Allodi, "Impersonation-as-a-service: Characterizing the emerging criminal infrastructure for user impersonation at scale", Technical report, arXiv:2009. 04344v1, 2020.

K.M. Carley, M.M. Malik, P.M. Landwehr, J. Pfeffer and M. Kowalchuck, "Crowd sourcing disaster management: The complex nature of Twitter usage in Padang Indonesia", *Safety Science*, 90:48–61, December 2016.

S. Carton, J. Helsby, K. Joseph, A. Mahmud, Y. Park, J. Walsh, C. Cody, E. Patterson, L. Haynes and R. Ghani, *Identifying Police Officers at Risk of Adverse Events*, in: *KDD '16*, 10pp, 2016.

N.A. Christakis and J.H. Fowler, "The spread of obesity in a large social network over 32 years", *New England Journal of Medicine*, 357:370–379, 2007.

N.A. Christakis and J.H. Fowler, *Connected: The Surprising Power of Our Social Networks and How They Shape Our Lives – How Your Friends' Friends' Friends Affect Everything You Feel, Think, and Do*, Little Brown, 2009.

F.R.K. Chung, *Spectral Graph Theory*, Number 92 in CBMS Regional Conference Series in Mathematics. American Mathematical Society, 1997.

L.E. Cohen and M. Felson, "Social change and crime rate trends: A routine activity approach", *American Sociological Review*, 44(4):588–608, August 1979..

K. Chen, D. Skillicorn, X. Li, "Reversing the asymmetry in data exfiltration", *CoRR*, abs/1809.04648, 2018.

B.M. DePaulo, J.J. Lindsay, B.E. Malone, L. Muhlenbruck, K. Charlton and H. Cooper, "Cues to deception", *Psychology Bulletin*, 9:74–118, 2003.

"Designing out crime", Design & Technology Alliance against Crime, 2015.

C. Frydensberg, B. Arial and M. Bland, "Targeting the most harmful co-offenders in Denmark: a social network analysis approach", *Cambridge Journal of Evidence-Based Policing*, 3:21–36, 2019.

H. Goldstein, *Problem-Oriented Policing*, Temple University Press, 1990..

J.E. Hoover, "Criminal identification", *The Annals of the American Academy of Political and Social Science*, 146:205–213, 1929.

C. Jacob, N. Guéguen, A. Martin and G. Boulbry, "Retail salespeople's mimicry of customers: Effects on consumer behavior", *Journal of Retailing and Consumer Services*, 18:381–388, 2011.

M. Jain, J. Tsai, J. Pita, C. Kiekintveld, S. Rathi, M. Tambe and F. Ordò nez, "Software assistants for randomized patrol planning for the LAX Airport Police and the Federal Air Marshal Service", *Interfaces*, 40:267–290, July–August 2010.

J.L. Jenkins, J.G. Proudfoot, J.S. Valacich, G.M. Grimes and J.F. Nunamaker Jr, "Sleight of hand: Identifying concealed information by monitoring mouse-cursor movements", *Journal of the Association for Information Systems*, 20(1):1–32, 2019.

J.W. Johnsen and K. Franke, *Identifying proficient cybercriminals through text and network analysis*, in: *18th International Conference on Intelligence and Security Informatics*, 2020.

K.C. Lee, B. Ladizinski and D.G. Federman, "Complications associated with use of levamisole-contaminated cocaine: An emerging public health challenge", *Mayo Clinic Proceedings*, 87(6):581–586, 2012.

N.K. Katyal, "Architecture as crime control", *Yale Law Journal*, pp. 1046–1149, 2002.

M. Kenney, "The architecture of drug trafficking: Network forms of organisation in the Colombian cocaine trade", *Global Crime*, 8(3)233–259, 2007.

O. Kudlacek, T. Hofmaier, A. Luf, F.P. Mayer, T. Stockner, C. Nagy, M. Holy, M. Freissmuth, R. Schmid and H.H. Sitte, "Cocaine adulteration", *Journal of Chemical Neuroanatomy*, 83–84:75–81, 2017.

C.E. Lamb and D.B. Skillicorn, "Extending textual models of deception to interrogation settings", *Linguistic Evidence in Security, Law and Intelligence (LESLI)*, 1(1):13–40, December 2013.

L. Lessig, *The laws of cyberspace*, in: R.A. Spinello and H.T. Tavani, (eds.), *Readings in Cyberethics*, pp. 134–145. Jones & Bartlett Learning, 2004..

C. Leuprecht and A. Aulthouse, "Guns for hire: North America's intra-continental gun trafficking networks", *Criminology, Criminal Justice, Law & Society*, 15:57–74, 2014.

B. Loveluck, "The many shades of digital vigilantism. A typology of online self-justice", *Global Crime*, 21(3–4):213–241, 2020.

U. Luxburg, "A tutorial on spectral clustering", *Statistics and Computing*, 17(4):395–416, December 2007.

J. Martin, *Drugs on the Dark Net: How Cryptomarkets are Transforming the Global Trade in Illicit Drugs*, Palgrave Macmillan, 2014.

S. Milgram, "The small world problem", *Psychology Today*, 1:61, 1967.

C. Morselli and K. Petit, "Law-enforcement disruption of a drug importation network", *Global Crime*, 8:109–130, 2007.

R. Munksgaard, D. Décary-Hétu, A. Malm and A. Nouvian, "Distributing tobacco in the dark: assessing the regional structure and shipping patterns of illicit tobacco in cryptomarkets", *Global Crime*, 22:1:1–21, 2021.

R. Murataya and D.R. Gutiérrez, "Effects of weather on crime", *International Journal of Humanities and Social Science*, 3:71–75, 2013.

P.R. Murphy, L. Purda and D. Skillicorn, "Can fraudulent cues be transmitted by innocent participants?", *Journal of Behavioral Finance*, 19, 2018.

M.L. Newman, J.W. Pennebaker, D.S. Berry and J.M. Richards, "Lying words: Predicting deception from linguistic style", *Personality and Social Psychology Bulletin*, 29:665–675, 2003.

O. Newman, "Architectural design for crime prevention", Institute of Planning and Housing, New York University, 1973.

B. Nick, C. Lee, P. Cunningham and U. Brandes, *Simmelian Backbones: Amplifying Hidden Homophily in Facebook Networks*, in: *Proceedings of Advances in Social Network Analysis and Modelling ASONAM, ACM & IEEE*, August 2013.

A.V. Papachristos, "Murder by structure: Dominance relations and the social structure of gang homicide", *American Journal of Sociology*, 115:74–128, 2009.

A.V. Papachristos, A.A. Braga and D.M. Hureau, "Social networks and the risk of gunshot injury", *Journal of Urban Health*, 89:992–1003, 2012.

A.V. Papachristos, A.A. Braga, E. Piza and L.S. Grossman, "The company you keep? the spillover effects of gang membership on individual gunshot victimization in a co-offending network", *Criminology*, 53:624–649, 2015.

J. Patrick, *The Scamseek Project – Text Mining for Financial Scams on the Internet*, in: *Data Mining: Proceedings of the 4th Australasian Workshop on Data Mining*, Springer LNCS 3755, pp. 295–302, 2006.

L. Purda and D.B. Skillicorn, "Accounting variables, deception, and a bag of words: Assessing the tools of fraud detection", *Contemporary Accounting Research*, 2014.

M. Reichhoff, "The effect of weather on crime: An investigation of weather and annual crime rates", Speciale, University of Wisconsin Whitewater, 2017..

L.W. Sherman, "Repeat calls to police in Minneapolis", Technical Report 4, Crime Control Reports, Crime Control Institute, Washington D.C., 1987..

D.B. Skillicorn and B. Simons, *A Bootstrapped Model to Detect Abuse and Intent in White Supremacist Corpora*, in: *IEEE International Conference on Intelligence and Security Informatics*, 2020.

D.B. Skillicorn, Q. Zhen and C. Morselli, "Modeling dynamic social networks using spectral embedding", *Social Network Analysis and Mining*, 4, March 2014.

D.B. Skillicorn and F. Calderoni, "Inductive discovery of criminal group structure using spectral embedding", *Information and Security*, 31:49–66, 2015.

D.B. Skillicorn and L. Purda, *Detecting Fraud in Financial Reports*, in: *European Conference on Intelligence and Security Informatics*, 2012.

D.B. Skillicorn, F. Spezzano, V.S. Subrahmanian and M. Garber, *Understanding South Asian Violent Extremist Group-Group Interactions*, in: *FOSINT 2014 at ASONAM 2014*, August 2014.

K.P. Smith and N.A. Christakis, "Social networks and health", *Annual Review of Sociology*, 34:402–429, 2008.

B. Snook, K. Luther, J.C. House, C. Bennell and P.J. Taylor, "The violent crime linkage analysis system: A test of interrater reliability", *Criminal Justice and Behavior*, 39(5):607–619, 2012.

J.W. Streefkerk, M.P. Esch-Bussmakers and M.A. Neerinc, *Field evaluation of a mobile location-based notification system for police officers*, in: *MobileHCI '08: Proceedings of the 10th International Conference on Human-Computer Interaction with Mobile Devices and Services*, pp. 101–108, September 2008.

J. Tiihonen, P. Halonen, L. Tiihonen, H. Kautiainen, M. Storvik and J. Callaway, "The association of ambient temperature and violent crime", *Nature Scientific Reports*, 7:6543, 2017.

S. Towers, S. Chen, A. Malik and D. Ebert, "Factors influencing temporal patterns in crime in a large American city: A predictive analytics perspective", *PLOS One*, 13(10), 2018.

J. Travers and S. Milgram, "An experimental study of the small world problem", *Sociometry*, pp. 425–443, 1969.

R.B. van Baaren, R.W. Holland, B. Steenaert and A. van Knippenberg, "Mimicry for money: Behavioral consequences of imitation", *Journal of Experimental Social Psychology*, 39:393–398, 2003.

C.J. Vilalta, R. Muggah and G. Fondevila, "Homicide as a function of city block layout: Mexico City as case study", *Global Crime*, 21:2:111–129, 2020.

L. Zhou, J.K. Burgoon, D.P. Twitchell, T. Qin and J.F. Nunamaker Jr, "A comparison of classification methods for predicting deception in computer-mediated communication", *Journal of Management Information Systems*, 20(4):139–165, 2004.

L. Zhou, D.P. Twitchell, T. Qin, J.K. Burgoon and J.F. Nunamaker Jr., *An exploratory study into deception detection in text-based computer mediated communication*, in: *Proceedings of the 36th Hawaii International Conference on Systems Science*, 2003.

Index